F106 .M664 2013
Tangled roots :
33663005309774
CYP

DATE DUE

D1452766

WEYERHAEUSER ENVIRONMENTAL BOOKS

William Cronon, Editor

Weyerhaeuser Environmental Books explore human relationships with natural environments in all their variety and complexity. They seek to cast new light on the ways that natural systems affect human communities, the ways that people affect the environments of which they are a part, and the ways that different cultural conceptions of nature profoundly shape our sense of the world around us. A complete list of the books in the series appears at the end of this book.

TANGLED ROOTS

The Appalachian Trail and

American Environmental Politics

Sarah Mittlefehldt

FOREWORD BY WILLIAM CRONON

University of Washington Press

Seattle and London

Tangled Roots: The Appalachian Trail and American Environmental Politics is published with the assistance of a grant from the Weyerhaeuser Environmental Books Endowment, established by the Weyerhaeuser Company Foundation, members of the Weyerhaeuser family, and Janet and Jack Creighton.

Printed and bound in the United States
Composed in Mill Sorts Goudy, a typeface designed by Barry Schwartz, inspired by the original typeface by Frederic W. Goudy

17 16 15 14 13 12   5 4 3 2 1

University of Washington Press
PO Box 50096, Seattle, WA 98145, USA

www.washington.edu/uwpress

Library of Congress Cataloging-in-Publication Data

Mittlefehldt, Sarah.
The Appalachian Trail and American environmental politics / Sarah Mittlefehldt.
pages cm—(Weyerhaeuser environmental books)
ISBN 978-0-295-99300-3 (hardback)
1. Appalachain Trail—History. 2. Trails—Public use—Appalachain Trail—History. 3. Environmental policy—United States—History—20th century.
4. Nature conservation—Political aspects—United States—History—20th century.
5. Environmentalism—Political aspects—United States—History—20th century.
6. Eminent domain—United States. 7. MacKaye, Benton, 1879-1975. I. Title.
F106.M664 2013   363.700973—dc23   2013015519

The paper used in this publication is acid-free and meets the minimum requirements of American National Standard for Information Sciences—Permanence of Paper for Printed Library Materials, ANSI Z39.48–1984.∞

Frontispiece and half-title illustrations courtesy of the Appalachian Trail Conservancy. See pp. 43 and 107.

For those who have worked to build and maintain the Appalachian Trail

CONTENTS

STATE OF THE TRAIL

William Cronon

THERE ARE FEW MORE BEGUILING SYMBOLS OF AMERICAN WILDERNESS than the Appalachian Trail, which extends some 2,180 miles from Springer Mountain in Georgia to Mount Katahdin in Maine. Most Americans who have ever seriously backpacked have spent at least a few moments imagining what it would be like to walk its entire length. Although it is neither the oldest nor the longest such trail in the United States, it has few rivals in the scale of daydreaming it provokes. Each year, two to three million people walk at least a segment of its route, though only a tiny fraction ever attempt to walk from Maine to Georgia (or vice versa—the more common direction for seasonal reasons). Even among the thousands who try each year to join the elite group of "2,000-milers" or "end-to-enders," as they are known, only about one in four ever completes the journey. Probably the best-known hiker who ever *failed* to complete the full hike was the writer Bill Bryson, whose hilarious *A Walk in the Woods: Rediscovering America on the Appalachian Trail* sat near the top of the *New York Times* best seller list for months after it was published in May of 1998—and Bryson no doubt provoked thousands of daydreams among readers who were tempted to follow in his footsteps, if not in his mishaps.

Fewer than a thousand hikers manage to traverse the full route each year, and the ten thousandth person to do so in the history of the trail completed the trek only in 2008.

Sarah Mittlefehldt, the author of *Tangled Roots: The Appalachian Trail and American Environmental Politics*, joined those ten thousand in 2007. While making a very long honeymoon hike with her newlywed husband, she did much of the research and interviewing that has gone into this first-ever scholarly history of the trail. She knows the AT very much at first hand, but the thought-provoking historical narrative she has pieced together will likely surprise even those who know the trail on the ground as well as she does. In Mittlefehldt's skilled hands, the story of how the trail came into being and how it has evolved over time is nothing less than the story in microcosm of American environmental politics over the course of the twentieth century. Indeed, one could go further still: the Appalachian Trail may have as much to teach us about the *future* of those politics as it does about their past.

Those familiar with the trail will know the story of its unlikely origins in an article published by the urban and regional planner Benton MacKaye in 1921 in the *Journal of the American Institute of Architects*. Entitled "An Appalachian Trail: A Project in Regional Planning," MacKaye's essay proposed the construction of a two-thousand-mile trail along the high watershed divide of the Appalachian Mountains to serve not just as a long-distance recreational opportunity for hikers but also as a source of economic prosperity for isolated rural communities that would thereby be connected with the wider world. A series of camps along the route would create nodes for farming, craftwork, and study, functioning as much-needed retreats from an urban-industrial world. Although this aspect of MacKaye's vision is often forgotten today, the trail was intended to be as much a community development project as it was a form of environmental protection.

Most articles like MacKaye's are speculative and utopian enough that they vanish into oblivion. This one had a different fate. MacKaye was taken enough by his own idea that he used his extensive personal and professional networks to recruit allies to make the trail a reality. Less than four years later, he and the Regional Planning Association had convened an Appalachian Trail Conference to recruit volunteers to start building the trail, and a young Washington, D.C., lawyer named Myron Avery went to work organizing hiking enthusiasts along the eastern seaboard to begin construction. Gaining permission from landowners for the trail's informal right of way to cross their property and then organizing small armies of volunteers to clear the route, trail advocates moved with astonishing swiftness to achieve their vision. They accomplished in just over a decade and a half what still feels like a miraculous feat. On August 14, 1937, the Appalachian Trail Conference announced that it had succeeded in creating a continuous footpath from Maine to Georgia . . . and Myron Avery the year before managed to become the first 2,000-miler.

This part of the story is well known and has long served as an almost mythic source of inspiration for those who know and care about the Appalachian Trail. Mittlefehldt lays out its particulars and its larger significance as well as anyone ever has, but the most compelling part of her book begins once the trail had been completed. Organized and run by private citizens on a volunteer basis, the state-based nonprofit organizations whose activities were coordinated by the Appalachian Trail Conference still had to maintain what they had created. They erected shelters for long-distance hikers, published maps and guidebooks, and tried to make sure that landowners remained content about people they had never met traversing their properties in growing numbers. Some owners decided they didn't really like the idea after all, so the route had to be renegotiated when permission to use the original right of way was lost. Volunteerism, citizen action, public-private cooperation—these were what built the trail and kept it going for its first half century.

By the 1950s and 1960s, the explosion of interest in outdoor recreation was putting ever-increasing pressure on the trail corridor. The through-hikers weren't yet a big problem—only five people completed the full hike in the 1930s, three in the 1940s, fourteen in the 1950s, and thirty-seven in the 1960s—but many thousands of others were using the trail for shorter hikes. Trail advocates began to believe that the lands along the route should be permanently protected by having the government purchase the properties through which the trail ran. The opportunity to begin doing so on a large scale came in 1968 with the passage of the National Trails System Act, which gave the AT federal protection as a national scenic trail. Just as importantly, the Federal Land and Water Conservation Fund, which had been created in 1965, provided money for land purchases, with at least the possibility that the federal power of eminent domain could be used to force recalcitrant landowners to sell. Overseen by the National Park Service as the agency with responsibility for coordinating all this protective activity, the Appalachian Trail moved quite definitively away from the period of voluntarism that had characterized its early history and into a period of government oversight that proved far more tumultuous than before.

By now, I trust, my sketch of Sarah Mittlefehldt's far subtler book-length narrative and analysis should be feeling uncomfortably familiar. The angry fights over property rights and the claimed abuses of federal power that followed in the wake of the 1960s legislation—even as trail advocates worked as they had in the past to protect what they rightly saw as an incomparable national treasure—parallel disturbingly what would emerge during the

1970s and 1980s as a conservative backlash against environmentalism in the name of liberty and property rights. Who would have thought that so venerable and beloved a national wilderness icon might become the epicenter of such controversies? Yet that is what happened, and that is what makes *Tangled Roots* such a fascinating book with such important implications for conservation politics in our own time.

I won't give away Mittlefehldt's conclusions other than to note that the turning point in her story comes in 1984, when the National Park Service delegated to the Appalachian Trail Conference (which in 2005 changed its name to the Appalachian Trail Conservancy) responsibility for managing the trail, with the Park Service retaining a crucial oversight role. Both practically and symbolically, this represented a leaning back toward public-private partnership, a kind of institutionalized remembering of the volunteerism that had built the trail in the first place. Extreme partisans on either side of past environmental controversies could no doubt read their own preferred morals into this story: at one end of the spectrum, government cannot be trusted to protect private property, and at the other, private volunteerism cannot be trusted to protect wild nature. But I prefer to join Sarah Mittlefehldt in thinking that a better moral lies somewhere in between: government power is essential for protecting a natural resource as complex as the Appalachian Trail, but government alone cannot create the volunteerism and community caretaking that created the trail in the first place and that sustain its stewardship today. If this in-between reading of the trail's lessons is correct—and I believe it is—its implications extend much further even than the two thousand miles between Katahdin and Springer Mountain.

LIKE THE APPALACHIAN TRAIL ITSELF, THE PATH TO COMPLETING THIS book was long and tortuous. I would never have reached the end if it weren't for the support of my mentors and colleagues, the assistance of archive staff and members of the trail community, and the encouragement of my friends and family. This book grew out of my research at the University of Wisconsin–Madison, where I had the opportunity to work with two great scholars—Nancy Langston and William Cronon. From conversations in Russell Labs to kayak excursions on Lake Superior, Nancy helped me clarify my ideas for this project and encouraged me to think about the broader implications of historical scholarship. This manuscript greatly benefited from her experience, wisdom, and constructive criticism on earlier drafts. Like Nancy, Bill Cronon also maintained faith in my ability to pull this manuscript together even when I struggled to clarify its central purpose. As an advisor and then as editor, Bill's gentle guidance helped me craft a story that I hope will appeal to a broad community of scholars and policy makers, as well as hiking and conservation aficionados across the country.

In 2007, my research assistant and newlywed spouse and I left Madison to begin a ten-month field expedition and honeymoon along the Appalachian Trail. As we hiked from archive to archive, starting in Georgia and heading north to Katahdin, we met with a number of trail volunteers, public officials, hikers, landowners, and community leaders to learn about the human history hidden in this wilderness footpath. We were often overwhelmed by the generosity of strangers, who shuttled us to archives in the backs of their pick-up trucks, fed us ice cream and pancakes, and told us their intimate life histories. The list of people who provided logistical and emotional support for this project is longer than I can acknowledge here, and I am grateful to them all.

There are a few individuals and organizations, however, without whom this book would not have been possible. Staff members at the Georgia Archives, the Maine State Library, the Jones Memorial Library, and the Wisconsin Historical Society were all extremely helpful. Staff members at the Dartmouth College Library displayed grace and tolerance of our unprofessional odor and attire when we literally walked a hundred yards off the trail to use the Rauner Special Collections. Helen Wykle of the D. H. Ramsey Library at the University of North Carolina–Asheville was particularly enthusiastic about the project, as was Ed Goodell, the executive director of the New York–New Jersey Trail Conference. Ed let us search through the organization's filing cabinets, took us out to lunch, and introduced us to trail volunteer Gus Vasiliadis, who let us stay at his home while we worked in the archive in New Jersey.

In Cumberland County, Pennsylvania, Barb Bartos, the county archivist, let us into the cells of the old county jail, where the county keeps boxes of retired files. Barb was extremely generous with her time and energy. Warren Doyle, who teaches at Lees-McRae College in Banner Elk, North Carolina, was also exceptionally helpful and generous. Warren and his wife Terry invited us to stay in their home while we worked in the collection at Lees McRae. I am also indebted to Brian King, archivist for the Appalachian Trail Conservancy (ATC). Sources at the ATC provide the basis of this analysis, and Brian very graciously opened the ATC archives to us. Brian also knows more history about the trail than I will probably ever absorb; I always appreciated hearing his stories when I visited the archive.

One of the most enjoyable aspects of the project was talking with the people who helped create the trail. Although there are too many to name individually, there were several people who were especially helpful in shaping this research. Don Owen, formerly of the National Park Service's Appalachian Trail Project Office, provided helpful constructive criticism on early drafts of the research. Conversations with landowners such as Don and Pam Fenicle, who were involved in organized resistance against the relocation of the trail in the late 1970s and early 1980s, reminded me of the need to incorporate the voices of those affected by federal policies. By incorporating voices from a wide range of perspectives, I aim to tell a balanced story of one of the most complicated initiatives in the history of the National Park Service.

Several employees of the Appalachian Trail Conservancy were very generous with their time and knowledge. I am exceedingly grateful to Bob Proudman, Caroline Dafur, and Laurie Pottinger for sharing their insights on various aspects of trail development. Special thanks to Todd Coyle and Sarah Cargill, who shuttled us back and forth between the ATC archives in Charlestown, West Virginia, and the headquarters in Harpers Ferry. Regional ATC staff members were also very helpful, including Morgan Sommerville in Asheville, and Sally Naser, Karen Lutz, Todd Ramaley, and Michelle Miller in Boiling Springs. US Forest Service rangers Beth Merz and Candice Wyman also supplied useful information about current challenges and contemporary initiatives.

Our hosts at many of the hiker hostels along the trail also shared interesting perspectives on the history of relationships between trail workers, local communities, and state agents. I am particularly grateful to Jeff and Nancy Hoch at the Hike Inn at Fontana Dam; Payson Kennedy at the Nantahala Outdoor Center in Wesser, North Carolina; Dave Patrick of Mount Rogers Outfitters in Damascus, Virginia; and John "Uncle Johnny" Shores in Erwin, Tennessee. A special thanks to "Sunny" and Elmer Hall at the Sunnybank Inn in Hot Springs, North Carolina; our multiple-course vegetarian dinner and the lively conservation there was one of the most refreshing dining experiences of the field research.

Spending Easter weekend trapped in a blizzard at Bob and Pat People's Kincora Hostel and helping to prepare a feast for twenty-plus hungry hikers was also a memorable moment. In addition to running the hostel, Bob has spent over a decade volunteering for the trail and organizing work parties. Pat passed away in 2008, and this book is dedicated to all of the people like Bob and Pat Peoples—the volunteers who give so generously of their time, energy, and spirit to protect a place for future generations. Their passion and commitment inspired me and motivated me to write this history.

Fieldwork for this project would not have been completed without the financial support of the Garden Club of America, the American Society for Environmental History's Hal K. Rothman Dissertation Fellowship, and the Vilas Travel Fellowship program at the University of Wisconsin–Madison. The University of Wisconsin–Madison's Center for Culture, History, and Environment (CHE) and the Nelson Institute for Environmental Studies also provided research funds and supportive colleagues.

At meetings of the American Society of Environmental History, I was grateful for the encouragement and constructive advice I received from colleagues. Sara Gregg and Paul Sutter were particularly helpful in thinking about ways in which this project would contribute to the field. Jim Feldman and Kathryn Newfont painstakingly reviewed this manuscript and offered great insights that I had not considered in earlier drafts. Marianne Kedding-ton-Lang at the University of Washington Press provided much-needed guidance and helpful advice throughout the publication process. I am also thankful to the other members of my dissertation committee: Ray Guries, Arne Alanen, and Sam Dennis, for their feedback on earlier drafts of this research. Friends and colleagues from the Environmental History Caucus at the University of Virginia, including Laura Kolar and Katy Shively Meier, also provided intellectual grounding and helpful feedback as I wandered the lonely abyss of dissertation writing in Charlottesville. I am also grate-ful to new colleagues in Vermont who provided insightful comments on this manuscript, including Jen Powers at Green Mountain College and Eric Hansen. My undergraduate research assistants, Ben Sweet and Erin Hardy, also gave their time and talents to help prepare this manuscript. Despite all of the organizations and individuals who contributed to this research, how-ever, any errors are my own.

Finally, I give my warmest thanks to friends and family who provided emotional and logistical support. I thank anyone who ever attended Whis-key Friday in my living room or backyard. Making music with friends remains one my favorite ways to recharge my mental batteries. We partic-ularly enjoyed traveling through Maine's Hundred-Mile Wilderness with Michael "5-String" Hawkins, a fellow troubadour with a banjo, and we were extremely grateful for the Subway sandwiches that his parents, David and Martha Hawkins, provided after our descent of Katahdin. The Hawkins also shared moving stories about how the creation of the Fontana Dam and Great Smoky Mountains National Park affected David's grandfather's homestead in the Appalachian Mountains in the 1930s and 1940s.

My family has been the bedrock of my support throughout the process of creating this book. My father-in-law, Doug Gillette, helped to facilitate the field research by meeting us at the Atlanta airport, dropping us off near the trail's southern terminus, and then driving our car back to the Gillette home in Connecticut. There, Beth Gillette kept a bottle of chilled wine and an easy laugh on tap until we reached their place several months later and took a much-needed respite. When the White Mountains started to wreak havoc on my left knee, Matt, Petra, and Josephine Gillette welcomed us into their New Hampshire home. Throughout all stages of this project,

I received the solid, steadfast support of my brother, Noah, and his wife, Rhonda. I look forward to introducing my nephews, Ryan and Joran, and my new niece, Amelia, to the Appalachian Trail one day. Bill Mittlefehldt has been a father unmatched in his willingness to do anything for those he loves—including canoe across the Great Lakes. I am especially grateful to my mother, Pamela, for her exceptional editorial skills on this manuscript, the countless hours she spent reading messy drafts, and her insistence that words and ideas can have a radical effect on the world.

Finally, I acknowledge the one person who helped facilitate every aspect of this project—my husband, John Gillette. I know of no other person who would agree to a honeymoon that involved walking 2,180 miles, sitting through countless interviews, sifting through old documents at archives, and listening to me pontificate for hours about my analytical center. His patience, humor, and music sustained me through this long journey—poison ivy and all—and I look forward to walking beside him on many adventures to come.

TANGLED
ROOTS

THE TORTUOUS PATH TOWARD PUBLIC-PRIVATE PARTNERSHIP

IN 1921, PROGRESSIVE FORESTER BENTON MACKAYE PROPOSED A PLAN TO build a footpath along the spine of the Appalachian Mountains that would run from Georgia to Maine. When later asked what the purpose of this Appalachian Trail might be, MacKaye replied that there were three objectives: "(1) to walk; (2) to see; (3) to *see* what you see."[1] MacKaye probably meant that a hiker should remain alert to her surroundings, absorbing the landscape around her and contemplating its meaning and beauty. Yet, two months into my ten-month field season on the trail in 2007, I realized that most hikers, particularly through-hikers (those who walk the two-thousand-mile trail in one season), spend the majority of their waking hours staring at the ground two feet ahead of their boots. We see dirt, mud, rocks, snow, and mile after mile of tangled roots. Every once in a while, the trail pops us out at an overlook, where we take in some scenery and enjoy that snack we've been thinking about for the past two hours.

Occasionally we take note of the changes in the landscapes through which we traverse. Those of us who walk the Appalachian Trail (AT) from south to north are intoxicated by the smell of blooming mountain laurel in Georgia and humbled by the towering giants of old-growth forest in the Great Smoky Mountains. We stride alongside wild ponies in Virginia's Grayson Highlands and slide through golden cornfields in Pennsylvania's Cumberland Valley. In the mid-Atlantic area, we dash across road crossings and drool over the scents coming from backyard barbeques as we skirt around some of the most populated parts of the country. In Connecticut and Massachusetts, the signs of suburbia along the trail begin to recede, replaced by thousands of acres of lush mixed-hardwood forests. These vast woodlands continue through Vermont and New Hampshire, but shift in composition to a greater percentage of northern species as we move toward the boreal forests of Maine. Although astute hikers might carefully observe changes in the physical landscape, seldom do we get a sense of the complicated political dynamics involved in creating the simple footpath that we tread on and the scenic views that surround us. This book aims to reveal that unseen story.

Like the tangled roots that hikers encounter along the trail, for those involved in building this famous footpath, the tangled political roots of the Appalachian Trail were frustrating and difficult to navigate at times but were ultimately an essential part of the broader system they support. Just as the tangled roots along the trail sustain surrounding forests, the trail's diverse political structure provided the foundation for trail-building efforts, and made the Appalachian Trail one of the most successful land stewardship projects of the twentieth century and a model for environmental protection in the twenty-first century. Over the course of nearly a century, the AT project has combined the horizontal, dendritic roots of grassroots social action with the strong central taproot of federal authority. These two sources of political power evolved in dynamic interaction with one another, tipping at times toward one side or the other, but never fully separate. The history of the AT reveals a complex, relational view of power and authority between the state and private citizens. Viewing power in this way—not purely as a top-down hegemonic force or a bubbling up from the grassroots but as a much more interactive process—enriches our collective understanding of twentieth-century conservation efforts in the United States, and has important implications for the future of environmental protection.

In some ways, the history of the Appalachian Trail reflects a broader story about land management and protection in the eastern United States that will be familiar to environmental historians. The trail was initiated at the end of the Progressive Era, when conservationist Republican Theodore Roosevelt found himself in the Oval Office after president William McKinley's assassination, and Congress began to establish federal land managing agencies such as the US Forest Service and the National Park Service. Members of a growing urban population began to "get back to nature" through a variety of outdoor activities such as hiking and camping, and by means of influential outdoor organizations, such as the Appalachian Mountain Club and the Appalachian National Park Association, began working with state and federal representatives to expand recreational opportunities throughout the eastern hinterlands.[2] By the time the second President Roosevelt came to power in 1933, Americans' interest in protecting natural resources and preserving wild places for recreation had spread throughout the country, and the political machinery that was necessary to support such efforts had been put in place.

When the Great Depression rocked American families—hitting urban populations hard and amplifying the existing problems of rural communities—president Franklin Roosevelt responded with a suite of programs that would forever transform the American political landscape. The New Deal ushered in an era of federal power that would grow and evolve throughout the rest of the century. Although at that time, the Appalachian Trail remained predominantly under the purview of the Appalachian Trail Conference—a nonprofit, nongovernmental organization—federal programs such as the Civilian Conservation Corps and the growing authority of agencies such as the National Park Service and the US Forest Service played a critical supporting role in the early development of the Appalachian Trail.

The AT did not officially become part of the national park system until 1968, when Congress passed the National Trails Act, but during the late 1920s and 1930s, the emerging footpath physically and politically intersected with other federal land management initiatives that were being planned and developed at that time, such as the Shenandoah National Park and Skyline Drive, the Great Smoky Mountains National Park, the Blue Ridge Parkway, and a handful of Tennessee Valley Authority projects. As well-intentioned government agents attempted to promote the public good by creating new recreation resources and through large-scale regional planning projects, rural residents—particularly in the Southern Appalachian Mountains—were sometimes forced to leave their homes. Although many were grateful for relief from years of struggling to farm steep slopes and poor soils, others resisted the government's efforts to take their homes and property.[3]

Unlike the broad federal land reforms and efforts to create the nation's first eastern national parks of the 1930s, however, the AT lacked the official authority of the federal government. Instead, private volunteers with the Appalachian Trail Conference relied on oral "handshake" agreements with landowners. Because trail use was minimal and relatively local, most landowners were willing to have a few weekend adventurers cross their properties. Although many of the early AT advocates were connected with the broader national conservation movement and with efforts to create national parks, the AT initially relied on volunteers' status as quasipublic servants, and was ultimately established along the path of least political resistance.

Informal agreements with landowners began to erode after World War II, when the landscapes surrounding the trail underwent dramatic environmental, economic, political, and cultural changes. When soldiers returned home, many were eager to move to the suburbs to live out the American Dream. The growing demand for new housing construction put additional pressure on the forests through which the trail passed. In some areas, urban sprawl forced hikers from the woods onto pavement. In addition, as leisure time and disposable income increased during the postwar era, Americans began flocking to the hinterlands in droves, not only for recreation but also to build vacation homes and resort developments. As a result of these pressures, many miles of the original AT were obliterated or relocated onto roads.

Trail advocates realized that in order to maintain the continuity of the footpath, they would need stronger support from the federal government. Their lobbying efforts reached fruition when Congress passed the National Trails Act in 1968 as part of a broader response to the skyrocketing demand for outdoor recreation and an expansion of the national park system in the 1960s and 1970s. This expansion marked an important shift from the National Park Service's primary focus on developing park and recreation areas out of the public domain in the West, to the much more complicated task of building new types of park and recreation areas in the East—closer to where the bulk of the population lived, worked, and owned land.

The growth of the National Park System in the 1960s and 1970s reflected the desire of American citizens and their representatives to protect the nation's resources and to preserve wild and scenic areas from the postwar economic forces that continued to have dramatic environmental effects.[4] Some historians point to this as the formative era of the modern environmental movement, when the older conservation movement of the Progressive Era expanded its priorities from protecting parks and forests to include a wider range of "new" environmental issues, such as human health and pollution, and, in the process, began to incorporate a wider range of political strategies to achieve environmental protection.[5] Public participation became an even greater force in making decisions about resource management, and environmental groups such as the Sierra Club and the Wilderness Society became powerful players in Washington politics. Environmental issues received strong bipartisan support throughout the 1960s, and some of the most robust pieces of environmental legislation to date were signed by president Richard Nixon in the 1970s, including the Clean Water Act, the Clean Air Act, and the Endangered Species Act.[6]

Although most Americans—Republicans and Democrats alike—supported environmental legislation in the 1960s and 1970s, there was also a growing number of citizens who were concerned about the federal government's influence on land management and the regulation of private property. People whose businesses had been negatively affected by new environmental regulations and property owners who felt they were losing control over their land began to organize in resistance to the federal largesse that had been growing since the New Deal era. In the West, a new kind of conservative grassroots movement emerged—one that sought the protection of property rights and freedom from an expanding federal bureaucracy.[7] This rousing of resistance culminated in what some scholars have called the "antienvironmental movement." This antienvironmental, pro-property rights movement was characterized by the Sagebrush Rebellion in the late 1970s, in which ranchers, farmers, loggers, and miners advocated for state control over western public lands, and the "wise use" movement in the 1990s, which sought to give greater control to individual property owners. The movements to protect states' rights and individual property rights gained national significance when self-proclaimed Sagebrush Rebel Ronald Reagan became president in 1980, bringing strength and legitimacy to a growing conservative constituency.[8]

In 1978, the same year that Congress amended the National Trails Act to give more power to the National Park Service to acquire land for the AT, the National Park Inholders Association formed in California to protest the expansion of the National Park System. The organization's leader, Charles Cushman, traveled around the country helping landowners who believed that the National Park Service had violated their constitutional rights. Cushman's organization helped bring the growing resistance to federal control of public lands in the West to like-minded property rights advocates in the East. When the National Park Service launched an aggressive land acquisition program for the Appalachian Trail in 1978, Cushman helped landowners up and down the AT to organize to protest the acquisition program. Through organized resistance, AT landowners were able to link their concerns to a broader political movement that sought to limit the power of the federal government and to defend the rights of private interests.

Yet the National Park Service's land acquisition program for the AT was unlike any other in the history of federal land management in the United States. To broker federal power and to develop support for the acquisition program, the Park Service relied on the participation of citizen advocates and encouraged local and state governments to play a leadership role in the project. The agency's private partners helped scout and map new relocated sections of the trail off of roads and private land. Citizen volunteers also helped to locate land ownership data, discuss options with landowners, and eventually helped to blaze the new federally protected footpath. Never before had an agency relied so heavily on an army of knowledgeable and highly motivated citizens to help facilitate an incredibly complex land acquisition program. Part of this decision was pragmatic; the agency understood that in many cases, long-time volunteers and trail workers had a deep understanding of the physical and political landscapes surrounding the trail. But the Park Service also hoped that continuing the project's history of grassroots involvement, and relying on the knowledge and experience of citizen volunteers, would overcome growing concerns about the protection of property rights and the heavy hand of the federal government. The agency hoped to prevent the negative image of federal acquisition programs that had begun to be spread in the national media by property rights advocates.

Members of communities along the AT reacted to citizen advocates' involvement in the federal acquisition program in a variety of ways. In many cases, citizen coordinators for the acquisition program helped ease potential hostility to the project. For example, in parts of New York, long-term volunteers such as Elizabeth Levers were able to demonstrate genuine concern for landowners' ideas and opinions. This helped advocates to frame the program as more of a community-based initiative and to avoid the image of the project being a federal mandate. In other places, however, reliance on citizen coordinators led to political complications. For example, in Pennsylvania's Cumberland County, the involvement of citizen coordinators added to the program's complexity, and to landowners' hesitancy to support the project.

As communities along the trail struggled to come to consensus on a final route for the corridor, President Reagan appointed James Watt as the secretary of the Interior in 1981. While he served as director of the Bureau of Outdoor Recreation in the mid-1970s, Watt had frequently cited the AT project as an example of the power of private citizens to achieve national conservation goals. He lost any allies he may have had among the trail community, however, when he called for an immediate moratorium on all funding for federal land acquisition in 1981. Instead of protecting land through

large-scale federal acquisition, the Reagan administration was more interested in keeping land in productive, private ownership, and on the local tax
rolls. Under the mantra of "creative conservation," the administration supported the delegation of responsibility for conservation efforts to the private sector and to local and state authorities. Environmental advocates who
had grown accustomed to relying on the power of the federal government
that had been growing since the New Deal era realized that they would have
to take a somewhat different approach to environmental protection. The
Appalachian Trail offered an ideal opportunity to explore the power and
possibilities of public-private partnerships.

As financial and political support for large-scale federal land acquisition projects diminished and the property rights movement gained traction in the 1980s, the National Park Service delegated the responsibility for
managing newly acquired public corridor lands to the Appalachian Trail
Conference—a nongovernmental, largely volunteer-based organization
(the organization changed its name to Appalachian Trail Conservancy in
2005 but maintained the same acronym—ATC). In 1984, the ATC eagerly
accepted the challenge, and through many years of learning and cooperation, the initiative became one of the most successful examples of public-
private partnership in the conservation arena. The formalization of a
long-standing partnership between private trail organizations and public
land managing agencies reflected new attitudes toward large-scale federal
projects that evolved in response to broader economic and political changes
in the 1980s and 1990s.

By the end of the twentieth century, the Park Service's land acquisition
program for the AT slowly neared completion. Now, in the twenty-first century, the ATC has begun to explore new opportunities for conserving the
corridor and surrounding landscapes. The organization has resurrected
Benton MacKaye's ideas about regional planning, and the trail has become
even more integrated into the fabric of local land-use plans. The purpose of
such initiatives has been to expand the range and variety of landscapes protected, and to encourage greater participation from residents of local communities in land-use decision making. Through new programs such as the
Appalachian Trail Community program, the ATC has worked with local
officials and residents from towns along the AT to plan for sustainable economic development and to engage local citizens in environmental stewardship initiatives.

The historic arc the Appalachian Trail reveals that at every stage of the project's past, the diversity of the project's partners has increased and the zone of collaboration has expanded. From its initial conception by Benton MacKaye to a handful of eager volunteer trailblazers to new generations of trail users, advocates, and critics, the number of participants in this public-private partnership has grown. As the diversity of project participants increased, so, too, did the range of ideas about the project's purpose. This has, at times, led to ideological conflict among trail partners. For many advocates, the trail was an icon of wilderness, a protected swath of natural land, untrammeled by human development, to be used for primitive forms of recreation. For many others, however, managing the trail and surrounding corridor lands provided a vehicle for protecting certain land uses such as grazing and small-scale farming and forestry activities. Although the Appalachian Trail is known as a "footpath through the wilderness," the project has also involved conserving hundreds of acres of working lands that surround the trail in addition to the wild ones. Because of the AT's unusual linear shape and its close proximity to towns and cities in the East, the trail's history reveals important nuances in the debates about wilderness protection and eastern land management.[9]

The history of the Appalachian Trail also demonstrates that land conservation in the United States has often involved both the strong central taproot of the state, as well as several strands of horizontal, branching roots of grassroots social action. Just as supporters of the AT found strength in organizing through an extended network of local clubs and private associations, those who resisted the project also gained momentum through grassroots organizations, and by linking up with a growing conservative movement that was based on the protection of property rights and freedom from federal control. Understanding why people protested something that was supposed to be, in the famous words of conservationist and first chief of the US Forest Service, Gifford Pinchot, "the greatest good, for the greatest number, for the longest time," is an essential part of understanding the struggle for environmental protection. By examining conflict and resistance to the AT project we develop a deeper understanding of the origins of antienvironmentalist sentiment and how the growing power of the New Right influenced environmental politics.[10]

Environmental historians such as Karl Jacoby and Sara Gregg have recently begun to unveil "hidden histories" of American conservation initiatives by examining the voices of people who were affected by federal conservation policies.[11] These new perspectives have raised important questions about the role of social justice in large-scale environmental protection initiatives. This history of the AT builds on these insights and presents a complex view of the relationship between the centralized state and decentralized citizen actors. An exploration of the dynamic interaction between grassroots organization and state-based authority involved in the creation of the Appalachian Trail reveals another "hidden history" of the American conservation movement. Instead of being a story about elite outsiders imposing a national agenda on poor rural inhabitants, the history of the Appalachian Trail demonstrates a much greater range of interactions—resistance as well as support and cooperation—between disparate groups. The AT was supported by Southern Baptist ministers and Ivy League professors, industrial workers and radical environmentalists. At the same time, however, the project was resisted by property rights advocates and chicken farmers, land developers and libertarians. Efforts to blaze the trail were often the result of complicated negotiations over land use, power, and control between a large number of public and private agents. By exploring how different dendrites of grassroots action interacted with centralized powers throughout the twentieth century, and illustrating how the movement to establish this sylvan swath across the eastern mountains shaped—and was shaped by—growing antienvironmentalist sentiment, I hope to provide a deeper understanding of the history of environmental politics in the United States.

Many authors have written about the Appalachian Trail from a variety of perspectives. In addition to the tomes of informal hiker narratives, scholars have examined the social dimensions of through-hiking the trail, the effects of technology on the trail, and the trail as an educational resource.[12] Other investigations have explored the Appalachian Trail as a cultural symbol, as a totem of twentieth-century America's growing passion for wilderness, and as an administrative anomaly among public lands.[13] Yet no author has explored the social, political, or material factors within local communities that have contributed to the trail's existence. This book examines these dimensions by analyzing the exchange of power and ideas between different individuals and groups involved in conceiving, constructing, legislating, acquiring, and conserving the Appalachian Trail corridor.

Writing a history of a landscape that crosses 2,180 miles, 250,000 acres, eight national forests, seven units of the national park system, over seventy state-owned reserve areas, and 287 local jurisdictions is an ambitious task, especially when one is hitchhiking to archives and interviews, and camping along the trail during ten months of field research. Perhaps the greatest limitation of this study is its expansiveness. Fieldwork for the project, including visits to ten archives; the oral histories of local residents, volunteers, and public land managers; and a countless number of informal discussions with others produced a stunning abundance of material—more than could ever be included in a single book. My arguments are based on examples from the research that were representative of general trends and patterns. It was not feasible to detail relations in every community between Georgia and Maine. Instead, I use a range of examples to explain the political dynamics involved in blazing the trail.

These examples and stories demonstrate that the Appalachian Trail ultimately relied on civic engagement and the negotiation of disparate worldviews. The project was, and continues to be, based on an interaction of power and authority—a tangle of centralized and decentralized roots. Although signs of political struggle and alliance may not be obvious to hikers wandering along this famous footpath, these tangled roots have sustained the trail and continue to ensure its longevity. The history of the AT illustrates the complicated relationship between state-based and citizen-based environmental action during the twentieth century. Moreover, by establishing important precedents for public land policy and by serving as a premier example of public-private partnership during the twentieth century, the Appalachian Trail helped to blaze the way for twenty-first-century environmental policy.

The Appalachian Trail holds a powerful place in the American imagination. As I walked from Georgia to Maine in 2007, I was struck by the passion people feel for this famous footpath. My conversations with volunteers, public land managers, landowners, and hikers made me profoundly aware that the Appalachian Trail is not merely a thin continuous strip of dirt across the eastern United States. Rather, this long, linear landscape is a reminder of Americans' commitment to land conservation and a demonstration of our ability to work through conflict to achieve large-scale goals. In an era in which the environment has seemingly become a polarizing bipartisan issue, the history of the Appalachian Trail reminds us of the necessity of seeking common ground. It also reveals the tortuous path it sometimes takes to get there.

CHAPTER I

A PROGRESSIVE FOOTPATH

WHEN BENTON MACKAYE CLIMBED STRATTON MOUNTAIN IN SOUTHERN Vermont in 1900 on the trip that would inspire him to propose an Appalachian Trail, the landscape that surrounded him looked much different from the one hikers encounter today. Where we see a thriving ski resort and a lavish condominium development on the north side of the mountain, MacKaye saw a devastated rural community attempting to eke out an existence from subsistence agriculture and logging. Since the 1780s, European settlers had transformed old-growth forests into a scarred and eroded landscape as they struggled to turn the hills of central Vermont into an agricultural Eden. In the 1880s, new pressures were placed on the region's forests when several small lumber mills opened to provide jobs to a struggling population of farmers in the Stratton area. The success of these local mills was short-lived, however, as wealthy out-of-state lumbermen bought up land and put the smaller operations out of business. The new lumber barons ramped up production and set up camps for migratory workers. By 1920, a year before MacKaye proposed his plan for an Appalachian Trail, over a third of the people living in Stratton were migrant lumbermen, and the area's economic future looked uncertain.[1]

The story of Stratton was not unlike that of many other communities throughout the Appalachian Mountains. In both northern and southern ranges, thin soil, relatively steep slopes, and inaccessible markets limited European settlers' attempts at farming and ranching. Furthermore, the "cut-and-get-out" forest practices of large timber barons left both land and rural populations literally uprooted. By the turn of the nineteenth century, many rural people left for greener pastures out West or for industrialized urban areas, where they faced new problems associated with public health, unemployment, and worker safety. For MacKaye, the problems of the city and of the countryside were inseparable. When he came to Stratton for adventure and recreation in 1900, climbing a tree on the top of the mountain for a better perspective on the landscapes below, he began to envision a project to not only preserve scenic vistas and natural resources along the spine of the Appalachian Mountains but also to protect the people who lived and worked in the surrounding areas and in distant cities.

At the heart of MacKaye's proposal for an Appalachian Trail was the desire to solve "the problem of living," which, in his view, was an economic one. He wrote, "Living has been considerably complicated of late in various ways—by war, by questions of personal liberty, and by 'menaces' of one kind or another."[2] These menaces included unemployment, class antagonisms, the degradation of natural resources, and a kind of spiritual malaise that came from being disconnected from nature. MacKaye had begun to witness mental health problems spreading among his urban friends and family—most devastatingly exemplified by his wife's suicide in 1921. By putting people's spare time to productive use through voluntary service in the out-of-doors, MacKaye believed that the Appalachian Trail project would help ameliorate the angst of modern life.

According to MacKaye's plan, the Appalachian Trail would provide common ground for different parts of American society to come together to create opportunities for recreation, health and recuperation, and employment. When volunteers came together to build this skyline path and surrounding camps, MacKaye claimed, "Industry would come to be seen in its true perspective—as a means in life and not as an end in itself. The actual partaking of the recreative and nonindustrial life—systematically by the people and not spasmodically by a few—should emphasize the distinction between it and the industrial life."[3] As an alternative to the path of industrialization, MacKaye believed that the project would "put new zest in the labor movement. . . . The problems of the farmer, the coal miner, and the lumberjack could be studied intimately and with minimum partiality."[4]

MacKaye's 1921 proposal for an Appalachian Trail included a multitiered plan for developing "outdoors community life" that essentially amounted to the construction of a social utopia in the eastern wilderness, where "cooperation replaces antagonism, trust replaces suspicion, emulation replaces competition."[5] The trail itself would lead adventurers along the ridgeline of the Appalachian Mountains from Maine to Georgia, and provide a "strategic camping base" for the country's work and play.[6] Next would come shelters and huts modeled after those built in the White Mountains of New Hampshire and the Green Mountains of Vermont. The following phase—part of MacKaye's proposal that never reached fruition—was the creation of community encampments where people would collectively own acreage along the trail and live in private homes located in small, clustered settlements. Like all phases of the project, MacKaye insisted that these collectives would be established on a not-for-profit basis. He argued that the community camps "should become something more than a mere 'playground': it should stimulate every line of outdoor non-industrial endeavor."[7] Camps along the trail would be used for education, recreation, and spiritual and mental healing.

The final component of MacKaye's plan involved camps for food production. Like other aspects of the trail, the government would lead efforts to plan these agricultural centers, but private citizens would be instrumental in their development and maintenance. Although the trail became a conduit for the protection of agricultural lands in and around the Appalachian Trail corridor in the late twentieth and early twenty-first centuries, the kinds of federally planned farm and food camps that MacKaye had in mind did not materialize as he envisioned.

In the 1921 proposal, MacKaye acknowledged that all of these extra economic developments would come after the trail was established. The idea was that the same cooperative spirit and coordinated actions used to blaze the trail, build the shelters, and organize the camps could be channeled to create small agricultural-based communities that would produce food for hikers and rural families. In the valleys below the ridgeline, MacKaye envisioned an "experiment in 'getting back to the land.'" These centers of production would provide employment and "opportunities for those anxious to settle down in the country."[8] People might come to the trail and, upon finding spiritual fulfillment, would never want to leave the hinterlands. Thus, MacKaye believed that the AT could help reverse the trend of rapid urbanization and the problems of modern American life.

MacKaye's 1921 article was a bit vague about how to achieve the ambitious goals he proposed; he wrote, "Organizing is a matter of detail to be carefully worked out."[9] Not long after the proposal was published, however, MacKaye suggested that the AT project would require new forms of political engagement—a combination of decentralized and centralized power.[10] Like many of his Progressive counterparts, MacKaye believed in state-supported, technocratic solutions to natural resource problems. He felt that federal

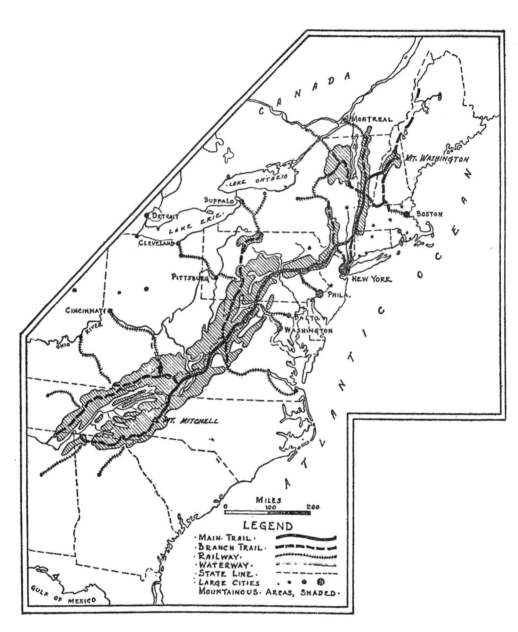

Map 1   MacKaye's 1921 map. When Benton MacKaye first mapped
the idea for an Appalachian Trail in 1921, he envisioned much more
than a recreational path. As one of the first major regional planning projects of the Regional Planning Association of America,
the AT was to address fundamental problems associated with labor
and resource management. Map first published in the *Journal of the
American Institute of Architects*, October 1921.

foresters, engineers, architects, and planners should all be involved in developing the AT. Yet he maintained that the Appalachian Trail project would be successful only if private citizens played an active role. He emphasized that the AT would ultimately rely on citizen volunteers and amateur "out-of-doors people":

> For without the will-to-do that comes from the people at large the technician's hands are tied. The amateur, as a representative of the people, is needed quite as much as the technician. He is needed not to look on, but to take part, to take his hand in planning and surveying. And if he goes astray the expert can correct. The professional should guide, but the amateur should do.[11]

Although MacKaye suggested that "some sort of general federated control" of local volunteers could be established to build the trail, he did not outline explicit plans as to how development should proceed. MacKaye's lack of detail was intentional; he wanted to first stir people's imaginations, not bore or alienate them with logistics. He believed that "people seem to be more interested in something which they do themselves than in what someone else does for them."[12] In light of this realization, MacKaye thought that the project "should grow and ripen rather than be suddenly created" by outside forces.[13] The notion that ordinary outdoors people should lead trail development efforts reflected MacKaye's desire to balance the trained professionalism of government experts with the everyday knowledge of local people. This balance and exchange of knowledge and authority lay at the heart of trail-building efforts not only during its early days in the 1920s and 1930s but throughout the course of the trail's history.

This system of entwined decentralized and centralized authority was part of MacKaye's broader political objective for the AT. For MacKaye, the project would not only promote the environmental and economic health of the country, but by promoting citizen involvement in natural resource management, it would also contribute to the political health of the nation. For MacKaye, the AT provided a place to empower American citizens and workers while at the same time exploring the possibilities of federal planning. Although MacKaye became less involved with the day-to-day development of the trail in the late 1920s and 1930s, his vision for an Appalachian Trail inspired a small group of committed citizens to complete an initial route by 1937.

Historians such as Larry Anderson, Robert Gottlieb, and Paul Sutter have begun to peel apart the many layers of MacKaye's eclectic mind and illustrious career. They have pointed out MacKaye's important—and often overlooked—ideological contribution to American environmental history, and have used his ideas to challenge conventional interpretations of the conservation movement during the Progressive Era.[14] While many historians have portrayed Progressive conservationists as being primarily interested in economic efficiency, watershed protection, wilderness, and wildlife, recent scholars have demonstrated that MacKaye and a handful of his colleagues, such as Raphael Zon and Bob Marshall, were also concerned about social justice and labor issues. Embedded in MacKaye's regional plan for an Appalachian Trail was a radical call for a reawakening of civic America; he believed that through collective engagement in nature and cooperative trail building, citizens of all sorts could work together with the state to build this important national resource. In addition to protecting the nation's natural heritage, the Appalachian Trail would be a symbol of the country's rich political capital. To understand how the Appalachian Trail unfolded in the twentieth century, we must first dive deeply into MacKaye's ideas about the political mechanisms for building the Appalachian Trail and the broader social objectives that he hoped the project would help achieve.

PRELUDE TO THE FOOTPATH

Understanding the origins of the Appalachian Trail proposal requires an examination of the political and cultural influences that shaped Benton MacKaye's thinking during the Progressive Era. As the environmental and human effects of industrial progress became evident at the turn of the twentieth century, critics of industrialization became more vocal. Preservationists and conservationists sought to protect America's forests from the plunder of large timber companies. Labor advocates campaigned to promote the health and financial security of workers. Urban reformers struggled to cope with the slumlike conditions associated with expanding urban populations. By the early 1920s, regional planners were working to mitigate the effects of agricultural depression in rural areas while urban workers began seeking places to get away from it all and reconnect with nature. Each of these movements—wilderness preservation, outdoor recreation, forest conservation, labor activism, urban reform, and regional planning—have distinct histories. Yet they were also linked in complex and unusual ways.

Underlying each of these movements was an emerging idea that the centralized government should take a stronger lead in efforts to protect the nation's resources. At the same time, this era also saw the growth of private organizations devoted to recreation and land preservation, such as the Appalachian Mountain Club in the Northeast and the Appalachian National Park Association in the South, and these organizations began to work closely with federal partners to achieve broad goals. The AT project was similar to other conservation projects undertaken during the Progressive Era in that it involved the technical expertise of federal bureaucrats, while at the same time engaging a growing number of private citizens interested in experiencing and protecting America's hinterlands. Unlike related projects, however, the AT differed in the form and degree of partnership between public and private players. From its origins, the AT project involved a range of different private groups and a variety of governmental agencies.

Perhaps the most obvious audience for MacKaye's Appalachian Trail proposal was a growing number of advocates for outdoor recreation and wilderness preservation. By the mid-nineteenth century, Americans began to view wilderness less as a frightening place that needed to be subdued and more as a place to explore nature's beauty.[15] Poets, artists, and philosophers began to seek inspiration from America's scenic landscapes, and by the 1870s, well-to-do easterners became interested in active forms of recreation—hiking and climbing mountains—instead of passively soaking in sublime scenery.[16]

Many of these early American outdoor enthusiasts were inspired, in part, by European examples. By the early nineteenth century, walking had become a pleasurable ritual for working people in England and in other European countries. The York Footpath Society was established in 1824, and in the 1930s its members had worked with the Manchester Society for the Preservation of Ancient Footpaths (established in 1826) to develop and maintain local trails in the British countryside. These early footpath preservation movements were made possible by changing economic conditions and the emergence of a working class.[17]

MacKaye and his colleagues believed that a similar movement could take place on American soil. Just as American planners had been influenced by European counterparts such as Ebenezer Howard and Patrick Geddes, MacKaye and other trail enthusiasts were inspired by English ideas about developing trail systems. In the 1860s, professor Albert Hopkins of Williams College was the first American to organize a hiking club—the Alpine

Club of Williamstown, Massachusetts—primarily for the extracurricular education of his students. In New York, botany professor John Torrey soon followed by forming the Torrey Botanical Club at Columbia University. In 1876, professor Edward C. Pickering organized a group of MIT and Harvard affiliates and established the Appalachian Mountain Club (AMC). The AMC is still active today and is the nation's oldest continuously operating mountain club. Before the twentieth century, the early mountain clubs primarily served social functions. The clubs were generally exclusive—professors of elite institutions and other powerful figures with long summer vacations were common among their ranks. Early club members tended to be more interested in socializing and walking on trails than in building them and, for the most part, paid laborers built the first recreational trails in remote areas like the Presidential Range in New Hampshire.[18]

As the demand for recreational trails increased, leaders of hiking clubs throughout New England realized that they needed to develop more extensive routes and new organizational models that would involve more people in the trail-building process. In 1910, James P. Taylor, headmaster of the Vermont Academy for Boys, suggested a new approach for building footpaths. Instead of the circuit routes developed by hired hands or the trails built on public lands by public officials, he proposed organizing a group of volunteers—the Green Mountain Club—to build a "through trail" across Vermont from the southern Massachusetts border to Canada. Known as the Long Trail, Taylor explained that the footpath would expose hikers to different kinds of local places with unique combinations of topography, vegetation, and cultural elements within the state. He played on Vermonters' sense of independence and autonomy by emphasizing that the state's citizens would control the project's destiny; the Long Trail would be something unique to Vermont—a symbol of Vermonters' self-reliance and an expression of regional identity. These ideas were echoed in MacKaye's plans for the Appalachian Trail. In fact, although he never met with Taylor, MacKaye was deeply influenced by older trail-building initiatives in New England, and by Vermont's Long Trail in particular.

The through-trail concept slowly caught on among hiking enthusiasts in New England, and momentum for building long-distance trails was fueled by the introduction of the automobile. The mass-production of the Model T Ford around 1913 allowed greater numbers of people access to the mountains. Not only did cars open up distant terrain to adventurous recreation seekers, they also allowed hiking enthusiasts to experiment with new trail geographies. Automobiles made it easier for hikers to move from point A to point B, and enabled the creation of longer linear routes, as opposed to shorter loop trails. All aspects of trail making—from scouting and planning new paths to maintaining existing pathways to simply enjoying Sunday afternoon saunters—became easier with the widespread introduction of cars to the American landscape.[19]

To coordinate trail-building efforts throughout New England, members of the Green Mountain Club, the Appalachian Mountain Club, and the Society for the Protection of New Hampshire Forests gathered on December 15, 1916, to discuss how they might begin to link up their respective trail systems. At this first meeting of the New England Trail Conference, US forester William L. Hall even suggested extending the trails of the Northeast into the Southern Appalachians. Members of the New England Trail Conference had years of trail-building experience, and it seemed to be only a matter of time before an extended Georgia-to-Maine route would be proposed.[20]

Although MacKaye was not involved in the organizational leadership of the early New England hiking clubs prior to his work on the AT, several of his closest friends and colleagues, such as James Sturgis Pray, were leaders in the hiking community. During their undergraduate years together at Harvard, MacKaye and Pray embarked on several expeditions throughout the New England countryside, and MacKaye learned much from his bearded companion. Working for the AMC in 1902, Pray had helped to create an extended network of trails through the White Mountains, and he developed a policy to delegate the responsibility for maintaining the main paths and subordinate trails. After graduation, Pray worked as a landscape architect for the Olmsted brothers and eventually returned to Harvard to teach the subject. Pray's ideas about land planning resonated with MacKaye's own philosophies. Through his personal and professional relationships with Pray and others, MacKaye was influenced by trends in trail development and by the broader land conservation initiatives of the New England mountain clubs.

As citizen conservationists gained greater access to free time and money during the Progressive Era, organized groups such as the AMC became powerful players in conservation politics in both the public and private arenas. In the Northeast, the AMC helped to launch the first land trust in the United States—the Trustees of Reservations—in 1891. The trustees' founder, Charles Eliot, partner of Frederick Law Olmsted's landscape

Hikers at Pinkham Notch Camp, 1920. The nation's first hiking clubs began in the Northeast in the late nineteenth and early twentieth centuries, when outdoor enthusiasts—like those pictured here at Pinkham Notch Camp—flocked to the northern Appalachian Mountains in search of adventure and recuperation from urban industrial life. Courtesy of the Appalachian Trail Conservancy.

architecture firm and son of the famous Harvard president, correctly predicted that influential preservation-minded members of the AMC would help the young land trust gain the capital it needed to start purchasing land for protection.[21] In Maine, Eliot's father, Charles W. Eliot, worked with wealthy preservationists to purchase land on Mount Desert Island. The land they bought served as the nucleus of what would become Acadia National Park in 1919—the nation's first national park in the East.[22]

In the Southern Appalachians, a movement to preserve land and create national parks was also stirring. In 1899, a group of local business leaders met in Asheville, North Carolina, to form the Appalachian National Park Association. The purpose of the organization was to advocate for national parks and forest reserves in the Southern Appalachian Mountains, and its efforts resulted in Congress allocating five thousand dollars for an initial investigation of forest conditions in the region.[23] When Congress passed the Weeks Act in 1911 and conservationists gained the legal authority to create national forests in the East, this research proved to be invaluable for the thirty-five forest examiners responsible for acquiring land for the new eastern national forests.[24] By 1916, the federal government had acquired enough land to establish the first federal forest reserve in the East—the Pisgah National Forest. In 1918, Congress established the Shenandoah (now part of George Washington), Natural Bridge, and White Mountain National Forests, followed by the Boone, Nantahala, Cherokee, Unaka, and Monongahela National Forests in 1920.

In addition to advocating for national forest reserves in the Southern Appalachians, members of the Appalachian National Park Association also worked with state and federal officials to establish national parks in the region. In 1925, Congress authorized the secretary of the Interior to begin an investigation to determine the boundaries of what would become the Great Smoky Mountains and Shenandoah National Parks in the 1930s—a process that will be discussed in greater detail in chapter two. These federal initiatives were, in part, motivated by a growing interest in forest-based recreation in the East and by the ability of powerful citizens' groups to influence national conservation policies.

Like other leaders within the emerging conservation movement, MacKaye was particularly effective because of his connections with influential private groups as well as his professional positions within the federal government. MacKaye was among the first class to graduate from Harvard with a degree in forestry, and after graduation, he went to work for the US Forest Service in 1908. US forest chief Gifford Pinchot and his enthusiastic cadre of young foresters such as MacKaye believed that the application of scientific forestry and the power of government experts could be used to ensure a sustainable yield of timber and protection from flooding and erosion.[25] Yet MacKaye developed a view of forest management that aimed not only at natural resource protection and economic efficiency but also at social well-being. Historian Paul Sutter explains that MacKaye "was after a brand of social efficiency tied to equity, not business efficiency and profit maximization, and local control was always his goal."[26] MacKaye routinely expressed concern about woods workers and frequently criticized the forestry profession for not addressing the social aspects of the industry. He felt that the profession lacked compassion for "the lumberjack and the very human problems that go along with him," and he argued that if foresters wanted to

Cutover Land in Wisconsin. MacKaye's work with the US Forest Service and later the Department of Labor brought him to rural communities across the country, including the cut-over forest in northern Wisconsin. There, he saw the effects that logging in the late nineteenth and early twentieth centuries had on rural land and people. Courtesy of the Wisconsin Historical Society.

promote the physical integrity of the forest and maintain a sustainable yield of timber, they must also consider the needs of the workers who provided that supply.[27]

In his work with the US Forest Service, MacKaye observed the connection between the exploitation of land and labor. While surveying the cutover lands of northern Wisconsin and Minnesota in 1914, MacKaye witnessed the legacy of commercial lumber operations that had transformed the northern forest landscape into a sea of stumps. Large land-owning timber companies had moved on, taking with them a transitory labor force and leaving a few rural families to farm a relatively inhospitable area.[28] In November 1916, MacKaye went to work in the Snoqualmie National Forest in Washington. While he was surveying forest conditions near the mill town of Everett on the Pacific Coast, members of the International Workers of the World (IWW) arrived from Seattle to assist local mill workers in their demands for fair wages. The owners of Everett's mills controlled regional politics and were quick to squelch worker uprisings. When the union organizers attempted

WORKERS REMEMBER YOUR DEAD!

In Memory of

Felix Baran
Hugo Gerlot
Gus Johnson
John Looney
Abe Rabinowitz

Murdered by the Master Class in Everett Wash. on
Sunday Nov. 5th 1916
They died fighting for Free Speech. They Gave up--
their lives in the struggle of our Class for Freedom.

They are dead
BUT THEIR DEEDS LIVE ON!

Poster following Everett Massacre, 1917. Just a day before MacKaye arrived in the mill town of Everett, Washington, during a survey of forest conditions in 1916, a bloody shoot-out ensued between members of the International Workers of the World and Pinkertons who had been hired to squelch the labor uprising. MacKaye's visit reinforced his belief that good forestry meant protecting not only trees and soils but also the people who worked in the woods and mills. Courtesy of the Everett Public Library.

to dock their boat, a wild shootout between gunslingers on the boat and on the dock ensued, and several men were killed. MacKaye arrived on the scene a day after the incident, and was shocked to witness the extent to which labor conflicts had escalated. He believed that such events would continue if those in public office failed to take into account the interests of America's workers.[29]

To avoid bloody labor uprisings and land speculation by large profit-motivated timber companies, MacKaye proposed that the federal government should work in cooperation with workers. Although he believed that workers should have a say in management decisions, he argued that it was the federal government's responsibility to make sure that "local *public* interests, rather than local private interests," were served.[30] MacKaye had become all too aware of the consequences of neglecting labor interests, and urged government experts to understand and incorporate the ideas of "everyday folk" in their planning decisions.

MacKaye was transferred from the US Forest Service to the Department of Labor in 1918, and in the following year, he published one of the most substantial works of his career—*Employment and Natural Resources*. In it, MacKaye wrestled with two fundamental questions: Could the technical expertise and political authority of the federal government be balanced with the empowerment and democratic participation of local communities? How could planners effectively design programs that would combine civic engagement and federal leadership to promote the long-term stewardship of the nation's resources?[31]

On one hand, MacKaye understood the power of federal leadership to coordinate interregional projects. The federal government had access to the nation's most competent, scientifically trained engineers and technicians. MacKaye believed that decisions affecting the public welfare should be based on rational, scientific study. This would protect the public from the power of profit-driven special interests. Giving sole power to local or state governments would lead to myopic decisions and the squandering of the nation's resources. Because "natural resources are national resources," he argued, "what happens to the soils, the forests, the ores, or the water powers in any one State affects the people of the entire Nation."[32] MacKaye also argued that the federal government was generally more effective at raising "clean" money—funds that were able to promote the local public good and not the interests of a handful of powerful local industrialists. After witnessing how local mill-owning authorities in Everett had hired Pinkertons to suppress the labor revolt, MacKaye had grown concerned about what he viewed as the corruption of local politics by small groups of wealthy capitalists. He felt that the federal government was in a much better position than states or local groups to ensure economic justice and democratic decision making.

On the other hand, however, MacKaye also acknowledged the danger of giving sole authority to a single federal agency. He was concerned that agencies might become absorbed in the "arbitrary power and inefficiency which we call 'bureaucracy'" and could become unresponsive to the genuine needs of local communities as a result.[33] He also pointed out that bureaucracy was not limited to the federal government and that state and local governments, as well as private corporations, were just as likely to prioritize their own needs over local communities' needs.

The best way to manage the nation's natural and cultural wealth was not the complete decentralization of all aspects of the federal government but a system of cooperation between different levels of government and between private citizens and state agents. As MacKaye wrote in *Employment and Natural Resources*, "Cooperation, coupled with constructive criticism both from within and from outside the Government, marks a definite line along which we can work to reduce, and finally abolish . . . bureaucracy."[34] For MacKaye, the Appalachian Trail would be a physical manifestation of this line. In its ideal form, the AT was a path not only through the mountain wilderness but also through the wilderness of political decision making. The proposal reflected MacKaye's belief that a strong federal government depended on strong autonomous local communities and that, in turn, local communities required federal protection from would-be exploiters. MacKaye, at his core, was simultaneously a committed patriot, an outspoken regionalist, and a promoter of local "indigenous communities."[35]

Given MacKaye's ultimate goal for the AT project—environmental protection and social and economic reform through comprehensive regional planning—it is not surprising that the initial proposal was published by the American Institute of Architects in 1921 and supported by the Regional Planning Association of America. The Regional Planning Association of America began as a handful of like-minded architects, planners, economists, and writers, including several of MacKaye's closest friends and colleagues—Clarence Stein, Charles Whitaker, Stuart Chase, and Lewis Mumford. The association's founding members each believed that their field would play an important role in addressing contemporary social issues, including the sprawl of cities, the decline of rural communities, and the growing economic disparity between rich and poor. The Appalachian Trail was one of the group's first tangible projects and provided a particular context through which to start defining the common dreams and agendas of the nation's first regional planners.[36]

Before publishing his proposal for an Appalachian Trail, MacKaye worked with his regional planning colleagues to refine the radical residue of earlier drafts. MacKaye realized that some of his broader objectives—the redistribution of population and power—might be too revolutionary for one of his primary audiences: upper-middle class hiking enthusiasts who tended to benefit from the very forces of industrialization that MacKaye was trying to reform.[37] In an essay that preceded the AT proposal entitled "Regional Planning and Social Readjustment," MacKaye outlined three potential plans for projects along the Appalachian spine. In the first plan—Plan A— the government would establish communities devoted to producing timber, raising stock, growing wheat, or manufacturing textiles or metals. These industries would be carefully planned and regulated by the federal government. MacKaye imagined that labor and other "advanced liberal" groups would support this plan. He speculated that "middle-ground people would be acquiescent. The ultra-conservatives would be hostile. If they did not call it 'visionary' they would say it was 'bolshevistic' and 'dangerous.'"[38]

MacKaye toned down the overt socialist ideas embodied in Plan A by proposing a second plan for community development in the Appalachian range. Plan B involved the creation of a series of "nonindustrial communities" or recreational camps connected by a mountain trail to be built by private and public agents. On the surface, these community camps appeared to be free from a radical social agenda. Yet because hikers and campers would require food and shelter on their sojourns, MacKaye believed that small, distributed markets would eventually be established. Creating the recreational aspect of the project would essentially lay the foundation for the planned natural resource development that would come later.

MacKaye understood that Plan A and Plan B would probably appeal to two separate groups: radical reformers and urban recreationists. To achieve the greatest amount of political support for the project, he proposed a third plan: Plan C. As a hybrid of Plans A and B, Plan C consisted of a series of industrial communities as well as a series of nonindustrial communities. Both types of communities would be linked by a main recreational trail stretching from Georgia to Maine and networks of local paths at various points along the route. The government would help coordinate the project, but private volunteers would play a central role. MacKaye suggested that a popular title for this plan might be "The Appalachian Trail: A Project for Developing a New Type of Community."

Although members of the Regional Planning Association eagerly endorsed the project, MacKaye was concerned that other "red friends" may consider the project to be irrelevant, indulgent, and potentially superfluous. He recognized that on its surface, the idea to link concerns about labor and natural resource conservation through a system of recreational trails seemed somewhat far-fetched. Yet MacKaye emphasized that one of the primary purposes of the Appalachian Trail was to help establish connections between disparate groups. The construction of this national trail would help to build relationships between technicians and amateurs, laborers and professionals, conservatives and liberals, rural people and urban dwellers, citizens and state agencies. The political infrastructure and social capital developed during the initial recreational, nonindustrial phase of the project would eventually shift to address other pressing social and economic issues. The project would help develop "popular understanding of—and interest in—fundamental (and in this sense radical) solutions of industrial questions."[39] These "industrial questions" involved issues about injustices in the workforce, a failing agricultural economy, mismanaged forests, and a massive redistribution of the American population from rural areas to overcrowded cities.

Furthermore, MacKaye believed that establishing these cooperative relationships would also provide a partial answer to the fundamental question of whether or not the power of federal authority and technical expertise could be reconciled with the local needs of American citizens and workers. He believed that "for every technical 'head' there must be a 'body' of amateurs if we are in truth to be a social organism."[40] By having different segments of society work together on a common goal—a seemingly simple and straightforward recreational path—MacKaye hoped to inspire civic engagement in conservation politics, rural revitalization, and a widespread environmental awakening.

A PROGRESSIVE PATH

MacKaye's desire to transform an increasingly profit-motivated capitalist society into a series of small-scale egalitarian farm and forest communities never materialized exactly as he had planned. Yet his vision for the Appalachian Trail helped to establish an important political model for grassroots environmental action that relied on citizen involvement and support from federal experts. The model, in practice, was fraught with idiosyncrasies, paradoxes, and surprises that this book explores in later chapters.

For MacKaye, the political structure of the project was central to the

Appalachian Trail's ultimate mission to protect human welfare and physical landscapes. For better or for worse, the project brought together different segments of society to work toward a common goal. It provided a new avenue for involving citizens in natural resource decision making, and demonstrated the power of local knowledge in those decisions. This was as much a part of MacKaye's ultimate aim for the project as was his desire to protect the physical environment or promote a social revolution, though, presumably, he was in favor of all three. For MacKaye, the project was as much about the conservation of a particular *political* nature as it was about the conservation of *physical* or *social* nature.

MacKaye also believed that achieving these conservation goals would require balancing the power and tools of the central state with the decentralized needs and knowledge of private citizens. To work toward this objective, MacKaye relied on his background as a professional forester, but he also emphasized his appreciation and knowledge of the material conditions of rural communities. Sociologist Charles V. Willie calls historical figures like Benton MacKaye "marginal" characters—individuals whose identities exist on the margins of different, overlapping social roles.[41] Willie argues that in pluralistic societies, it is often marginal figures that are most successful in sparking social change. This theory provides some grounds for understanding why the Appalachian Trail proposal gained traction in the 1920s. Because of the diversity of hats that Benton MacKaye wore throughout his lifetime—from hiking enthusiast to forester to labor advocate to regional planner to creative, unemployed writer living off of the hospitality of friends—MacKaye was able to reach a broad national audience. He seemed equally at ease chatting on the front porch of a logger's cabin as he was writing essays for national audiences, and he called on both to help create this new American landscape.

MacKaye wanted the AT to empower local communities through greater involvement in local land management decisions. Using local volunteers to build this national trail—what he often referred to as a new "empire"— would give Americans a deeper appreciation of the physical environment and make them better citizens. For MacKaye, an outspoken pacifist, "care of the country" was the most literal and powerful form of patriotism.[42] The Appalachian Trail was to be a national symbol of Americans' commitment to their homeland. MacKaye argued that building this symbolic link could not be left solely to the government experts. He wrote, "You cannot hire someone to build a new world for you. The actual doing of this job would constitute in itself a new kind of life."[43] The following chapters explore how attempts to create this "new kind of life" played out, and examine the tensions and challenges associated with building social utopia in the American wilderness. By examining the initial seed from which the tangled roots of the trail emerged—the idea for an Appalachian Trail that coalesced in MacKaye's mind as he sat in a treetop on Stratton Mountain—we gain a deeper understanding of how Progressive politics shaped the relationship between private citizens and federal bureaucracies involved in large-scale conservation projects in the early twentieth century. This seed would begin to blossom through the eager efforts of trail advocates and the broad federal initiatives of the New Deal Era—though not exactly in the ways that MacKaye had envisioned.

CHAPTER 2

THE PATH OF LEAST RESISTANCE

AS NORTHBOUND APPALACHIAN TRAIL HIKERS CROSS THE FONTANA
Dam, passing by Fontana Lake before entering the Great Smoky Mountains National Park, they walk over the drowned remains of several forest
towns—Fontana, Bushnell, Japan, Forney, Judson, Almond. To provide
electricity and resources for war efforts in the early 1940s, and to make a
new national park in the 1930s, federal agents destroyed these communities
and erased evidence of human habitation. By 1943, Proctor, one of the main
settlements in the area, had been reduced to derelict heaps of rotting lumber
destined to be burned by federal officials. One local resident recalled "standing on the graveyard hill in Possum Hollow and watching the Franklin store
and warehouse being put to the torch by the TVA. We children found this
very exciting, not realizing that a town and a way of life were dying."[1]

The torched Franklin store was owned by the great-grandparents of our
closest trail companion, Michael "5-String" Hawkins. Hawkins's grandparents grew up and courted along Hazel Creek—one of the tributaries on
the north side of Fontana Lake that was cut off when the Tennessee Valley
Authority (TVA) created Fontana Dam and Fontana Lake. As we walked
parts of the AT together on our respective through-hikes in 2007, first in the
barely budding forests of North Carolina, and then catching up again in the
height of summer in Maine, Hawkins explained how different members of
his grandparents' community reacted to the government's well-intentioned
efforts to build the massive dam in order to bring power to the people of
the Great Smoky Mountains and recreational opportunities to members of
an increasingly industrialized, urban-based society. Some families eagerly
accepted the government's offers to purchase their land, while others
resisted and fought bitterly to protect their access and rights to land.

Fontana Dam. As AT hikers cross the Fontana Dam, they travel over the submerged remains of several forest communities. In the 1930s and 1940s, the Tennessee Valley Authority and the National Park Service removed mountain residents in order to bring electrical power and recreational opportunities to the American public. These broad federal actions sometimes made local residents wary of early trail-building efforts, even though the first generation of AT volunteers had no official authority. Courtesy of the Appalachian Trail Conservancy.

The Fontana Dam and other TVA projects in the region were part of a broader federal response to the severe economic challenges facing rural communities in the 1920s and in the 1930s, when the Great Depression exacerbated hard times in America's hinterlands—particularly in the Southern Appalachians. In both northern and southern parts of the Appalachian Mountains, the government had been working with citizen partners to create public forest and recreation areas for several decades, and the large-scale plans for land reform embodied in president Franklin Roosevelt's New Deal programs built upon these earlier conservation efforts. Increasing pressures on thin mountain soils and a stagnant agricultural economy made many rural families receptive to large-scale land reforms in the early twentieth century. When government planners came to purchase land for new national forests, parks, and dam projects, many welcomed the economic relief and the opportunity to start anew. At the same time, however, many people resisted the government's efforts and expressed their desire to maintain local autonomy and self-determination. Mountain residents were often wary of the autocratic approach that federal planners often used to achieve grand plans for social reform in the Appalachians and of the low prices the government offered in exchange for their family homesteads.[2]

The stories that took shape in the late 1920s and 1930s about how federal land managers and their ambitious projects affected rural communities have had a long-lasting effect on people's relationship with the federal government, and, by extension, with the Appalachian Trail. The early development of the AT unfolded alongside the movement to bring federal dams and national parks to the eastern hinterlands. In some ways, early construction of the trail mirrored these broader federal initiatives. As volunteers associated with the Appalachian Trail Conference (ATC) began working to establish a thin footpath across the Appalachian Mountains, federal officials were also out in the woods surveying conditions for national parks and planning for large-scale land reforms that would blossom through Roosevelt's New Deal programs. Like federal projects at that time, the AT also involved private associations working in partnership with state and federal officials, and it relied on a growing national demand for outdoor recreation, conservation, and wilderness protection.

Yet in several important ways, the initial development of the AT differed from national park and federal planning projects during this era. The AT did not become part of the national park system until 1968, when Congress passed the National Trails Act. Because the project lacked official backing from the federal government, proponents of the AT had to rely on oral "handshake" agreements with rural landowners to establish the footpath that would run from Georgia to Maine. Unlike TVA projects and the construction of Shenandoah and Great Smoky Mountains National Parks, the AT did not require the removal of residents or dramatic changes in land use. Also, through the ATC, the nonprofit, volunteer-based organization that was responsible for developing and managing the trail, trail advocates sought to create a nested system of correspondence and control that was grounded at the local level while also promoting a broader national agenda.[3]

In a sense, the organization of the ATC was an experiment in voluntary federalism. Instead of official sanctions and laws, however, local affiliated clubs would be bound by informal agreements and shared goals. The project's center of authority would be distributed through a nested system of control that would involve multiple levels of "local" involvement, including urban volunteers from towns and cities near the trail as well as rural residents who lived in the Appalachian Mountains. Although volunteers would work with state and federal officials in expanding public jurisdictions, private citizens would be the primary drivers of trail development. Advocates hoped that this decentralized organizational structure would encourage ties with local communities and establish regional networks that would be linked to create a trail that spanned an entire nation.[4]

The story of the AT during the late 1920s and the 1930s builds on recent histories of national conservation efforts that preceded and unfolded during the New Deal Era, and offers a complex view of relationships between citizens and the state.[5] This chapter loosely follows the chronological development of the trail and explores the dynamics between rural people and largely urban-based outdoor enthusiasts in different regions along the spine of the Appalachians—from the first official white blaze of the AT in the mid-Atlantic area to the Southern Appalachians, particularly in and near the Great Smoky Mountains National Park in North Carolina and Tennessee, and the Shenandoah National Park in Virginia—and ending in northern New England, where the Civilian Conservation Corps (CCC) blazed the final swath of trail in Maine in 1937. An exploration of the development of the Appalachian Trail in the 1920s and 1930s—a period known for the expansion of government authority and the centralization of power—reveals a blurry boundary between public and private conservation efforts. It also demonstrates how different levels of local involvement—from trail-building volunteers in the scattered towns and cities of the East to residents of the Appalachian hills and hollows—helped to shape conservation politics during this formative era of environmental policy.

In 1922, advocates blazed the first six-mile section of the Appalachian Trail between the Ramapo River and Fingerboard Mountain in New York. Like several other areas along the initial 2,050-mile route, trail-building efforts often occurred in conjunction with the development of public parks and forests. As public land managers in the East struggled to cope with new responsibilities associated with expanding jurisdictions, they welcomed volunteer labor to help build recreational trails. For example, when Mary Harriman donated ten thousand acres to the Palisades Interstate Park to help establish the Bear Mountain and Harriman State Parks in New York, the jurisdiction of the Palisades Interstate Park Commission dramatically increased. At that time, the area was not the picturesque hillside that hikers see today. It was heavily quarried, burnt over, and hunted to the near extirpation of several wildlife species. When Major William Welch became manager of the Interstate Park Commission in 1912, the need to first restore the area to a condition that would attract visitors overrode Welch's desire to build recreational trails, and he encouraged the growing number of outdoor enthusiasts to assist with the creation and maintenance of trails.

By the early 1920s, there were at least seventy-five different hiking organizations in the New York metropolitan area.[6] In addition to New York chapters of the Adirondack, Green Mountain, and Appalachian Mountain Clubs, the area hosted a wide array of hiking and outdoor clubs with a variety of agendas and affiliations. There was a group of working-class Germans who called themselves Naturfreunde and "practiced a mild form of Socialism."[7] In the Bronx, the Young Men's Hebrew Association started its own hiking club for Jewish members. In Greenwich Village, a communist hiking club called the All-Tramp Soviet formed.[8] The increasing number and diversity of trail clubs in the 1920s and 1930s reflected a growing public interest in hiking and trail building in the New York–New Jersey area.[9]

Outdoor enthusiasts in the New York metropolitan area learned about trail-building opportunities and followed conservation-related issues in Raymond Torrey's column the "Long Brown Path," which was published every week in the *New York Post*. Through his column and leadership in the field, Torrey played a key role in organizing volunteer trail-building

2.2 Women's Hiking Club at Palisades Interstate Park. Women played an important role in the early trail clubs. Here, an all-women's hiking club takes a break at a shelter in the Palisades Interstate Park. Courtesy of the Appalachian Trail Conservancy.

activities in the New York–New Jersey area.[10] In 1920, he worked with Major Welch to form the Palisades Interstate Park Trail Conference. The name of the organization was changed to the New York–New Jersey Trail Conference in 1922 as enthusiastic volunteers began working to incorporate their "scattered and local" trails into a network that would extend beyond the boundaries of the interstate park.[11] To build trails outside of the park, volunteers reached beyond their comfortable partnerships with state agents to solicit cooperation from private landowners—a task that proved to be more challenging than building trails within the boundaries of public parks and forests.[12]

On private property, volunteers had to find titles to land and get consent from owners. Once marked, the trail's security depended on the good reputation of hikers; a shift in landowners' attitudes toward them could mean the end of a particular section. Although several landowners refused permission to use their land during the 1920s and 1930s, more often than not, they supported the project and allowed hikers to walk across their property. Volunteers developed and maintained the trust of landowners through informal face-to-face interactions and the use of handshake agreements. As hiking historians Laura Waterman and Guy Waterman wrote, "The AT maintainer had to be one-third trail worker, one-third organizer of other trail workers, but three-fourths diplomat among the landowners."[13]

Because advocates initially had no legal backing to establish trails, shelters, or camps, early developments were established only where diplomacy was successful. One example that typified the careful relationships that early trailblazers cultivated with rural residents involved a volunteer named Joseph Bartha who worked with a property owner near Mombasha High Point. The trail crossed Franz Kloiber's farm, and the owner occasionally offered lodging and meals to hikers. Kloiber's cattle had been getting loose, so he had strung double barbed wire around his property. Despite his efforts to contain the animals, both the cows and the barbed wire created trouble for hikers. When Bartha tried to explain the need to relocate the trail to a different part of his property, Kloiber just smiled and said, "Why, this is all on my property; you need not do any re-locating and just do what I tell you to do." In response, Bartha did the only thing he could do: "I listened."[14]

Instead of banishing hikers who presumably enabled the bovine exodus, Kloiber suggested that Bartha build steps over the wire using stones from a nearby wall. He also requested that hikers not tamper with his gates, fences, or ornery cattle. Bartha complied and posted signs along the trail that read: "By courtesy of Mr. F. Kloiber." Such signage was a common way of displaying gratitude during the early years of trail building. After he made the improvements, Bartha asked Torrey to write a notice in his weekly column in the *Post* requesting that hikers take special care in the area. He emphasized that "in doing so we may remain in his esteem and he will never have a cause to cancel his permit."[15] During the initial phase of AT construction, these "permits" were simply informal verbal agreements between volunteers and landowners, and they could be revoked at any time.

This example was typical of trail development in the late 1920s and 1930s, and provides insight into why oral agreements with landowners were generally successful during the trail's early stages. First, Bartha realized that the section ultimately relied on Kloiber's willingness to have it cross his property. Then Bartha did one very important thing to maintain Kloiber's trust and support—he listened. This allowed Kloiber to set the terms of the arrangement. Bartha abided by the landowner's terms and modified the trail to respect existing land uses. Finally, Bartha sought means to publicize the good-natured and kind cooperation of the landowner. Public displays of positive relationships with landowners helped to cultivate a sense of shared interest in the project. Advocates hoped that this public recognition would have a snowball effect: when other landowners witnessed successful precedents, they would be inspired to commit their property to the common good and allow hikers to cross their land. These strategies were generally effective during the early stages of trail development.

Not all landowners in the Palisades Interstate Park area lived on their rural properties, however. Many properties were owned by wealthy absentee landowners and natural resource companies. For example, the Harriman family owned large acreages near the Palisades Interstate Park, and the Vanderbilt-Webb family owned a large estate in Putnam County, New York. Both families had several other homes where they spent most of their time, so as long as hikers behaved themselves, the landowners generally did not protest the creation of trails on their property.[16] Industrial landowners were also usually willing to let hikers walk on their property. Along the Wawayanda Plateau west of Greenwood Lake, the New Jersey Zinc Company gave volunteers permission to mark the trail. On Pochuck Mountain, Raymond Torrey obtained permission from the Standard Oil Company to run the trail through a swath of land that had been cleared for a pipeline.

Sometimes determining who owned or used a particular property proved difficult. On vast properties that were seemingly unoccupied, Torrey encouraged volunteers to "go ahead and make the trail without asking, for the owners would never see it."[17] Arthur Perkins, a trail enthusiast and judge from Connecticut who served as the second chairman of the Appalachian Trail Conference, made similar suggestions. Perkins emphasized that while it was "desirable" to get permission from the landowner, if the trail was so remote and far away from dwellings that no one would even notice, he suggested that volunteers simply mark the path.[18] Because absentee owners controlled many remote parts of the trail and those areas received fewer visitors, early trail-building efforts in isolated areas generally went uncontested. For the most part, though, the early trailblazers sought—and secured—permission from private landowners in the New York–New Jersey area and throughout New England.

To expand AT development from its relatively well-established home in the northern Appalachian Mountains to the southern states, Major William Welch called for a "federation of trail making agencies all along the Atlantic Coast."[19] On March 2, 1925, a handful of trail enthusiasts from cities throughout the Atlantic seaboard gathered at the Hotel Raleigh in Washington, DC, to discuss the future of the Appalachian Trail. Participants at this first Appalachian Trail Conference (ATC) agreed that trail-building efforts should be organized as a "true federation and not a 'combine'—a pooling of common interests and not a compromise of conflicting interests."[20] As a result of a lack of funding, existing commitments on the part of individual members, and the great distances between sections of trail to be built, enthusiasm for expanding the trail waned in the three years following the first ATC meeting in 1925.[21] According to an ATC report in later years, the project was "practically moribund" until the ATC had its second meeting in 1928 and Judge Arthur Perkins was appointed as a key New England representative.[22]

As a leader of the Connecticut chapter of the AMC and member of the New England Trail Conference's executive committee, Perkins had scouted and marked the entire stretch of the Appalachian Trail through his home state during the summer of 1926. He was deeply committed to extending the work of the northern clubs to southern regions, and was more aggressive than previous leaders in his attempts to do so.

Despite Perkins's leadership and enthusiasm, the campaign to blaze the AT through the southern Appalachians presented a new set of political and cultural challenges for northern advocates. The relatively congenial relationships between trail advocates and landowners that developed in the northern states occurred in a much different political and economic context than in their southern counterparts. As explained in chapter one, several large and powerful mountain clubs in the Northeast had already established trails in remote places like the White Mountains where few people lived. Throughout New England and the mid-Atlantic region, private organizations and local governments had been actively involved in conservation politics. The Northeast also had a relatively strong economic foundation based on urban industries rather than rural resource extraction. At the same time, in the 1930s, the Southern Appalachian Mountains provided testing grounds for the power of centralized solutions to problems associated with rural development. Although communities in the Northern Appalachians were also affected by federal land reforms during this era, the government's experiments with large-scale planning initiatives especially affected rural resource-dependent communities in the Southern Appalachian Mountains. Understanding the movement to bring the Appalachian Trail through the southern states—and how different people and communities responded to this initiative—requires a deeper examination of the broader land reforms and large-scale recreation and regional planning projects in the late 1920s and 1930s.

BLAZING TRAIL THROUGH THE SOUTHERN APPALACHIANS

Unlike the rapid industrialization and urbanization that occurred in the Northeast in the early twentieth century, many parts of the South remained tied to a rural, agriculturally based economy. The agricultural depression of the 1920s that had devastated farm communities across the country hit this agricultural region particularly hard. Farm foreclosures reached unprecedented rates as inflated expectations of post–World War I prosperity led to overproduction. Falling prices on crops like corn, unanticipated changes in mortgage rates in rural places, increases in taxes, diminished power in an expanding global market, and severe drought in the early 1930s exacerbated the century-long trend of farm consolidation in the southern valleys and across the nation. As farmers sold their land to pay the bills, the average farm size grew and rural populations declined. Many who left the farm seeking job opportunities in the city in the 1920s returned home in the 1930s when the Great Depression extinguished their dreams of finding urban employment. Back home, they continued to face a suite of economic challenges.[23]

These trends affected rural communities in the South in different ways. The rural South is a diverse region, and the demographic patterns and economic context of the Appalachian lowlands differed from the conditions facing communities at higher elevations. Rural settlements in the highlands of the Appalachian Mountains were especially isolated from markets, and, unlike their lowland counterparts, many families in the Southern Appalachians remained self-sufficient until the 1930s. According to a 1930 census, a third of the United States' total population of self-sufficient farmers called the Appalachian Mountains home. As populations in the mountains grew during the early part of the twentieth century, farm sizes decreased as new generations plunged deeper into the hollows. Unlike the pattern of farm consolidation in the southern lowlands and across the nation, the average farm size in the mountains decreased from 187 acres in 1880 to 86 acres in

1930.[24] Despite the differences between the lowlands and the highlands, however, poverty in the southern Appalachian region was widespread. Some areas, such as the Tennessee Valley, had the lowest per capita income levels in the country.[25]

As northern trail advocates began to plot strategies to bring the Appalachian Trail to the southern states, federal land managers were working out large-scale plans for economic reform in the Southern Appalachian Mountains. As a result, the context in which the movement to bring the AT to the South unfolded was one that was increasingly controlled by state and federal power. Although the AT did not initially develop under the auspices of a federal agency, nor did it require the dispossession of land or dramatic changes in land use, the project reflected a growing national interest in the management of rural resources and the ability of private conservation groups to partner with public authorities on large-scale land projects. At the same time, the path depended on the willingness of rural inhabitants to allow urban hikers to tramp across their property. Northern trail advocates also had to recruit volunteers from the towns and cities near the Appalachian spine to help build and maintain the trail once it was completed. Trail-building efforts required multiple levels of local involvement—from southern towns to the remote highlands—in addition to emerging partnerships with public officials.

In some ways, cultivating local interest in the AT project proved to be more difficult in the South than it had been in the North. By 1927, members of the northern trail clubs had mostly blazed the trail down to Harpers Ferry, West Virginia. Outside of the Smoky Mountains, however, most of the southern states lacked a history and tradition of volunteer trail building. Northern hiking enthusiasts felt that the biggest problem facing AT development in the region was that southern "out-of-doors people" were simply "not trail conscious."[26] Newspapers in southern communities, such as the *Asheville Times*, the *Gainesville Eagle*, and the *Lynchburg News*, reported that local residents were "ignorant" of the recreational opportunities in their backyards.[27] Before their work in the Blue Ridge Mountains, many northern trailblazers believed that the area was "as little used as the White Mountains when in 1819 Abol Crawford cut the first path to Mt. Washington."[28] For northern hikers who were eager to open up the mountain wilderness to the nature-starved masses, the South was the new frontier.[29]

To explore the possibilities of extending the trail into Virginia and West Virginia, Myron Avery, Homer Corson, J. Frank Schairer, and H.

Avery and crew on Katahdin. Myron Avery (top right), never without his trail-measuring wheel, leads a group of trail workers up Katahdin. Avery served as the tireless leader of the ATC from 1931 until 1954. Courtesy of the Appalachian Trail Conservancy.

C. Anderson began scouting routes in the Shenandoah Mountains and north to Harpers Ferry in 1927. Along with two others, the men formed the Potomac Appalachian Trail Club (PATC)—the club that would lead efforts to bring the trail through much of the South.[30] The group, based in Washington, DC, was organized and led by Myron Avery, a young lawyer who had worked in a law office in Connecticut with Judge Perkins. If Benton MacKaye was the conceptual father of the Appalachian Trail, Myron Avery was the trail's physical father. No single individual in the history of the AT did more actual construction and promotion of the trail than Avery. Like MacKaye, Avery was originally from New England; Maine was his home state. Also like MacKaye, Avery worked for the federal government—the US Maritime Commission, where he specialized in admiralty law. Avery served in two world wars as a naval officer, and he brought his passion, attention to detail, and impressive work ethic to lead early trail-building efforts. As president of the Potomac Appalachian Trail Club for thirteen years and as chairman of the ATC for twenty-one years—from 1931 until his death in 1952—Avery led an aggressive campaign to spark southern interest in the AT project.

Avery's approach to trail development was first to build the trail and then extensively promote it to local and national audiences. He believed that once the trail was on the ground, public interest would sprout.[31] Avery worked with Judge Perkins to actively recruit interest in the trail from members of existing influential organizations—such as chambers of commerce or service organizations—that could help champion the cause. For example, in 1930, six members of the Potomac Appalachian Trail Club planned a public meeting with several members of the Lynchburg Lions in Lynchburg, Virginia. The Lions' secretary, Fred Davis, encouraged fellow members and friends to come to the meeting to hear "well-known government scientists and naturalists" talk about the Appalachian Trail project.[32]

Shortly after this meeting, the Lynchburg Lions sponsored the formation of a new AT club—the Natural Bridge Appalachian Trail Club. The group became responsible for trail development from Rockfish Gap, across the Peaks of Otter, and down through southwestern Virginia.[33] In total, the new club was responsible for approximately three hundred miles of trail in Virginia in what Avery called the "terra incognita" of the AT project.[34] Like other clubs that worked under the then-rickety umbrella of the ATC, the Natural Bridge Appalachian Trail Club was an autonomous group. Yet members were deeply influenced by the Potomac Appalachian Trail Club. When the Natural Bridge Club formed, members decided to simply adopt the Potomac group's constitution and bylaws, and they worked closely with members of the PATC to develop the trail in Virginia.[35] In this way, trail leaders based in Washington, DC, were able to tap the leadership and influence of a powerful local organization—the Lynchburg Lions. Using their status as outsiders from Washington and their demonstrated expertise in building the trail, members of the PATC developed networks of new recruits who were often eager to learn about existing trail-building procedures and protocol.

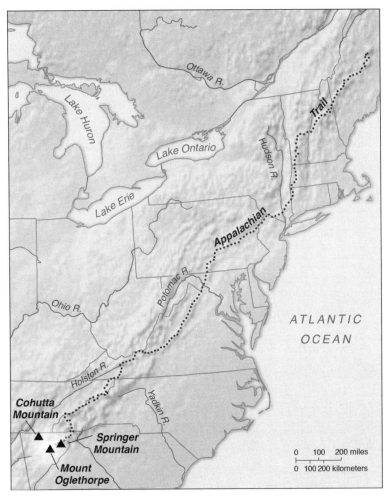

Map 2 Map of Contested Area in the Southern Appalachians.
In planning the original route of the AT, different groups had conflicting
ideas about where the southern terminus should be. The Smoky Mountain Hiking Club wanted it to be on top of Cohutta Mountain, in Georgia
but close to the Tennessee state line. The Potomac Appalachian Trail
Club and ATC wanted the AT to end on Mount Oglethorpe, which lay
deeper in Georgia. The original southern terminus was eventually blazed
on Mount Oglethorpe, but when private development began to encroach
on the trail after World War II, the southern terminus was moved to
Springer Mountain, which lay safely in the Chattahoochee National
Forest.

It is important to note, however, that while the PATC was trying to establish a decentralized system of local control, trail development in the 1920s and 1930s was not the perfect picture of social justice and equality. One needs only to consider the constituency of the Lynchburg Lions in 1930 to realize that the trail leaders from Washington were strategic about the kinds of local leaders to whom they would delegate trail-building responsibility. Like civic organizations in other areas at that time, the Lynchburg Lions was largely composed of educated white men—people who had the time and resources to spend weekends and even longer periods building the trail in America's hinterlands. Yet by developing a decentralized system of control, PATC and ATC leaders helped to establish an organizational structure that provided opportunities for citizen involvement in land-use decision making, or at least decisions about the AT. The kind of civic engagement in recreation and conservation projects embodied in the early development of the AT served as an organizational seed that would grow in the latter half of the twentieth century with the blossoming of the modern environmental movement.

In some ways, trail advocates' status as outsiders helped motivate trail work in the Southern Appalachians, but in other contexts, it created barriers to construction. For example, efforts to blaze the trail through the Smoky Mountains became entwined with deeper conflicts over how to most effectively manage land. When one of Avery's foot soldiers in the southern regions, Roy Ozmer, a young forester from Georgia, attempted the first through-hike of the trail with the intent to mark the trail as he went, his efforts sparked a local dispute about who should lead trail-building efforts in the southern states—particularly through the Smoky Mountains. Members of the Knoxville-based Smoky Mountain Hiking Club, one of the oldest hiking clubs in the South (established in 1924), contested the route that Ozmer marked, which ran from Siler's Bald, just west of Clingmans Dome on the Tennessee–North Carolina border, down through North Carolina to Standing Indian Mountain, and ended in Georgia at Mount Oglethorpe. The Knoxville club wanted a route that would end at Cohutta Mountain near the Tennessee state line, providing the Knoxvillians an easier point of access to the Smoky Mountains.

Members of the Knoxville group felt that the young Georgian was trespassing on their trail-building turf and were angry that articles in the *Knoxville Sentinel* that recounted Ozmer's trek gave the impression that outsiders were leading trail development in the area instead of the Smoky Mountain

Hiking Club. So while Ozmer's trip generated useful data for the AT project, determining how that data was to be used and who would lead local trail efforts became another challenge for the movement.

Tension between trail enthusiasts in Knoxville soon spread across borders. As Ozmer began looking to publish a comprehensive volume on his 1929 expedition, conflict erupted between outdoor enthusiasts in North Carolina and Tennessee. The Carolinians wanted to change the name of a prominent peak along the trail from Mount Collins to Mount Kephart, after the Great Smoky Mountains National Park booster Horace Kephart. After struggling with a drinking problem, Kephart had left his job as a librarian in Saint Louis, Missouri, in 1904 and went to live a healthier life in the hills of western North Carolina. He wrote extensively on the area's history and culture, and his work was used to support the movement to establish the Great Smoky Mountains National Park.[36] Like Kephart, Robert Lindsey Mason, another leader of the Smoky Mountain Hiking Club, also wrote several volumes on the history of the Smokies. Mason was "appalled, shocked, astounded" when he learned about the desire of "the ignorant *Asheville Times* and other North Carolinians" to change the name of Mount Collins to the name of a man who was "not native."[37] That Ozmer looked to Kephart for definitive knowledge about landmarks in the Smokies and used this information in his reports to Avery added to the Smoky Mountain Hiking Club's opposition to Ozmer's proposed AT route.

The incident was part of a larger controversy about mapping and determining precise locations for landmarks along the AT in the southern Appalachians. As different groups attempted to understand, define, and name features in the Smoky Mountains, long-standing regional cultural divisions arose. Mason wrote, "North Carolinians really are very ignorant about the actual Smokies because they are so far away. We are right under them every day and ought to know about these things."[38] In this sense, the Appalachian Mountain range not only divided watersheds, it divided cultures as well. Local newspapers in northern Georgia claimed that up until the twentieth century, people living on "the northern and southern sides of the Blue Ridge were total strangers. . . . Inhabitants on one side scarcely knew one another."[39] Issues about naming mountains and locating the AT required decisions that crossed rocky political boundaries, and consensus was not always easy to achieve. Doing so required the careful negotiation of local politics and regional differences.

As an opportunistic leader, Avery used regional disputes to incite potential collaborators to action. In the case of blazing a trail in the Smoky Mountains, Avery felt that Ozmer's and Kephart's direct experience gave them a better grasp of the local terrain than anyone he knew at the Smoky Mountain Hiking Club. Although Ozmer's attempted through-hike ended in southern Virginia when a severe spinal injury sent him to an operating table at Johns Hopkins University Hospital, Avery felt that he had the kind of temperament necessary to get the job done. Ozmer was an eager young man who was "anxious to let that New England bunch know that the South is not entirely lacking in active interest!"[40] He wrote to Avery to "tell the boys north that only 'Rigor Mortis' would keep him from making it."[41] Avery appreciated this kind of dedication and ultimately sided with Ozmer's plan. He wrote candidly to Perkins that "no one of us know that country and I think in the final analysis we should be governed by the views of Ozmer."[42] In this way, Avery delegated responsibility to the individuals who he felt had the best grasp of local knowledge. These individuals were not always trained scientists or prominent local leaders, but they were dedicated outdoor enthusiasts who Avery thought would be the most capable of turning local knowledge into action.

Avery tried to motivate Ozmer by writing that "some of the Smoky crowd seemed to resent you having blazed a route along the Smokies. They said that it was their territory and you should have kept your profane foot out of it. . . . as you know, the people who would say this are those who never would or could do anything themselves." Avery emphasized that the AT movement was relying on Ozmer to continue his work. If the young man didn't press on and mark the section of trail between Grandfather Mountain in North Carolina and the Peaks of Otter in Virginia, no one else would. Avery concluded by telling Ozmer not to be concerned about local antagonism against his work; he was beholden to no one and didn't "have to bunk with anyone."[43] Working as an outsider to the dispute in the Smokies, Avery simply went ahead, singled out an effective leader to get the project going, and avoided being drawn into the regional conflict.

Sometimes northerners' outsider status helped ameliorate local situations. In the case of the dispute about the trail's location in the Smoky Mountains, Paul Fink, a trail advocate from Jonesboro, Tennessee, felt that he and Avery could "work from the outside, without getting drawn into the racket," and thus help the project come to some "advantageous" solution.[44] Even without official status, the Potomac Appalachian Trail Club's base in Washington and its political influence through members' professional affiliations and experience in trail construction often allowed its members—and particularly its leader, Myron Avery—to play a special role in negotiating local politics.

In other situations, however, northern trail advocates' outsider status stalled trail development and led to conflict between northerners and southerners. For example, Ozmer was not the only one blazing trail in the southern Appalachians in 1929. In October, Judge Perkins left his home in Connecticut and joined Fink, Ozmer, and a handful of others to mark the trail through northern Georgia. The judge's condescending manner, demanding tone, and negative attitude toward the southerners offended the local volunteers and created a barrier to trail development. Claud C. Boynton, a pastor at the University Baptist Church in Brookhaven, Georgia, led Perkins on an outing during his October visit. The pastor was stunned by Perkins's demeanor and complained about the visit to Avery:

> Perhaps it was Perkins['s] general attitude toward all things southern that caused our little friction. He realized that HE was from the North and HE was rich. And the heck if he would allow no one to forget those two insignificant fact[s] for even a moment! I tried to retain our vaunted 'southern hospitality' as much as possible and show respect for his years . . . but the process was exceedingly griping![45]

Boynton was especially upset by Perkins's insistence that volunteers must refuse money or equipment from corporate manufacturers. Perkins wanted to maintain the trail's "non-for-profit" status as instructed by MacKaye's 1921 proposal. Boynton felt that since he was "no bloated millionaire," he needed to be compensated for the "vast quantities of beans and bacon consumed enroute." Without compensation, Boynton would be forced to give up his work on the trail. Boynton explained that southerners were a peculiar and "foolishly sensitive folk. When one approaches them rightly one will find co-operation to be readily obtained." But if northern advocates approached them with the attitude of "sarcastic superiority" displayed by Judge Perkins, they would have "a hard lot to accomplish anything!"[46]

Boynton was not the only would-be collaborator who was offended by Perkins's conduct and opposition to financial reimbursement. Ozmer received no compensation for his 1929 scouting trip, and while he loved the volunteer trail work, he told Avery that he needed some means to feed himself and his young family.[47] Ozmer had great respect for the work that

Perkins had accomplished on the trail, but he was "not prepared for the attitude he displayed" when he met him in the fall of 1929. He referred to the judge as "a true, natural-born dyed-in-the-wool diplomat," but, like Boynton, noted that Perkins's leadership style did not mesh well with potential collaborators in the southern sections.[48]

Paul Fink also chimed in on the incident involving Perkins and the southern volunteers. Like his fellow southerners, Fink did not share Perkins's concern about the project becoming tainted by commercialism by accepting donations from equipment manufacturers; he felt that such donations would provide good publicity for the project and much-needed economic opportunities for local people. He also expressed his disappointment in Perkins and the barrier to cooperation that the northern judge's attitude had created. Fink wrote,

> For generations we of the South have been patronized by those of the East, who come with the idea that the poor, ignorant southern mountaineers have never been nowhere nor seen nothing, and instead wishing to cooperate for the good of both parties, insist on running the whole show, in as much as they know all about it and possess more dollars, as well. This has bred in us something of a spirit of depending on ourselves, and resenting outside interference. So if Perkins seemed inclined to insist that everything be done just as it was in the East, not taking into allowance the complete change of conditions existing, both physical and financial, there was no wonder that Roy resented it. I should have done so myself. Most of us who are interested in trail work down here have little leisure and not much more means, and have to get the work done as best we can.[49]

Fink's remarks summarized a general attitude that many southern volunteers held toward the movement to blaze the AT through the southern states. While many were eager to prove that the South was ready to blaze the Appalachian Trail through their backyards, they wanted to do it according to their own styles and customs. Moreover, Fink's comments about the "complete change of conditions existing, both physical and financial" reveal important differences in regional economies. Although the agricultural depression of the 1920s and the Great Depression of the 1930s affected all parts of the country, the South was hit particularly hard because of its less developed industrial base and its predominant rural organization. For families living at higher elevations in the Southern Appalachian Mountains where the trail traversed, the struggle for self-sufficiency became increasingly difficult as soils were depleted and family sizes grew.

To aid economic development, federal planners, sociologists, and other scholars descended upon the Southern Appalachians in the 1930s. In their studies and plans, experts frequently perpetuated the idea that rural people were culturally backward, economically incompetent, and generally uncivil. In doing so, they reinforced stereotypes that had pervaded popular media since the late nineteenth century by depicting southern mountaineers as violent illiterates who sat around guarding their stills with a .44 rifle strapped around them and a banjo on their knee. Because of the region's prolonged physical isolation up until the 1930s, many viewed Appalachia as having its own social order—or disorder—and federal experts sought to help these mountain families integrate into the dominant cultural norms and land-use practices of mainstream America.[50]

When outdoor enthusiasts from eastern cities went into the hills to build the Appalachian Trail, they not only encountered new physical terrain but also discovered unfamiliar cultural terrain. In a sense, they encountered another level of "local"—not would-be collaborators in nearby urban centers like Knoxville or Asheville, but the people who lived and worked in the hills and valleys of the Appalachian Mountains. In some ways, interactions between urban outdoor enthusiasts and mountain families helped dispel popular myths; in other ways, they reinforced cultural stereotypes. In their reports to Avery, most volunteers spoke positively about their encounters with moonshiners and mountain residents. For example, on his "first real adventure of the trip" near Neels Gap in Georgia, Roy Ozmer discovered mule tracks and figured the only reason for having a mule high in the mountains was to make whiskey. As he continued his walk through the woods, he began to notice freshly chopped trees along the trail and sensed that he was getting close to the moonshine operation. In an article in the *Atlanta Journal*, Ozmer described his encounter as follows:

> Realizing that it would be poor policy indeed to brush upon the moonshiners unawares, I began singing in a very loud and very unmusical voice. . . . Suddenly I rounded a large, dense holly tree and found myself almost in the midst of a huge distilling plant. Before me appeared dozens of kegs and barrels. . . . Not a soul was in sight. My ruse had worked, and the moonshiners had discreetly cleared out. . . . [I] stepped boldly up to the still and carefully placed a few fagots on the smoldering fire . . . by that simple act I had become

equally guilty with them in making the liquor and so could not report what I had seen. . . . A hundred yards later, I called out 'That's all right, fellows. You needn't worry about me.' Somewhere down the ridge below me a cheerful voice answered: 'O.K. stranger, no harm done.'[51]

Ozmer's interaction with the moonshiner demonstrates the sort of uncomfortable alliance that was commonly forged between trail advocates and residents of the southern mountains—or at least the way advocates understood their relationship with mountaineers and wanted others to perceive it. The mountains frequently lay at the boundaries between governmental jurisdictions, and the county seats in which laws were passed and enforced were often far removed from the lives of rural people. Throughout the Prohibition Era, the national media reported stories about violence, corruption, and illegal activity permeating America's hinterlands.[52] Such stories fostered a popular conception of rural people as being exotic and dangerous, and many urban hikers feared encounters with the people who resided in the hills.

When they did meet, trail workers were often quick to prove that they posed no threat to mountain families' way of life. The respect they displayed was typically reciprocated, and relationships between the two groups were generally amicable. Occasionally, hillside encounters between urban and rural residents led to lifelong friendships. In an article in the *Gainesville Eagle*, Georgia Appalachian Trail Club member Charlie Elliott wrote, "Some of the finest friends I have ever known have been among these mountaineers of northern Georgia."[53] Elliott challenged conventional stereotypes and claimed that most of the insulting stories told about mountain residents were simply not true. Instead of trying to understand the residents of rural Appalachia, he felt that the "outside world has never associated or even tried to associate with them."[54] Like many of the other early trail advocates, Elliott's passion for hiking and camping was based on a desire to escape the trappings of modern civilization and live a more simple life in nature—albeit for short periods of time. Elliott had a great respect for mountaineers' self-reliance and their traditions of wearing homespun clothes, raising cattle, and growing their own food. He claimed that those who lived in the mountains were "cultured with the culture of the eighteenth century" and lamented the fact that their way of life was slowly changing as new summer resorts were built throughout the Appalachian Mountains. New developments were "gradually mixing these sons of the hills with the outside world"—an influence that, somewhat ironically, Elliott did not con-sider himself to be part of.[55]

In northern Virginia, when twenty-six members of the Washington-based Potomac Appalachian Trail Club went to build a section of trail near Mount Marshall in October 1928, a group of local inhabitants joined them at their evening campfire. In an account of the occasion, club historian David Bates wrote that "these folks, who were restricted in their activities by the demands of farm work and by poor roads, were hungry for outside com-pany and were very friendly." Club members told the locals that they would return for a weekend in November. When they came back, they found a well-arranged campfire area, stacks of firewood, and baskets of apples wait-ing for them. That evening, Frank Schairer, a close friend of Avery and a leader of the Potomac Appalachian Trail Club, led a "rousing song fest," and "congeniality was complete between the city hikers and the hill farmers."[56]

Schairer was particularly good at building strong relationships with rural residents. Although he had a PhD in chemical geology from Yale and worked for the Carnegie Institute in Washington, he was equally comfort-able sipping whiskey with mountaineers. Several mountain families—the Dodsons, Corbins, Micholsons, Weakleys, and Sisks—all enjoyed his company and welcomed him into their extended social network. Schairer helped to build a school near Hazel Hollow and, like many other trail advo-cates, frequently brought donations of food and clothing to struggling rural residents.[57] Because of his diplomacy and friendships with local people, Schairer was often able to procure oral agreements with landowners who owned or worked land in the southern Appalachians.

Of course, relationships between mountain residents and trail advocates were not always carefree and easy. Rural people who lived in the hills some-times resented the intrusion of outsiders into their territory, particularly in and near sections of the trail that became part of the Great Smoky Moun-tains and Shenandoah National Parks. In 1929, the Tennessee Park Com-mission, a state agency charged with acquiring land for the Great Smoky Mountains National Park, filed its first condemnation suit. As was typical of the condemnation proceedings involved in the acquisition of land for these two national parks, the landowner did not believe that the government was offering "just compensation" for his property and that the action was thus a violation of his Fifth Amendment rights. John Oliver, a resident of Cades Cove, one of the small communities located within the proposed boundar-ies of the Great Smoky Mountains National Park, had been offered twenty dollars per acre for his land, but Oliver insisted that the property was worth forty to fifty dollars per acre. When he contested the constitutionality of the action, the Blount County Circuit Court agreed with his protests, but the Tennessee Supreme Court decided in favor of the state.[58] Similar actions took place in Virginia, where landowners also protested the state's efforts to condemn their land to create the Shenandoah National Park.[59]

When government authorities removed thousands of families from the mountains to create national playgrounds that would primarily serve urban populations, a sense of resentment grew among members of adjacent communities.[60] Despite the promise of economic benefits from the new national parks and the growth of the recreation industry, many people were left feeling bitter toward the government and toward outdoor-adventure-seeking outsiders. Local authorities were concerned that instead of being an economic boom, the creation of national parks would encumber their jurisdictions with long-term poverty as the local tax base was sacrificed to create the country's common play space. In places such as Swain County, Tennessee, home of the Fontana Dam and the Great Smoky Mountains National Park, the federal government eventually purchased approximately 80 percent of the land base. Although this provided the foundation of a recreation industry that would blossom in the later twentieth century, many local people felt as though this shift in land ownership undermined the full development potential of the area and infringed upon their constitutional rights.[61]

Although many of the early Appalachian Trail blazers were not directly involved in the efforts to create the eastern national parks, when they went to the hills to build shelters and cut trail, local residents associated the hardy volunteers with broader park efforts, and trail workers occasionally encountered the anger that had been stirring in the hills. For example, in 1933 when members of the Potomac Appalachian Trail Club started to build the Range View shelter near the AT in what would soon be designated as the Shenandoah National Park, they encountered local resistance. On June 13, Otis Gates, the chairman of the PATC's Shelter Committee, reported several incidents of vandalism to Rappahannock County sheriff Keyser. The shelter was being constructed near the border of Rappahannock and Page Counties, so when Keyser didn't offer to remedy the situation, Gates sent letters to authorities in the adjacent county. Like Keyser, Sheriff Edwin Lucus of Page County had little inclination to address the problem. Gates felt that the local officials viewed club members as "outsiders" who did not pay taxes or vote in either county. The perpetrators of the crime, however, were constituents. Gates suspected that "Votes at elections mattered to these lawmen, and they were possibly reluctant to arrest local citizens on the complaints of non-residents."[62]

The perpetrators grew bolder when they realized that local authorities were not going to get involved. When PATC members came to work on the shelter during a weekend outing in December, a local gang led by Jerry Sowers harassed, cursed, and insulted the volunteers. Angry mob members threw stones at the trail volunteers and stole construction materials when they left. According to PATC accounts, gang members "repeatedly said they wanted no 'outsiders' in that part of the country, that city hikers and campers were not welcome."[63] Instead of going back to local authorities, the PATC decided to hire their own local help—a notorious tough guy named Charlie Sisk. Sisk was not only a very talented mason, he was also well known in the area for recently killing a man in a drunken fight. Leaders of the trail club waited for Sisk to serve his jail term and then hired him to help build the Range View shelter. When the gang came out to harass trail workers at a work party, Sisk and a fellow worker slowly unpacked their trail tools: mortar, trowels, and a couple of shotguns. "Silence fell quickly on the group of delinquents; rocks in hand were dropped to the ground.... Construction of the cabin proceeded without hindrance."[64] In this way, trail volunteers successfully manipulated local dynamics to promote the project; resistance from one local group was overcome by aligning with another.

Early trailblazers associated with the PATC and the ATC were often most successful when they were able to create favorable perceptions of and attitudes toward the Appalachian Trail. Although many were well connected in Washington, cultivating local support for the project was not done by flaunting their connections with high-powered state agencies and institutions but by cultivating positive relationships with other advocates, landowners, and rural residents. In order to establish an effective national grassroots campaign, advocates relied on local knowledge and tried to enlist local leaders in the movement. This process involved establishing relationships between northern advocates and southern collaborators as well as influencing political dynamics within a particular locale.

Understanding the cultural and political issues that arose during advocates' attempts to extend a grassroots network also requires a deeper exploration of the how the AT project interacted with New Deal programs, and the increasingly significant role that the federal government began to play in the 1930s. For this, we move from the hills of the Southern Appalachians

Pulpwood in the Androscoggin River, 1926. In the late 1920s and 1930s, it was not uncommon for AT hikers to see logging operations such as this raft of pulpwood in the Androscoggin River in 1926. At that time, logging was one of the primary ways in which Mainers earned a living. Courtesy of the Appalachian Trail Conservancy.

to the trail's northern terminus in Maine to investigate how the deepening Depression and the rising power of the central government affected local-outsider dynamics in the construction of the trail's final link.

FEDERAL INVOLVEMENT ON
THE APPALACHIAN TRAIL'S FINAL FRONTIER

Similar to conditions in the Southern Appalachians, the AT project in Maine initially suffered from a general lack of awareness among potential collaborators. The Depression and the remote location of the trail added to the list of challenges facing trail development in the 1930s. As economic conditions worsened across the nation, trail leaders tried to solicit the support of local leaders by emphasizing the financial benefits that the AT project would provide to rural communities. When efforts to organize local volunteers failed, trail advocates began to seek support from state and federal agencies in a more systematic manner. Bringing government officials and federal programs into the project shifted the interplay of power and authority between the state and citizens, and between locals and outsiders. It also indicated the direction the project was headed in future years.

As initially planned by Benton MacKaye, the trail was to enter Maine near Gorham, New Hampshire, extend across the Bigelow Range, cross over Moxie Bald Mountain to the town of Monson, wind through what is today known as the "Hundred-Mile Wilderness," and end on Mount Katahdin. In the late 1920s and 1930s, forest production remained one of the state's largest industries, and timber companies owned large tracts of land through which the AT was to cross.[65] Although owners of these large operations were generally favorable toward the trail, recreation was not a priority at the time. While the timber companies were usually willing to let volunteers blaze the trail on their land, they were not willing to have the path interfere with their plans to harvest timber.

Furthermore, the proposed route of the AT was far away from the state's major population centers such as Portland, Lewiston, and Augusta, where the project's most likely collaborators lived. Transporting volunteer trailblazers to the inland ranges required surpluses of energy, time, and money—resources that were becoming increasingly scarce in the 1930s. In Portland, a group of about forty outdoor enthusiasts tried to organize a hiking club in 1930. Due to "subnormal business conditions" and their distance from the mountains, however, their leader, Arthur M. Fogg, told Avery that the group had little to offer the AT movement. Although they were excited about the project, their membership was "mostly composed of young working men, who do not have large incomes, and who cannot take time away from work."[66] During the 1930s, this scenario became increasingly common. Most of the existing trail clubs saw membership growth rates slow; some declined. Many potential volunteers simply could not afford the expense of travel and the time off from work that a trail-building trip often involved. Because of economic limitations and geographic constraints in places such as Maine, AT advocates began to consider new strategies for trail development.

When Avery approached leaders in local communities, he was able to find people who would do the work—for a price. In 1933, Harry Davis, the fire warden of the town of Monson, told Avery that if there was compensation involved, he knew of some folks that would do the work. He stressed that "we are in a depression and I hardly think you could ask a young man to give up a position in these times that payed . . . to work on the trail."[67] If the ATC could ensure a "low wage of not over 2.00 per day" to local woodsmen, Davis volunteered to oversee the workers free of charge.[68] Avery could not promise an hourly wage but offered a total of eighty-five dollars for someone to build the trail from York's Camp at Long Pond to West Chairback Mountain—much of this cash he personally contributed.

Trail advocates also tried to appeal to local camps and resort businesses as a base of support for the project. Like Monson's fire warden, resort owners had to be convinced of the financial benefits of local participation in the project. In letters to Leon E. Potter, proprietor of the Antlers Camp on Lower Jo-Mary Lake, and Mrs. Robert McDougall, who ran a resort on Mahmakanta Lake, Avery explained how the trail would generate business. In return, he asked for the proprietors' permission to have the trail cross their properties.[69] Walter Greene, an actor from New York City who spent his summers in the Maine woods and was a strong advocate for the AT, also tried to garner support from local resort business owners. Greene used local media to "awaken" Mainers to the AT project and to the recreational possibilities of Maine's forests. Although wood pulp production continued to be an important component of the state's economy, Greene pointed out that the lumber industry had "drifted of late years." He emphasized that the state needed "every additional source of revenue" it could muster, and he argued that the AT would be the "initial wedge" to open Maine's economy to the economic benefits of outdoor recreation.[70] While camp and resort owners generally supported the creation of a long-distance recreational trail through the state, like most other individuals in the 1930s, they were economically strained and could not offer financial assistance.

While Greene felt that trail advocates owed it to the rural business owners to "use their influence" as outsiders to help promote private recreation-based tourism in Maine, Avery disagreed.[71] Avery felt that the state should be more involved in leading trail-building efforts. He pointed out that one of the greatest problems of garnering popular support for the AT project in Maine was the fact that it was such an expensive endeavor. First, would-be trail users had to pay the relatively large transportation costs to get there. Second, private camps were the only available accommodations in Maine at the time, and they cost more than the free lean-tos and shelters that had been established in other parts of the AT. On top of these expenses, according to Maine law, out-of-state campers had to hire a local guide.[72] The law was strictly enforced, and Avery pointed out that during the previous summer, a "chap from Washington" was fined a hundred and twenty-five dollars for camping without a guide. He wrote to Greene, "Your letter sounds as if the project were for the benefit of the camp owners. We didn't build this for them." In Avery's estimation, private camp owners had been unfair to trail workers: "Already 50 per cent have started to gouge us by raising prices. . . . None of the campowners really lost anything or did much for this. When you consider what it could do, the campowners helped very little."[73]

Furthermore, Greene was an actor from New York City who claimed that as "an adopted son of the Pine Tree State," he was intimately familiar with local conditions.[74] Greene's claims to local knowledge irritated Avery, who was born and raised in Lubec, Maine, went to college at Bowdoin, spent the summers of his college years working for the State Forestry Department, and claimed state residency in the 1930s. Expressing his frustration, Avery wrote to Greene, "I know the local angles and arguments so you won't have to write me any more of this."[75] Unlike Greene, Avery thought the construction of public campgrounds would not only benefit trail users but would also open up new avenues for cooperation with public authorities.

As a result of the economic challenges in Maine and elsewhere, Avery began to push harder for government involvement in the project. From the beginning of his involvement with the AT, Avery had supported the idea of enlisting state power, but conditions during the 1930s provided additional justification and more opportunities to do so. The AT project benefited from President Roosevelt's New Deal programs, such as the CCC and the TVA. Such programs opened the door for stronger federal involvement in the project, a presence that would grow in the postwar era.

Many Americans considered the CCC to be one of the most successful New Deal programs because it created opportunities and benefits for rural residents and urbanites alike.[76] In the early 1930s, CCC crews built public campgrounds, bridges, shelters, and hundreds of miles of trail in the southern national forests, including much of the AT and many of its side trails. In contrast, Maine's hinterlands were mostly privately owned. In order to get Washington to approve the use of CCC crews to build the trail in Maine, advocates first had to secure permission from private owners. This put volunteers in an unusual position as intermediaries between federal officials and local landowners. As in other areas, many landowners were willing to have the trail cross their property but were wary of making formal arrangements, especially with the federal government. Simple oral agreements with citizen

Robert Fechner and Myron Avery on the AT. The CCC played a major role in blazing the AT through public lands in the 1930s—particularly in the southern national forests. CCC director Fechner (left), shown here with Avery (right), authorized CCC crews to blaze the trail on private land as well. Courtesy of the Appalachian Trail Conservancy.

volunteers were more flexible and gave landowners the power to change their minds at any time. For early trail building efforts, these flexible arrangements sufficed. As long as trail users were respectful and courteous, most landowners had no problem with letting a few nature lovers build a small path across their property. When advocates tried to get federal approval to use CCC crews to build trail on private land, however, they incorrectly assumed that the process would require more formal arrangements with landowners.

James W. Sewall, who worked as a forester for the CCC in Maine, was particularly interested in trying to get permission for his crew to build sections of the AT. He had procured oral permission from several landowners but, like Avery, had found that they were "reluctant to execute documents which might be construed as easements or in any way giving anything more than a bare license." Both men felt trapped by the situation. They didn't want to "frighten off the landowners," but at the same time they realized that unless they could get "at least a confirmation of the oral permission by letter," they would probably not be able to make much progress.[77]

In order to surmount this conundrum, Avery and Sewall did two things. First, they got creative with how they pitched the project. Second, they used the influence of powerful colleagues within the ATC to lobby for their cause. According to federal regulations, the CCC could perform work on private lands if the project was for the purpose of fire protection. Acting district forester Crosby A. Hoar pointed out that because the proposed AT route in Maine went across the tops of exposed mountains, it would be difficult to argue that the project was for fire protection. Sewell suggested that to build a case for using CCC crews on the trail, they could focus on the sections that ran between mountains. As the CCC workers cleared the trail, they would also remove flammable debris along the sides. The trail itself could also serve as a fire break. Not only would this fit the federal criteria, but it would allow the trail to be relocated off of old tote roads and in more scenic and densely wooded areas.[78]

Sewell was concerned that the proposal to use CCC crews on private lands "might meet some criticism further up in Washington."[79] In order to troubleshoot opposition from higher-ups, the ATC relied on some of its influential members. In April 1935, Major William Welch met with CCC director Robert Fechner to discuss the possibility of using CCC labor to develop trails on private land. The US Forest Service had issued an explicit order against having the CCC build truck trails on private property, a precedent that seemed somewhat akin to establishing hiking trails. After some conversations with Major Welch and others, however, Fechner approved the use of CCC labor for the construction of the AT on private land without formal easements or written permission.[80]

Sewall saw this as a great victory, and was soon coordinating crews of fifteen men at Millinocket, Greenville, Flagstaff, and Rangeley. He suggested that the CCC take over the development of the whole trail in Maine. His supervisor, Christopher M. Granger, argued that the CCC could perform the actual construction of the trail, if ATC volunteers would secure permission from landowners and maintain the trail once it was completed. This gave the project a "semipublic character" and demonstrated the strengthening relationship between the trail community and the federal government.[81]

Trail advocates tried to use the example of federal involvement to engage other levels of government—particularly the state. Avery wrote to the executive secretary of the Maine Development Commission, Everett F. Groaton, "Those of us who have been responsible for developing the Trail project in Maine . . . are interested in having the project rest upon a permanent basis with as much official State sanction as possible." He argued that since the federal government supported the project by authorizing the use of CCC labor, the state should take some responsibility and help volunteers keep the project maintained once the trail was constructed.[82]

While many state officials reacted favorably, others resented the intrusion of federal control into their jurisdiction. Tensions between state and federal conservation agendas flared when Representative Ralph O. Brewster proposed a bill to turn the Katahdin area into a national park. The proposal and the controversy it created reflected the different roles that local, state, and federal agents played in regional disputes about trail development and land management. The conflict in Maine also foreshadowed future debates about federalism and the appropriate balance of power between state and federal government that would arise after the AT became part of the national park system in the late 1960s.

Former governor Percival Baxter had been working to protect the Katahdin area for over fifteen years. Due to lack of support from the state, Baxter had begun to slowly acquire land on his own with the intention of donating the land to the people of Maine. When Baxter vehemently opposed Brewster's bill, Avery and the national park representatives were dumbfounded. They couldn't understand why the ex-governor would be against protecting the area through national park status. Avery attributed the opposition to personal resentment, ego, and messy state politics. He wondered what would have happened if instead of the "Katahdin National Park" the bill had been proposed as "the Baxter National Park."[83]

The issue inspired a flurry of heated exchanges between Baxter and Avery that was fueled by conflicting claims about local needs. Baxter felt that the people of Maine were perfectly capable of managing their own resources without the assistance of the federal government. He noted that

Maine's state parks were not as "big ... smartly kept up ... well policed ... nor as crowded as the National Parks." Mainers liked it that way, he claimed, and they were not interested in the "inevitable background of trailers, food stands and confusion" found at national parks. Baxter wrote to Avery,

> Maine people are proud of their mountain, and your worry about Katahdin's "fast approaching fate" is ridiculous. Its fate will be properly provided for under the control and guidance of Maine men and women rather than under those who live in the great centers of the country. We Down EASTERNERS will handle it ourselves. Maine is still a Sovereign State amply equipped both spiritually and financially for such an undertaking.[84]

Baxter acknowledged Avery's historical connection with the state, but the ex-governor pointed out that Avery had left Maine to pursue grander ambitions. Baxter felt that during his time in Washington, Avery had "lost confidence in the good sense and high ideals of the citizens of the Pine Tree State." According to Baxter, had Avery stayed in his home state, he may have "acquired some special knowledge of local men, conditions and motives."[85] Baxter eventually won the debate, and today through-hikers bound from Georgia end their journeys on Mount Katahdin in Baxter State Park.

Like the conflicts in the Smoky Mountains, the debate between Avery and Baxter demonstrated how claims of local identity and local knowledge influenced early decisions about the AT. These conflicts shed light on how regional politics shaped debates over state and national control in the conservation arena. Navigating these tensions was essential as trail advocates sought support for the project in communities along the Appalachian spine.

Like Baxter, some members of the trail community were concerned about increasing the role of the federal government in the project. In 1934, even though MacKaye was working for the Tennessee Valley Authority at the time and was "intensely interested" in having the ATC work with federal agencies, he was hesitant to hand the trail over to the federal government. Reiterating the project's grassroots spirit, MacKaye emphasized that "in all things it is persons and not agencies that do the real cooperating, and the basis of it all is mutual understanding."[86] Furthermore, he explained that the purpose of the AT "should not be confused with the purposes, varied and sundry, of the Federal government."[87] When the federal government invested money into a particular initiative, MacKaye argued, it expected to see results—"to have 'something to show for it.'" This "something" tended to come in the form of infrastructural developments. "If it is something *merely* physical then it must be *very* physical—and the tendency will be to manicure the wilderness. This is the opposite concept of the Appalachian Trail."[88] While most members of the trail community appreciated Avery's eagerness to gain support from the national government, others wondered if federal involvement might compromise the grassroots spirit and ultimate purpose of the project. Although many advocates struggled with this tension, they could not deny the important role that the CCC had played in getting the trail built in remote sections where it would have been difficult to send volunteers.

In April 1937, a crew of strapping CCC workers marked the last link of the Appalachian Trail—two miles between Spaulding and Sugarloaf Mountains in Maine. The shift from a handful of citizen volunteers to employed government laborers was a telling indicator of the coming transition for the AT project. When members of the ATC met for the annual meeting in 1937 in Gatlinburg, Tennessee, they celebrated the creation of a continuous 2,025-mile path. Yet at the same time, volunteers recognized that the trail's future was uncertain. ATC chairman Avery reported, "The fluctuation of interest in voluntary groups is too well known, as are the difficulties of all movements or organizations which depend on voluntary and amateur effort. The time has come to face the future and to establish the Trail on a permanent and lasting basis; to determine on a definite program."[89] Without changing the fundamental nature of the project or its commitment to grassroots voluntary action, Avery insisted that the ATC should enlist the support of state and federal agencies to secure the project's future.

In addition to members of the ATC's affiliated clubs, representatives of the National Park Service also attended the 1937 ATC meeting in Gatlinburg. Edward B. Ballard, a field coordinator for the Park Service, presented plans for an Appalachian Trailway Agreement. The Trailway Agreement consisted of a five-point program for future developments that included: (1) a protected zone that extended 100 feet on each side of the trail; (2) improvements to be made on the existing route by relocating certain sections on public lands; (3) the gradual extension of public holdings along the trail; (4) the acquisition of scenic easements; and (5) the development of a comprehensive shelter system. Ballard explained that instead of relying solely on the informal structure of the ATC, the Trailway Agreement would establish a "coordinated *public* policy and program for the trail project."[90] In essence, the plan represented a stronger commitment by the Park Service to support

Appalachian Trail building activities and foreshadowed the expansion in the federal government's role in future AT activities.

The new challenge, Ballard explained, was to fatten "the backbone of this skeleton network of trails ... with the flesh of enduring life by protective zones of publicly owned land."[91] The Trailway Agreement involved the cooperation of the National Park Service, the US Forest Service, and several state agencies. On June 26, 1936, Congress had passed legislation to promote cooperative agreements between two or more states in planning parks, parkways, and other recreational areas.[92] Ballard noted that this legislation would be particularly useful for the future development and protection of the AT. By replacing informal agreements and tenuous relationships with landowners with official sanctions and the support of state and federal government, Ballard emphasized that the trail would no longer have to follow the path of least resistance. Instead, its elevated legal status would enable the project to boldly blaze its way across the Appalachian Mountains.

AN EXPERIMENT IN VOLUNTARY FEDERALISM

Although participants initially came to the Appalachian Trail project with a wide array of goals and aspirations, they were generally able to work together because the stakes were not very high. Trail building was mostly regionally focused, recreational use was relatively minimal, and the project had not yet received the widespread national attention that it would attract in the 1960s and 1970s. Conflict along the trail was relatively rare. Occasionally different clubs got into territorial disputes or rural people expressed resentment toward outsiders in expensive attire. For the most part, though, trail construction was done by volunteers, and agreements with landowners were cooperative, informal, and revocable at any time. Because the project lacked official backing, it posed no major threat to property rights, land use, or rural ways of life. At a conference in Pennsylvania in the 1930s, volunteers described the effort as follows:

> The Appalachian Trail was the outgrowth of local and regional trail systems, in separate states, now being joined together in friendly cooperation ... men and women in widely separated regions have become warm friends by their work on this project ... in Easton, in Washington DC, in Virginia, Tennessee, and New York. Their work has been of a kind that could never be paid for in money. No public agency would ever have done it with the

same efficiency, nor without a cost which governmental agencies would have refused to pay, as for a chimerical and impossible idea. But beginning here and there, in isolated centers, where enthusiasm for the job was active early ... the trail grew in each direction, north and south, from these centers, and now, behold ... completion is in sight.[93]

This rosy interpretation of the AT's origins differs from historical interpretations offered by scholars such as Robert Foresta. In an article titled "The Transformation of the Appalachian Trail," Foresta argued that following MacKaye's 1921 proposal, an elite group of urban professionals and state conservation agents usurped MacKaye's project and transformed its mission. According to Foresta, the early trail aficionados had no interest in MacKaye's broader vision for the trail—economic justice and the empowerment of local communities. Instead, they stripped the project of its reformist goals and turned it into a mere pleasure path for urban elites. Foresta claimed that "because they benefited from the rise of industrial capitalism, the professionals were not revolutionaries."[94] They were content simply playing pioneer in the woods, enjoying their rugged individualism, and reinforcing sociopolitical boundaries in the process. Thus the Appalachian Trail became a mechanism of escape from the industrial society that MacKaye and his regional planning colleagues were trying to actively reform.

Foresta's argument is similar to recent histories of early conservation politics that have tended to portray power as a top-down process of control (and in some cases even oppression) of local people. Recent scholars have demonstrated how early state conservationists in the United States relied on scientific expertise and institutionalized bureaucracy and in doing so sometimes overlooked the ways in which local people understood and interacted with the natural environment.[95] Yet this investigation of the relationship between state power, private influence, and local communities involved in the AT project during the late 1920s and 1930s reveals a different interpretation of large-scale recreation and conservation initiatives in the early twentieth century.

Unlike the Great Smoky Mountains and Shenandoah National Parks, the Fontana Dam, and other federal land projects in the 1930s, early Appalachian Trail–blazers had no official power to authorize trail construction until the project gained legal status as a unit within the national park system in the 1960s. Instead, tacit forms of political power—influence and trust—initially helped to blaze the trail. Because of the project's geography, leaders of the Appalachian Trail Conference tried to create a system of organization that was simultaneously dedicated to a national agenda while also being responsive to the needs of local communities. Although many of the leaders of the AT movement worked as conservation agents with various government agencies, they understood that central state-based power was politically unfeasible at the time. Alternatively, they depended on local political dynamics to establish cooperative relationships in communities from Georgia to Maine.

As an experiment in voluntary federalism, the Appalachian Trail initially relied not on formal government mandates but on informal and cooperative agreements between disparate groups. Where advocates were successful in garnering local support, the trail was built; where their efforts failed, alternative routes were considered. Thus, in the project's beginning stages, out of legal necessity, the trail followed the path of least political resistance through a landscape that was increasingly shaped by the forces of federal policies and programs. Although meant to alleviate rural poverty, the large-scale planning and land reforms of the New Deal Era were greeted with a range of responses. Examples such as the Fontana Dam, where federal forces literally put rural people's homelands under water, and the creation of the Great Smoky Mountains and Shenandoah National Parks, where thousands of people were removed from their homes and land, left many feeling resentment toward the federal government. Collective memories of torched stores and rotted homes destroyed by the government would prove to challenge AT advocates efforts' to blaze the trail throughout the twentieth century.

CHAPTER 3

FEDERALIZING AMERICA'S FOOT TRAILS

WHEN SEVERAL HIKERS FROM CHATTANOOGA CAME TO ENJOY A REFRESH-ing weekend getaway along the Appalachian Trail in Georgia in 1955, their plans were soured by a pungent, black ooze that coated the trail. The area, located near Mount Oglethorpe—the trail's southern terminus at the time and the one section of the trail in Georgia that lay outside the national forest boundary—had been turned into a "dumping ground for manure" from a large chicken farm nearby. The Chattanoogans could find no way around the mess and had been forced to "wade through the filth . . . of thousands of chickens."[1] In an irate letter to the Appalachian Trail Conference (ATC), the leader of the group, Mrs. Leon Cross, reported that the trail was "so slimy that one of our group fell flat on her face in the stuff."[2] Several years earlier, local volunteers with the Georgia Appalachian Trail Club had found small mountains of rotting lumber, scattered brush, tar paper, and approximately fifty thousand beer and oil cans.[3] They also discovered that extensive logging operations had "ravaged" the last eleven miles of the trail near its southern terminus.[4] The conditions in the Mount Oglethorpe area ultimately led the Georgia club and the ATC to relocate the southern terminus to Springer Mountain, where it would be protected within the boundaries of the Chattahoochee National Forest.[5]

The chickens' filth not only offered an "indelicate olfactory salute" to hikers, as one local volunteer put it; the situation at the trail's southern terminus also revealed broader economic and environmental changes that occurred during the decades that followed World War II.[6] When the trail volunteers of the 1920s and 1930s returned to the Appalachian Trail after the war, they discovered that many sections had been obliterated by the expansion of forestry and agricultural operations, new housing developments, road construction, and hurricane damage. At the same time, Americans began flocking to the countryside for recreation and outdoor adventure. Between 1940 and 1965 visits to national parks and national forests doubled, and the Appalachian Trail became one of America's premier gateways for getting back to nature.[7] Simultaneous growth in the outdoor recreation, housing, and extractive resource industries led to new tensions over how to manage America's hinterlands.[8]

The movement to protect the aesthetic value of the countryside that had started in the early twentieth century with wilderness advocates like Benton MacKaye gained momentum during the postwar era, and new strategies and justifications for land conservation took root. As environmental awareness spread, with notable publications such as Aldo Leopold's *Sand County Almanac* and Rachel Carson's *Silent Spring*, public support for stronger federal environmental laws and policies also grew. Hiking trails, most famously the Appalachian Trail, served as key conduits for shaping Americans' relationship with the natural world and for galvanizing public support for federal conservation policies. When outdoor enthusiasts headed for the hills, they confronted the environmental consequences of a growing consumer economy. Like the Chattanoogans, many Americans became increasingly distressed by what they discovered, and they began to seek new institutional mechanisms—both public and private—to protect land from the ooze and sprawl of postwar industries.

Although the first attempt to create a national system of trails in 1945 failed, by 1968, the political climate was ripe for creating federal footpaths.[9] Environmental and cultural changes in the postwar era led to changing ideas about the purpose of land conservation and shaped decisions about the trail's future. The Appalachian Trail's path toward federal protection was guided by broader national debates about wilderness preservation, park development, and multiple-use management. Navigating this tortuous political route required the negotiation of authority between a large number of private and public agents who held different views about the federal government's role in controlling land and protecting natural resources. The movement to federalize America's footpaths—from the first failed attempt to create a national system of footpaths in 1945 to Congress's passage of the National Trails Act in 1968—demonstrates how a growing number of outdoor enthusiasts worked to transform a largely grassroots project into a new

Jim Hanson (left) and David Field (right) clearing away hurricane damage. Damage from the 1938 hurricane in Maine caused major hurdles for AT volunteers. Courtesy of the Appalachian Trail Conservancy.

two-thousand-mile unit of the national park system. The process helped to establish new ideas about the purpose of American's national parks and forests, and embodied new strategies for achieving large-scale conservation goals.

BATTLES ON THE HOME FRONT

In the decades that followed World War II, many AT volunteers reported being in constant battle with two distinct forces: nature and civilization. In 1961, Stanley Murray, the vice-chairman of the ATC who would later serve as the organization's chairman, reported that volunteers had spent the past two decades fighting "the encroachment of the forest, which tends to revert the Trail itself into wilderness" and the "encroachment of civilization, which tends to leave no wilderness at all, and in fact no Trail."[10]

Hurricane damage near Kinsman Mountain in New Hampshire, circa 1939. Courtesy of the Appalachian Trail Conservancy.

While volunteers fought new developments in one area, unruly vegetation and bulldozers annihilated the trail in other sections. Murray maintained that protecting the Appalachian Trail was "a fine line that we have to hold: keeping the wilderness out of the Trail by a carefully planned maintenance program, and keeping the Trail in the wilderness by maintaining constant alertness to impending developments of an incompatible nature."[11]

Although the AT was completed in 1937, nature soon began to reclaim the path. ATC chairman Myron Avery noted that once blazed, it didn't take long for the trail to revert back to "wilderness . . . in the form of storm damage, annual growth and the inevitable obliteration by Nature of routes created by man."[12] The first major interruption along the long-distance route occurred in 1938, when an infamous hurricane blasted New England's shores and ricocheted through the region's forests. Hikers today can still observe the damage caused by the 1938 hurricane while walking through forests in New England, and one can only imagine what the worst-hit areas must have

Log loading. After World War II, new technologies such as four-wheel drive trucks allowed for logging in remote mountainous regions. The growing postwar demand for forest products also increased production in the nation's forests. Courtesy of the Wisconsin Historical Society.

looked like before decades of decomposition and human efforts to tidy up after the storm.[13] In one section in Maine, a volunteer crew reported sixty-four blowdowns in 1.3 miles.[14] When Charles C. Hardy, a forester from north-central Maine, took two trail volunteers, Edward Meeich and Bartram Frost, to clear the trail from Maine State Route 16 to Little Bigelow Mountain in 1949, the group discovered that the trail was still covered with large blowdowns from the hurricane, and was nearly completely overgrown with hardwood sprouts. After only a couple of sleepless nights during which insects feasted on the men's flesh, the group abandoned the project. Hardy suggested that the ATC hire three or four paid workers to finish the job, as it was a task that would require more than a few days of volunteer labor.[15]

Volunteers discovered that nature had taken over the trail in many other places as well. A section of trail near Reeds Gap in central Virginia had become "an overgrown old field," and on top of The Priest, a popular peak in the area, the trail had simply vanished.[16] The notion of nature taking over the trail was somewhat ironic because, as one of the country's premier wilderness footpaths, the trail was intended to provide a place for people to connect with wild, untrammeled nature. Yet at the same time, the trail was designed and controlled by humans. Because blowdowns from the hurricane made walking difficult, and blighted forests resulted in unattractive scenery, trail volunteers felt that relinquishing too much control to natural forces could lead to unpleasant hiking experiences. Nature was what hikers sought to connect with on the trail, yet paradoxically, it was also a force that volunteers battled in order to maintain a clear pathway.

As problematic as damage to the trail caused by the hurricane and new vegetative growth was, however, it could not compare to the onslaught of human-induced changes that occurred in the decades following World War II. As the demand for new construction soared after the war, annual timber sales in the national forests grew from three billion board feet in the late 1940s to approximately twelve billion board feet by the 1950s.[17] In the eight national forests through which the trail passed, volunteers increasingly discovered that the AT had been turned into an access road for logging trucks. For example, in the Glenwood District of the Jefferson National Forest in Virginia, Avery found that service roads had been laid on top of four miles of trail. Erosion resulting from these backwoods roads sometimes became so severe that trail leaders relocated the AT away from gullied areas.[18] During the postwar era, private companies such as the International Paper Company in Maine also increased the production of pulp and paper products through the use of new forest technologies. The intensification of logging operations and the construction of forest roads affected not only the trail but also the landscapes that hikers saw from the trail—what land managers began to refer to as "the viewshed."

Civilization encroached on the Appalachian Trail in other ways as well. As leisure time and financial wealth became more abundant in the decades after World War II, second homes and luxury resorts began to sprout up along the trail. Between the first movement for national trails legislation in 1945 and the reintroduction of legislation in the 1960s, the ATC and its affiliated clubs endured many prolonged battles with real estate developers on private lands. By the 1960s, expensive new high-rise apartments threatened to take over land where the trail passed through the Palisades area between New York and New Jersey.[19] Throughout the mid-Atlantic region, second

Postwar highway construction. During the post–World War II era, new highways began to snake deeper into the countryside, and housing developments sprawled through America's hinterlands. These changes often threatened the integrity and continuity of the AT. Courtesy of the Appalachian Trail Conservancy.

homes, country clubs, and suburban sprawl began to force the trail onto undesirable routes and created breaks along the 2,075-mile footpath.[20] In the South, most of the trail passed through national forests or national parks, but in sections of private land—places such as Big Bald in Tennessee and Big Butt in North Carolina—southern clubs also faced new second-home developments.

Trail advocates had generally maintained friendly agreements with local landowners during the 1930s, but by the 1950s and 1960s, they found themselves struggling to gain support for the AT from a new generation of landowners. These new landowners lacked the history of trust and mutual respect with trail volunteers, and many had different visions of how they planned to use the land.[21] In the case of Big Bald, prior to World War II, Pearl Buck of Beelog, North Carolina, owned the mountain.[22] Buck had been friendly with the trail community and sought to protect the area from commercial development. When she sold the property to a man named

Edwards, the mountain's fate changed. Edwards sought to develop the area, and although he allowed the trail to continue to cross the mountain, by 1966, the ATC reported that the mountain's "original charm and any sense of remoteness from the activities of the mechanized world" had been lost and that the trail needed to be relocated.[23]

Developments such as the one at Big Bald became a frequent threat to the trail environment, and by the 1960s, even the remote woods of Maine succumbed to mounting pressures for luxury homes when realtors proposed a condo development on Mount Bigelow. To reach new vacation homes and ski resorts—and in less remote locations, to facilitate suburban growth—new roads were built. According to trail volunteer Laura Bliss, a section of trail that had been a peaceful country road walk in southern Virginia before the war had become a dangerous and unpleasant scramble where new housing developments had been built in the 1950s.[24]

In addition to the expansion of roads and housing developments, the nation's military operations also posed new challenges for the trail. With the eminent threat of the atomic bomb, national security trumped recreational use of America's hinterlands. By the mid-1950s, army rangers set up a training area along ten miles of trail in Georgia between Gooch Gap and Winding Stair Gap. They filled the area with mock mines and booby traps. Members of the Georgia Appalachian Trail Club warned hikers that accidental explosions would "startle but not harm" them as they sauntered through the area.[25] Also in the mid-1950s, when the air force began building an extensive communications system on Apple Orchard Mountain in the Jefferson National Forest in Virginia, the AT was relocated off the mountain.[26] In other areas, civilian communications systems, primarily radio towers and telephone lines, also "blotted out" sections of the trail.[27]

The development of new military complexes, roads, houses, and incompatible recreational facilities during the postwar era, combined with the intensification of logging and agricultural activities, threatened to destroy the trail—particularly on private land. Trail advocates correctly anticipated that these threats would increase in the coming decades. As a result, AT enthusiasts became more determined to attain greater support from federal partners and to get the trail on public lands through outright purchase or easements.[28]

Under Myron Avery's leadership in the late 1940s, the ATC focused on protecting the AT corridor and was less involved in promoting a broad environmental agenda. In 1946 Avery wrote, "Carrying the Appalachian Trail

Daniel Hoch, Earl Shaffer, and Murray Stevens, 1955. These men helped lead the AT toward
its federal status between 1945 and 1968. Representative Hoch (D-PA, left) introduced the
first bill for national footpaths to Congress in 1945, Shaffer (center) inspired thousands by
being the first person to hike the AT end-to-end, and Stevens (right) served as the chairman
of the ATC from 1952 to 1961. Courtesy of the Appalachian Trail Conservancy.

into public ownership is the primary and fundamental problem of the Conference. If this battle is not won, then all else is useless."[29] Although the
ATC focused primarily on protecting the AT corridor in the decades that
followed World War II, the organization's efforts to prevent development

and the regulation of industrial uses throughout the eastern mountains reinforced the work of a growing number of environmental organizations. Between the 1950s and 1970, national environmental organizations experienced a dramatic growth in membership.[30] Many members of the local trail clubs affiliated with the ATC were also listed among the memberships of national environmental groups such as the Sierra Club, the Wilderness Society, and the National Audubon Society.[31] In addition to the growth of private environmental advocacy organizations, the number of land trusts also began to increase. The country's first national land trust, what became known as the Nature Conservancy, began in 1946 and served as a model for protecting land through private acquisition.[32] AT advocates' efforts to protect a sylvan swath across the Appalachian Mountains echoed growing public support for both public and private approaches to environmental protection, and revealed new ideas about the purpose of land conservation.

FROM FOOTPATH TO CONSERVATION CORRIDOR: NEW IDEAS ABOUT THE NATURE OF THE TRAIL

To protect the Appalachian Trail from dramatic environmental and cultural changes in the postwar era, Daniel K. Hoch, a US Representative from Pennsylvania and officer of the Blue Mountain Eagle Climbing Club, first proposed a bill for a national system of footpaths in 1945. Hoch claimed that as a new type of recreational area, the national footpaths would be "just as novel as were the national parks and national forests when first proposed."[33] After a brief committee hearing in the House of Representatives in 1945, committee chairman J. W. Robinson concluded that there was no need to "federalize" the country's footpaths. He maintained that demand for such a system did not exist; trails were a "local affair," not a "national affair" and should be managed and developed by state and local groups. Myron Avery, who was then serving as chairman of the ATC, attended the hearing and argued that the ATC viewed the Appalachian Trail as "a national thing, as one project, rather than 14 separate projects which might have 14 different and varying policies."[34] Despite compelling arguments made by Hoch, Avery, and their allies, trail advocates were unable to convince Robinson that the bill was worthy of ratification. Hoch's congressional colleagues quickly dismissed the bill, and the movement to establish a system of national footpaths was set to the wayside for the next twenty years, until 1968, when Congress passed the National Trails Act.

During that time, between 1945 and 1968, members of the trail community began to view the AT not merely as a thin footpath but as a corridor of protected land to buffer hikers from the sights and sounds of civilization. AT advocates became increasingly eager to protect lands adjacent to the trail, but they had different ideas about how land within an AT corridor should be protected and what types of land uses would be appropriate. As a long, narrow pathway running through some of the most populated regions in the country, the AT faced a host of challenges associated with changes in land use and ownership. Yet it also possessed the flexibility to adapt to this changing mosaic—winding through remote forests in some areas and weaving between cultivated fields and suburban backyards in others.

For many trail advocates, the AT corridor would protect a thin strip of wilderness in the East. From its origins in the 1920s, the ATC promoted the Appalachian Trail as "a footpath through the wilderness," and many of the organization's members were active in the movement to pass the 1964 Wilderness Act, which protected nine million acres of federal land under a new legal definition of wilderness. According the 1964 act, wilderness areas were defined in contrast to "areas where man and his own works dominate the landscape." Wilderness was a place that was "untrammeled by man, where man himself is a visitor who does not remain."[35] Most of the new wilderness areas established by the 1964 act were created out of existing public lands in the West, and therefore did not have much effect on the AT until Congress passed the Eastern Wilderness Areas Act in 1975.

In some ways, the AT fit the definition outlined by the 1964 Wilderness Act. In most places, the trail seemed relatively pristine. Yet the history of land use and ownership in the eastern hills was much more extensive than in remote areas in the West. Also, many AT advocates believed that traditional land uses along the corridor added an important cultural dimension to the AT experience. Since the project's beginnings, trail volunteers had worked with landowners to accommodate a range of land uses, and they aimed to maintain these positive relations. Arguing in favor of the creation of a national trails system in the 1960s, Anthony Wayne Smith, president and general counsel of the National Parks Association, noted that trails could be established with relatively little difficulty because they would "disturb very few presently existing land uses."[36] Members of the ATC realized that in the East, where farming, logging, and mining had long influenced landscapes along the trail, trying to defend an idea of nature that excluded all human influence was an unrealistic goal. Outside of a few isolated patches

Park officials plan to remove a homestead in Shenandoah National Park. To create a sense of wildness in the national parks, the National Park Service removed traces of human history. Here officials have bulldozed an old farmhouse and outbuilding in Shenandoah National Park. Courtesy of the Appalachian Trail Conservancy.

Site of removed homestead in Shenandoah National Park. Courtesy of the Appalachian Trail Conservancy.

of old-growth forest on the tops of remote mountains, those types of land-scapes simply did not exist in the eastern United States. Instead, advocates sought to have the trail meander through a mosaic of existing landscapes and land uses. For some AT enthusiasts, "nature" meant pristine places untouched by human intervention, but for many others, it included farm fields, managed forests, and pastured hillsides.

AT advocates' ideas about wilderness were, in part, influenced by the economic geography of the eastern mountains. Instead of adhering to a defi-nition of wilderness that precluded all land uses, trails advocates and their allies within the National Park Service pointed out that expanding outdoor recreation opportunities in the hinterlands would bring much-needed eco-nomic development to rural areas. In 1964, a report by the National Park Service found that

the Appalachian mountain chain offers the most significant opportunity for supplying the needs for more remote natural areas. Lying near the east coast "megalopolis" and the growing urban, industrial complexes in western Pennsylvania and central New York, the mountains are even now relatively accessible to multitudes of people. If the public can act quickly enough, acquisition of recreational lands in the mountains can logically serve as the backbone of a concentrated effort to protect and develop important outdoor recreation resources.[37]

As in Benton MacKaye's initial vision of the AT, Park Service officials rec-ognized that the trail could provide a vital link for broader economic devel-opment and cultural resource preservation in the Appalachian Mountains.

In the midst of national debates over appropriate types of land use, trail advocates—many of whom were active in the national park, wilder-ness preservation, and conservation movements—argued that because of its shape, size, and scope, the Appalachian Trail was a resource that could provide protection of relatively untrammeled landscapes while also being consistent with well-planned recreational developments and working land-scapes. They promoted the AT—and later, other long-distance trails—as a project in which wilderness and park advocates, and even forest and agri-cultural industries, could work together to define a common agenda in an emerging framework of multiple use.[38]

When Congress passed the Multiple-Use Sustained Yield Act of 1960, it set a legal precedent for the management of national forests that

acknowledged the importance of outdoor recreation and wildlife protection while also maintaining traditional management goals, such as timber
production and watershed protection.[39] Like many well-intentioned land
management paradigms, defining "multiple-use management" was a difficult task. In the national forests, federal land managers sought to please the
growing number and diversity of users, but balancing competing interests
proved to be more difficult in practice than in concept.[40] Paul Vincent, a
long-time trail supporter and supervisor of the Forest Service's southern
region, argued that multiple-use legislation offered a way to "stretch our
states' acres to meet the many demands we must expect in the decades and
centuries ahead."[41] Like others, Vincent believed that that the trail could
help satisfy the growing demand for outdoor recreation without interfering
with plans for timber production, and in this sense the project was compatible with the goals of multiple-use management.

During the attempt to establish federal legislation in the 1940s and again
in the 1960s, trail advocates argued that national trails would help set aside
something akin to wilderness without having to fit an increasingly fixed
idea of pristine nature. In the New York–New Jersey area, advocates claimed
that small-scale farms, old cellar holes, and historic mining and milling sites
all added "personality to this country that a wilderness newly discovered
does not have."[42] Instead of being unsightly nuisances to erase from the
landscape, many viewed traces of historic work and old sites of industrial
production as interesting features to highlight along the trail. This differed from earlier national park policies that required human imprints to
be removed in order to create a sense of uninhabited wilderness for visitors.
For example, in Great Smoky Mountains and Shenandoah National Parks,
park officials had burned down homes and removed flowerbeds in order
erase traces of civilization in the parks.[43] To many trail advocates, these
traces of the past added to the experience of hiking; in a sense, for them,
the nature to be protected along the trail was both functional, and historical. Getting stronger federal protection for the trail would not necessarily
exclude the human history contained in the landscape or traditional land
uses such as logging, grazing, or farming but would create ways to regulate
these activities and prevent problems associated with resource exploitation
and pollution.[44]

Appalachian Trail advocates argued that the project would promote conservation efforts in other ways as well. Proponents believed
that hiking and camping along the eastern mountains would help

Americans gain a greater appreciation of the natural world. Although many forms of outdoor recreation became increasingly popular during the post-war era, there was a sense among trail advocates that simple activities like walking and camping in nature would more effectively promote environmental awareness than other forms of outdoor recreation. They claimed that people who hiked the trail would develop a deeper connection with nature than those who glanced at the same views through the windshields of their automobiles. An article in the *Lynchburg News* noted that most "people find that prolonged driving along the high mountain scenic drives becomes actually monotonous. On the other hand, the change of scenery while walking is slower and the mind accepts and records it better."[45] This idea was often expressed in literature produced by the trail clubs during the postwar era. In 1946, Jean Stephenson, editor of ATC publications, wrote that if "one is to know Nature, one must frequent the woods. One of the best ways to come to know the woodlands is to follow winding woodland trails."[46]

By sparking environmental awareness though slow-moving experiences in nature, advocates believed that the Appalachian Trail would promote environmental values among the nation's citizens and inspire them to take action. In his testimony to promote the national trails legislation in 1945, Representative Hoch spoke about the need for environmental protection and the importance of citizen involvement. He articulated a narrative of historic decline, explaining that there was a time when

> the wilderness was a nuisance, when man felt it their duty to destroy it. This was perfectly proper, for then farmers were establishing their farms, and homes were being hewn out of the wilderness. But man went too far with this destruction, and in doing so unbalanced nature. As a consequence man is suffering. His water supply has become depleted; insects, rodents, and blight attack his crops to a degree unknown when there was more wilderness. When man destroyed the wilderness, he destroyed his best friends—the birds and other wilderness creatures which were provided by nature to keep in check weeds, insects, rodents, which are so destructive to the grains and fruits of the farms.[47]

Hoch argued that the national trails would not only help protect remaining wild areas and provide opportunities for wholesome recreation but would also "teach people the value of the wilderness to the end that they may become interested in conserving it."[48] In this sense, he believed that national trails would help Americans develop an understanding of changes in the countryside while also motivating them to protect it.

Perhaps one of the most powerful statements that helped connect the Appalachian Trail project to growing concerns about environmental protection was president Lyndon B. Johnson's 1965 speech "The Natural Beauty of Our Country." In it, Johnson outlined a range of environmental concerns and proposed several steps to address the issues. Addressing such topics as the preservation of scenic areas in national parks, the protection of air and water supplies, the rejuvenation of urban spaces, and the proliferation of "technological waste" that affected human and environmental health, Johnson called for a "new conservation." He stated, "Our conservation must not be just the classic conservation of protection and development, but a creative conservation of restoration and innovation. Its concern is not with nature alone, but with the total relation between man and the world around him."[49]

Johnson's message reflected an emerging idea about the proper ethical relationship between humans and the environment that was popularized by Aldo Leopold, an influential conservationist and one of the founders of the Wilderness Society, along with Benton MacKaye. In his famous treatise on the land ethic, Leopold wrote that humans should not act as conquerors of nature but as plain members of the ecological communities that support civilization.[50] Like Leopold and many AT advocates, Johnson believed that understanding our inherent connection to the natural world required full-bodied immersion in nature—experiences that the Appalachian Trail would help facilitate. In concluding his 1965 speech, the president claimed that "we need to copy the great Appalachian Trail in all parts of America" as a way to promote awareness of the "total relation" between humans and the environment.[51]

Environmental awareness among American citizens did indeed swell in the 1960s, with the publication of paradigm-shifting works such as Rachel Carson's *Silent Spring* in 1962, and the passage of the early versions of key environmental statutes such as the Clean Air Act in 1963 and the Water Quality Act in 1965. Citizens' support for environmental causes gained momentum during the 1960s and culminated in the largest single day of grassroots demonstration in US history on April 22, 1970, when communities around the country celebrated the first official Earth Day. It was no mere coincidence that the man who helped to organize and establish Earth Day, Senator Gaylord Nelson of Wisconsin, was also the individual who

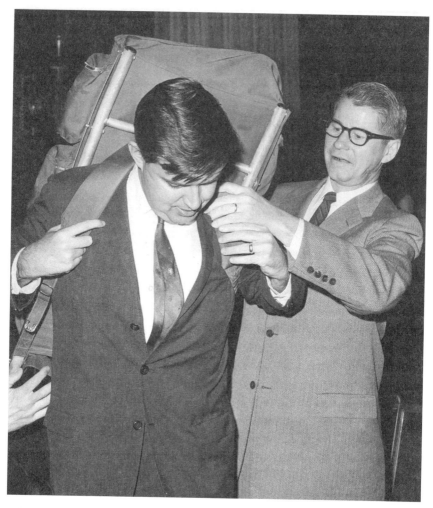

US secretary of agriculture Orville Freeman helps senator Frank Church (D-ID) with his pack. Church, who served in the Senate from 1957 to 1981, was a staunch advocate for wilderness legislation in the 1960s. Both men supported the 1968 National Trails Act. Courtesy of the Appalachian Trail Conservancy.

proposed national trails legislation in the 1960s. In a congressional statement in support of the Appalachian Trail, Nelson claimed that the AT would provide a means for people to experience "an intimate relationship" with the natural world and thereby be inspired to aid in its protection.[52]

Many supporters echoed Nelson's desire to use the AT project as a means to engage citizens in environmental protection efforts, and Nelson's bill received support from unexpected allies outside of the environmental community. Because of its thin shape and populist origins, the trail project did not pose a major threat to industry and was supported by several labor groups. In his statement supporting the National Trails Act, Franklin Wallick, an AT advocate and representative of the United Automobile, Aerospace, and Agricultural Implement Workers of America (AFL-CIO), argued that national trails would promote physical health, a sense of community, and an environmental ethic. He claimed, "Walking is a free and vigorous way for people of all ages to maintain good health, an alert feel for the world around them, and a sound appreciation of nature." Protecting lands that would be accessible to urban populations for recreation would help develop "a spirit of neighborliness" and community identity in places throughout the East.[53] Like many others, Wallick believed trails could serve as conduits to promote the well-being of workers and the health of communities connected to the trail. That union leaders such as Wallick supported the national trails legislation demonstrates surprising common ground between labor and environmental groups—interests that were often at odds in the late twentieth century—and signaled the persistence of MacKaye's vision for social collaboration along the trail.[54]

As Americans' desire to protect human health and the environment increased during the 1960s, widespread support for federal involvement in large-scale conservation initiatives increased. At the same time, the membership of the ATC grew and the organization became more savvy in its lobbying and public relations efforts. Trail advocates realized that protecting and maintaining the trail would require new forms of collaboration and cooperation between public and private groups, but some of the local clubs affiliated with the ATC were wary of handing the project over to the federal government. Some clubs, such as Vermont's Green Mountain Club, feared that the transfer of power might diminish the volunteer spirit and sense of local ownership that had characterized the project from its inception. Vermont's Long Trail, which overlapped with the AT in the southern half of the state, was a great source of state pride. Many Vermonters were concerned about the possible loss of autonomy and control.[55]

Other clubs were concerned about how federal involvement in the AT project might affect the physical characteristics of the trail itself. In the New York metropolitan area, advocates feared that federal control would cause local trail networks to be "gradually brought into conditions now obtained in some National Parks where they are widened and graded into near boulevards."[56] The New Yorkers' concerns echoed those of several increasingly powerful conservation groups, such as the Wilderness Society, the Sierra Club, the Nature Conservancy, and the Audubon Society.

Since the National Park Service's establishment in 1916, the agency had struggled to achieve its dual mission of providing park resources for the public while also preserving the integrity of those resources. When visitation to the national parks and forests surged in the postwar era, the National Park Service responded with an ambitious plan to improve the park system known as Mission 66. The plan, implemented in 1956, called for the construction of new buildings and roads within the national parks—an infrastructural renaissance to be completed by the agency's fiftieth anniversary, 1966.[57] But by the early 1960s, many conservationists became increasingly critical of new developments in the national parks, and argued that the federal government had failed to protect the integrity of the nation's natural resources in the face of competing postwar demands.[58] In 1962, ATC secretary Jean Stephenson reported that because the Park Service and Forest Service had experienced so much "sniping" by conservation organizations, many officials "dread[ed] to have any such groups display interest in any proposal before them." Stephenson regretted the lack of trust between the private groups and the federal partners, and acknowledged that in the case of the AT, volunteers had usually met with "splendid cooperation."[59]

Because of the ATC's long-standing relationships with the National Park Service and the US Forest Service, the organization occasionally found itself playing an intermediary role among private conservation groups, local trail clubs, and federal agencies. For example, in the 1960s, the National Park Service planned to extend the Blue Ridge Parkway into Georgia. With conflict looming on the horizon, the ATC worked with Park and Forest Service officials, local Georgia Appalachian Trail Club members, and members of the Audubon Society and the Nature Conservancy to try to find a route for the proposed parkway that would not negatively affect the forest ecosystem or interfere with the trail corridor. Although the extension was never created, the planning process revealed how trail advocates occasionally served as mediators between other increasingly critical conservation groups and federal land managing agencies.

The ATC and many of its affiliated local clubs tried to maintain positive relations with the National Park Service and US Forest Service by avoiding official stances against parkways and other recreational developments. Yet most trail advocates were not indifferent to these types of infringements along the trail. Instead of having the ATC take an official stance on a particular issue as an organization, trail volunteers often used their extensive social networks to encourage individual members to take particular actions. For example, when the Park Service announced its plans to build the Blue Ridge Parkway extension in Georgia, the ATC and the Georgia Appalachian Trail Club were concerned about the effects that the new road would have on the trail corridor. Yet members of both groups were also concerned about protecting their relationship with the National Park Service. Many felt that the agency would be an important ally in future initiatives, and they did not want to jeopardize their connections. Instead of taking an official stand against the proposed skyline extension as a group, Gannon Coffey, the president of the Georgia club, asked members to write letters to their representatives and bring publicity to the trail's cause, urging that they "write *in their own name*, speaking for *themselves*, to newspapers or Congressmen," and not to speak for the Georgia Appalachian Trail Club or the ATC. Coffey maintained that the trail clubs should not formally oppose the parkway project because they needed to "be able to save face" for future negotiations with the National Park Service.[60]

A similar phenomenon occurred between the trail clubs and the US Forest Service. In 1957 the agency had planned to lease approximately twenty acres of national forest land in the George Washington National Forest to the Potomac Conference of Seventh-Day Adventists. The church wanted to build a camp for kids at Crabtree Meadow that would include a swimming pool, baseball field, and a bunkhouse that would accommodate two hundred youngsters. Such camps were not uncommon; the Forest Service had permitted approximately six hundred similar camps throughout the national forests at that time. Several members of the Natural Bridge Appalachian Trail Club wanted to protest the camp, but they recognized that, like the Seventh-Day Adventists, their group benefited from policies that allowed private nonprofit organizations to extensively use national forest land. They also received pressure from the ATC not to press the issue. The secretary of the ATC, George Blackburn, wrote to Hester Hastings, the president of the Natural Bridge Appalachian Trail Club, to encourage her not to jeopardize the trail community's relationship with the Forest Service by objecting to the proposed church camp.[61] Hastings did protest the camp, however, but in her correspondence with Forest Service officials, she maintained that she spoke for herself and not for the ATC and its associated clubs. The permit was never allowed, and instead the church group purchased a tract of private land nearby.[62] Like the situation in Georgia, Hastings's actions demonstrated how individuals affiliated with the trail community used the fluidity of their private identities and the flexibility of the quasipublic status of the ATC to influence national land-management decisions.[63]

In addition to some citizens' concerns about federal projects, long-standing tensions between federal land management agencies also posed challenges to the AT project. Although the National Park Service and the US Forest Service had generally worked amicably with trail advocates in the 1920s and 1930s, postwar efforts to bring a stronger federal presence to the project caused historic tensions to resurface.[64] In their first attempt to get the AT designated as a national trail in the 1940s, trail advocates suggested that the US Forest Service be the primary federal leader on the project because more miles of the trail lay within the borders of national forests than within the boundaries of national parks. Outside of Shenandoah and Great Smoky Mountains National Parks—the two national parks through which the trail passed—trail advocates emphasized that the trail would "in no way" affect the Park Service.[65]

Before representative Daniel Hoch introduced his national footpaths legislation in 1945, the ATC gave copies of the bill to the superintendents of the two national parks, along with a memo that emphasized the cooperative nature of the project. Park Service officials who had apparently not seen the memo, and had not conferred with the ATC, mistakenly thought that the bill would give the US Forest Service jurisdiction over a strip of land in the national parks. In protest, the National Park Service submitted an adverse report to the congressional committee that was overseeing the trails legislation.[66]

Because ATC leaders had taken express pains to emphasize the cooperative nature of the project and avoid territorial disputes between the agencies, they were upset about the Park Service's damaging submission. After ATC chairman Myron Avery read the unexpectedly negative statement, he wrote to the director of the National Park Service, Newton B. Drury, and to the author of the report, Arthur Demaray.[67] Avery told the Park Service officials that their unfavorable account "was more detrimental to itself than to the project" because it would "be interpreted as premised on the 'feud' with the Forest Service, and would enhance the criticism which it experienced in the East from conservation circles."[68] Avery reminded the agency that despite many AT advocates' disapproval of new road construction and other recreational developments in the national parks, the ATC had publicly defended the agency against harsh criticism. Many of these long-time supporters of the Park Service would be offended by the agencies' adverse report. Drury called Avery within two days and told him that he would try to submit a supplemental statement to clarify the Park Service's general support for the AT project.

Not wanting to burn future bridges with the agency, the ATC wrote in its monthly newsletter to members, "While it is a situation which should not have occurred, *Appalachian Trailway News* feels that the National Park Service report should not be construed or interpreted as reflecting opposition to the Trail project or lack of support. It can best be written off as an unfortunate incident."[69] As an organization, the ATC again tried to maintain its relationships with the National Park Service and US Forest Service, and did not want misunderstandings or tensions in one decade to affect policies in another. When legislators killed the 1945 bill to create national footpaths, AT advocates realized that having full support from both the National Park Service and the US Forest Service would be essential for future legislative efforts.

Administrative differences occurred not only between federal partners but also increasingly among the various state partners involved in the AT project. As the following chapter will explain, collaborating with three federal land managing agencies—the US Forest Service, the National Park Service, and the Tennessee Valley Authority (on a very small section of the trail)—and with natural resource agencies from the fourteen states through which the trail passed became a major challenge to the AT movement. Yet because the project's locus of power had historically rested within its extended network of citizen volunteers, trail advocates were able to work with state and federal partners as independent agents not beholden to a particular administrative lineage or ideology.

AMERICA'S FIRST FEDERAL FOOTPATHS

Between 1945, when Representative Hoch first introduced a bill to create a national system of footpaths, and the passage of the National Trails Act in 1968, Americans' desire to recreate in the national parks swelled. Visits to the national parks jumped from fourteen million in 1955 to forty-six million in 1974.[70] In response to this growing demand, Congress passed several key pieces of legislation to improve existing parks and expand the national park system. In 1961, Congress began approving the appropriation of money from offshore oil leases to acquire land to create eastern national parks such

President Johnson at the signing of the National Trails Act, 1968. The 1968 National Trails Act, signed by President Johnson (center), created the Appalachian Trail and the Pacific Crest Trail as the first two national scenic trails in the United States. It also authorized the study of fourteen other trails to be included in the system. Courtesy of the Appalachian Trail Conservancy.

as the Cape Cod National Seashore. The Land and Water Conservation Fund, established in 1965, provided a necessary mechanism for funding land acquisition for several new types of national park units, including national seashores, recreation areas, trails, and wild and scenic rivers. These new kinds of national parks, including the national trails, reflected the agency's desire to bring the parks to the people—to locate new park units where the bulk of the population lived and, for better or for worse, where many Americans worked and owned land.

The expansion and improvement of park resources in the 1960s marked a broader transition in national park policy in which the agency shifted from carving parks out of the public domain in the West to the much more complex task of creating public recreational spaces in densely populated, privately owned land near the urbanized East.[71] The passage of the 1968 National Trails Act was not only part of this important transition in public land policy but was also a pivotal moment in the history of the Appalachian Trail. After half a century of advocacy and diplomacy, trail volunteers had successfully achieved federal protection for the project—at least on paper.

The purpose of the new national scenic trails was to provide the "maximum outdoor recreation potential" and "the conservation and enjoyment of the nationally significant scenic, historic, natural, or cultural qualities of the areas through which such trails may pass."[72] The 1968 National Trails Act designated the Pacific Crest Trail in the West and the Appalachian Trail in the East as the first national scenic trails in the country. The Pacific Crest Trail primarily lay on public land, so its development was relatively straightforward compared to the acquisition of new private lands that was required for the AT and for other eastern trails that would come later. In 1968, only about one third of the AT lay within the boundaries of existing public lands—much of which was in the southern national forests. The rest of the corridor existed on private land that was increasingly threatened by postwar changes.[73]

The goal of the AT program as outlined in the 1968 act was to create a public corridor that was approximately two thousand miles long and an average of two hundred feet wide. To promote local ownership of the AT project, federal officials encouraged state or local governments to initiate their own land acquisition programs. If state or local agencies failed to attain legal access to the trail right-of-way within two years, the act authorized the secretary of the Interior to take action. Congress appropriated five million dollars for federal acquisition efforts along the AT, and although condemnation was generally avoided, the 1968 act contained provisions that allowed the National Park Service to use the power of eminent domain on the acquisition of properties of up to twenty-five acres per mile. Project partners estimated that they would need to acquire about 630,500 acres in order to create a publicly protected corridor that was about two thousand miles long and an average width of two hundred feet.[74]

The act required the secretary of the Interior to organize an Appalachian National Scenic Trail Advisory Council (ANSTAC) that the Park Service would consult before making important decisions about land acquisition. A representative of the National Park Service was to lead the council, and the group would include officials from the US Forest Service and the states, members of the Appalachian Trail Conference and its local clubs, and landowners from areas through which the trail passed. The purpose of the advisory council was to maintain an open forum for communication among the different groups involved in the project. In this way, the federal government attempted to remain connected to the project's historic grassroots structure and to collaborate with a variety of public, private, local, and nonlocal partners.[75]

Many long-term advocates were curious about how the next phase of trail development would unfold and how stronger federal involvement might affect the project. In his testimony before the Senate in 1967, ATC executive secretary Ed Garvey asked, "Will the individual initiative and personal stewardship that have been vital to the Trail and [have] added their own unique flavor be lost? Will the government convert the Trail into something unrecognizable and undesired by those citizens who are now seeking its protection?"[76] Others wondered how landowners with whom volunteers had established relatively positive relationships would react to this shift in leadership. In the effort to pass federal trail legislation in the 1940s and again in the 1960s, ATC leaders such as Garvey insisted that the movement to federalize the trail was worth these risks because without federal assistance, they feared that there would soon be no trail left to protect.[77] The loose arrangements with landowners were proving to be no match for the dramatic environmental and economic changes that began in the postwar era and continued to erode the integrity of the trail during the 1950s and 1960s.

In the decades leading up to the 1968 National Trails Act, the Appalachian Trail project became a litmus test for how the country was going to respond to competing economic uses of America's hinterlands. As logging, farming, and housing pressures increased, so too did the demand for places to recreate in nature. In some ways, the AT project was tied to a larger movement to provide more recreational opportunities to the American public. The 1968 National Trails Act was part of a broader set of laws and programs that recognized outdoor recreation as a public good that needed to be protected by the government. As the National Park Service and the US Forest Service planned ways to improve and expand recreational resources through programs such as Mission 66 and Operation Outdoors, Congress established the Outdoor Recreation Resources Review Commission (ORRRC) in 1958 and passed the Outdoor Recreation Act in 1963. The 1963 act required the Department of the Interior to prepare a nation-wide plan for meeting Americans' growing demand for outdoor recreation and established the Bureau of Outdoor Recreation. Congress' passage of the

Wilderness Act a year later was another great victory for outdoor enthusiasts looking to experience the sublime in nature. All of these initiatives demonstrated the growing influence of the federal government in protecting the scenic experiences of outdoorsy Americans.

At the same time, however, because of its legacy of citizen involvement, its narrow shape, and its general location along ridgelines, the Appalachian Trail project offered a slightly different direction for the future of land management in the eastern United States. The project brought together all levels of government, from local municipalities to federal land management agencies; an array of private conservation groups; and a host of civic-minded individuals. This complex campaign involved adapting to certain existing land uses and ownership patterns while protecting a thin corridor of the Appalachian Mountains from destructive developments.

As debates about the appropriate use and control of land intensified during the postwar era, the AT became metaphorically, and sometimes literally, a line between different ideologies, policies, and approaches to conservation. The project maintained this liminal state by relying on its quasipublic status and its historically positive associations with government officials and local landowners. By building on this dynamic interplay of power between an extended grassroots network and a number of state and federal agencies during the movement to federalize America's footpaths, the AT project began to formalize long-term relations between public and private partners. Although advocates sought greater federal support, the project remained rooted in a growing grassroots constituency. Because of its unusual combination of centralized and decentralized authority, the Appalachian Trail helped to blaze a thin and somewhat tenuous path for public-private conservation partnerships in the 1950s and 1960s—a formative period for US environmental policy and the modern environmental movement.

Curious to see what had happened to one section of the AT that had not received federal protection during this critical period, my research assistant and I visited the trail's original southern terminus in 2007. Recalling the Chattanoogans' vivid descriptions of chicken filth and pungent oozes, we set out to see what had become of the one section of trail that lay outside the boundary of the Chattahoochee National Forest. Finding this historic endpoint proved more difficult than I anticipated. At a gas station in Jasper, just a few miles west of Mount Oglethorpe, we asked for directions to this once-celebrated summit. The attendant had never heard of Mount Oglethorpe, and two other customers asked if we meant Tate Estates—one of the developments that had threatened the wilderness character of the AT in the mid-twentieth century. Armed with vague directions, we headed for the tallest peak in the area. When we got to the top, we found no evidence of the trailside chicken coops that had once layered the trail with a coat of fecal slime. Instead, we found a winding road, a radio tower, and a series of expensive homes. Amid these decidedly unwilderness-like features, we discovered the decaying foundation of the original concrete obelisk that had once marked the AT's southern terminus.

Although there was no pungent ooze, nor any chickens in sight, the cracked concrete and encroaching brambles were a telling sight. Without federal protection, the trail had, as its mid-twentieth-century promoters foresaw, turned into a paved lot subject to the whims and wills of private developers. The path to federalizing this famous footpath—to completely protecting the trail through public ownership—was blazed during the two decades that followed World War II. Yet as the environmental and economic changes that began in the postwar era intensified in the late 1960s and 1970s, implementing the new federal legislation proved to be much more complicated than its advocates had predicted.

CHAPTER 4

FALLOUT FROM
FEDERALIZATION

IN THE DECADE THAT FOLLOWED THE 1968 NATIONAL TRAILS ACT, STATE
and federal authorities struggled to establish who would be responsible for
acquiring the 886 miles of Appalachian Trail that existed on private land or
roads, and trail advocates encountered new and unanticipated challenges.
In 1974, the Dartmouth Outing Club received a letter from a disgruntled
landowner who wrote that the next time he saw a snowmobile crossing the
AT on his land, he would "shoot their machine from under them."[1] Another
Vermont landowner complained of motorcycles on the trail and reported
that a negligent trail camper had recently burned an entire acre of her property. As a result, she wrote to the Dartmouth Outing Club: "we want the
trail off our land—NOW!"[2]

In addition to losing the support of these previously agreeable landowners, a growing number of new landowners—primarily second homeowners—were often unreceptive to having the trail on their property. In New
Jersey, a stretch of nineteen miles that had once been owned by a handful of
farmers and a few large absentee landowners had been turned into eighty-
eight separate holdings. These eighty-eight owners held "widely divergent
attitudes about everything from the behavior of backpackers to the moral-
ity of eminent domain."[3] In Massachusetts, fifty-six miles of trail were
converted into seventy-five individual parcels, transforming a once scenic
stretch of trail into a forest of "No Trespassing" signs.[4] This trend toward
parcelization—the splitting of large land holdings into many smaller parcels—added to the complexity of negotiating land acquisition for the trail.
By 1974, ATC chairman Stanley Murray noted that "for all the promise of

Landowner sign. In the decade after Congress passed the 1968 National Trails Act, hikers increasingly encountered signs warning against trespass and inappropriate uses. Despite the trail's new federal status—and in some cases because of it—AT advocates continued to struggle to maintain a contiguous trail. Courtesy of the Appalachian Trail Conservancy.

protection, the Appalachian Trail environment remain[ed] as fragile as a frayed rope—and it's taut against the cutting edge of entrenched private ownership and burgeoning public use."[5]

As government officials engaged in bureaucratic battles over which agency would lead the project, and developers continued to carve up the Appalachian hinterlands, an unprecedented number of hikers descended upon the trail. The growing number of inexperienced hikers brought with them new problems associated with pollution, erosion, vandalism, motorized vehicles, and drug use. In some cases, the new generation of hikers alienated many landowners who had once welcomed the trail on their property. New landowners who had no prior relationship with the project, whose numbers were also rapidly increasing, were often hesitant to allow the trail to cross their land. In addition, a stronger federal presence and the perception that the government was planning to take people's land caused many landowners—both old and new—to preemptively remove the trail from their land.

At the same time, many trail advocates began to lose faith in the government's ability to meet the goals of the 1968 act: to protect the Appalachian Trail and the Pacific Crest Trail as the first examples in a growing system of national trails, and to provide for "the conservation and enjoyment of the nationally significant scenic, historic, natural, or cultural qualities of the areas through which such trails may pass."[6] Some felt that the greatest threat to the project was the "lingering and time-wasting hope" that the federal government could be "spurred . . . to action sufficient to save the Trail."[7] Howard Brackney, ATC board member, pointed out that the outright purchase of land by the government was unlikely not only because the 1968 act had not allocated sufficient funds for such a program but also because "the number of people already occupying these lands [was] too great to make their divestment and evacuation by government edict either politically feasible or morally defensible."[8] Despite the provisions of the 1968 act, by 1974, approximately 850 miles of trail still remained unprotected on rapidly developing private land.[9]

Although AT advocates celebrated the passage of the National Trails Act in 1968, establishing the AT as one of the first national scenic trails did not solve all of the problems facing the project. Ironically, the act not only failed to protect the AT in the decade that followed its passage, but its implementation created a new set of challenges. Three key issues that prevented the effective implementation of the Act included: (1) the struggle between state and federal agencies; (2) the growing popularity and use of the trail, and landowners' reactions to the trail and its users; and (3) expanded visions about the purpose of the AT that were tied to broader changes in Americans' views of environmental issues. In the decade that followed the 1968 National Trails Act, these challenges had important implications for both the future of the AT and for environmental politics in general. Political debates about states' rights, property rights, and the purpose of land conservation not only shaped decisions about how to protect the AT but were also central to shaping reactions to environmentalism in the late twentieth century.

PASSING THE BUREAUCRATIC BUCK

The 1968 act designated the secretary of the Interior as the primary administrator of the AT project, but it encouraged the states to lead efforts to protect and acquire land for the trail. The secretary's first responsibility was to establish the official location of the trail. Because long-time volunteers were often more knowledgeable about the existing route than National Park Service officials, the agency relied on these volunteers during the initial mapping process.[10] The ATC served as a "storehouse of knowledge" about the trail's current course, existing standards, potential problem areas, characteristics about trail users, and what constituted a "good Trail environment."[11]

The mapping process began with the ATC and Park Service working together to determine the trail's initial location. Once the general location of the trail was outlined on maps, volunteers carried large white plastic panels into the woods and laid them along the current trail. The Park Service then hired professional aerial photographers to take pictures of the plastic slabs that lay along the entire route from Georgia to Maine. After several months of delay due to weather and logistical issues, Park Service officials gave long-term volunteers a complete set of images to ground-truth the photos and map the route. The ATC's first hired administrative officer, Lester Holmes, then wrote a report to authorities in the fourteen states and to the regional directors of the Park Service to validate the trail's location. After public officials scouted and confirmed the route, the information was filed in the *Federal Register* in 1971 for public review.[12] At that point, the more complicated processes of planning relocations and acquiring the right-of-way for the trail could begin.

One of the greatest challenges facing the implementation of the 1968 act was determining which agency would lead acquisition efforts. According to the act, the secretary of the Interior was to work with the Appalachian National Scenic Trail Advisory Council to encourage state or local governments to acquire land for the trail. If state or local agencies failed to attain legal access to the trail right-of-way either through the use of easements or by fee simple acquisition within two years, the act authorized the secretary to do so. When the Park Service tried to encourage the states to apply for grants from the Land and Water Conservation Fund to acquire land for the AT corridor, and thus take the lead on protecting the AT corridor, the fourteen states responded with varying degrees of initiative. One scholar found that the initial stage of the acquisition process went more effectively in states where strong channels of communication and close relationships existed between local clubs and state officials.[13] Conversely, politically weak links between volunteers and state governments resulted in physically weak links—and occasionally gaping holes—in sections of private land along the two-thousand-mile route.

Prior to the 1968 National Trails Act, some states had enthusiastically launched their own legislation to establish the corridor within their boundaries. Massachusetts adopted a statewide statute on trails as early as 1922, and was the first state to pass legislation to acquire land for the AT in 1968. Although the legislation provided state funding to acquire the right-of-way and to hire a state coordinator for the process, it also stated that local clubs would continue to be responsible for maintaining the trail in the newly acquired sections.[14] Led by a sense of state pride, political support for the project, and the financial wherewithal to take such proactive measures, Massachusetts was a model for strong state initiative on the AT.[15]

In other states, when officials realized that the National Park Service was required to take action and spend federal dollars if the states failed to act in two years, they did exactly that—failed to act. Planners from New York's Department of Parks and Recreation, Ivan Vamos and Michael Geiss, reported that the federal legislation and the Park Service's approach to implementation had "galvanized" their department "into inactivity."[16] If the AT was truly to be a national trail, they figured that the Park Service could spend federal money on it, while the state's resources should be used to satisfy increasing demands for local recreational projects.

For some states, the trail simply wasn't a priority. In an interview with Ann Satterthwaite, a consultant hired by the ATC to help plan the future of the AT project, three officials from Vermont's Agency of Environmental Conservation reported that "on no uncertain terms" was the agency interested in the Appalachian Trail.[17] Even if they did support such a project, they told Satterthwaite that they had no money to spend on it. They wanted the "Feds [to] stick to their own business and not interfere with state activities."[18] In West Virginia, Robert Mathis of the Division of Planning and Development for the Department of Natural Resources reported that "people in West Virginia are totally apathetic about the Trail."[19] In Maryland, the acquisition program was stalled by weak relations between the local club and the state, a lack of public enthusiasm for the trail, and state authorities' belief that in two years, the federal government would take over the land acquisition process.[20] This range of reactions—from firm defiance of federal involvement and an emphasis on state rights in Vermont, to sheer lack of political support in places like West Virginia, to a strong desire to let the feds foot the bill in Maryland—prevented several states from participating in the land acquisition process as outlined in the 1968 act.

When nearly 40 percent of the trail remained on unprotected private lands in 1975, seven years after Congress passed the 1968 Trails Act, ATC leaders began to sense that all levels of government were shirking responsibility. Long-term advocates became irritated by the "cycle of the Park Service passing the buck to the states and the states passing the buck back to the Park Service."[21] Ultimately, however, many volunteers blamed the National Park Service for failing to assert a stronger leadership role. Expressing their frustration at a meeting in 1974, ATC leaders claimed that there was no one in the upper levels of the Department of the Interior who was "really interested in the Trail today."[22]

This perception was supported by the trends in leadership of the Appalachian National Scenic Trail Advisory Committee (ANSTAC), the federal advisory council that was established in 1968 to help coordinate the land acquisition program. In a detailed administrative history, Charles H. W. Foster, the group's first nongovernmental chairman, who served between 1975 and 1978, recalled that ANSTAC was initially "the classic federal advisory committee, destined to be seen and not heard."[23] Within the first five years of ANSTAC's existence, the National Park Service transferred three different chairman of the council at three different times—giving AT enthusiasts the impression that the trail was not a priority for the Park Service. In 1973, Edgar L. Gray, the Park Service official who had been serving as the chairman of ANSTAC, was reassigned to the Philadelphia Regional Office for Petroleum Allocation. In response to his new assignment, Gray wrote to ATC chairman Stanley Murray to explain in a somewhat ironic statement that "the energy crisis ha[d] finally superseded environmental awareness."[24] When the country's domestic oil production peaked in 1970 and leaders of Middle Eastern countries announced an embargo on oil in 1973, the Park Service decided that Gray's time would be better spent working to find oil rather than helping to build a recreational footpath across the Appalachian Mountains.

The secretary of the Interior's indifference to ANSTAC and the AT project upset members of the advisory group, particularly state leaders such as Walter L. Criley, director of Tennessee's Department of Conservation's Division of Planning and Development. Criley complained to secretary of the Interior Rogers C. B. Morton that Gray's transfer "leads us to question the priority assigned to the Appalachian Trail and other national trails projects."[25] He claimed that "the work and dreams of thousands of citizens who [had] worked for the enactment and subsequent implementation of the National Trails Act" had been threatened by the slow erosion of the federal advisory council. Moreover, Criley noted that the energy crisis was causing a "major change in lifestyles" in the American people, and he believed that in response "the federal government should be promoting the acceptance of foot and bicycle travel, not downgrading it."[26]

Many within the National Park Service were also concerned about their own agency's inability to lead the land acquisition process. They attributed the slow progress in land acquisition to several factors: the complex administrative logistics of the program, the spatial configuration of the AT, and the lack of federal funds and authority available to acquire land for the corridor. Coordinating such a large number of agencies, organizations, and individuals across such a geographically dispersed area was an administrative nightmare, and it required a level of time, personnel, and funding that legislators in 1968 had not anticipated. Although the 1968 act allocated five million dollars for land acquisition, even in late-1960s dollars such a figure could not buy many miles, and most of the money had been spent on the mapping program.[27] Richard Stanton, the first Park Service coordinator for the AT, who had helped to organize the initial mapping campaign, was one of many who felt that the federal government—and his agency in particular—would have to allocate far more resources to the program than the act had authorized.[28] Because the Park Service was busy acquiring park inholdings and working on new developments in existing national parks, the agency was hesitant to launch a massive land acquisition program for the AT—a new kind of unit within the national park system that came with its own special challenges.[29]

The unusual spatial configuration of long-distance trails presented unfamiliar administrative challenges for the Park Service, and some suspected that the agency was eschewing its responsibilities for managerial reasons. Robert Eastman, head of the Division of Special Projects for the Bureau of Outdoor Recreation, sensed that the National Park Service "never had any interest in the Appalachian Trail" because the agency "did not believe that linear parks were manageable park units." Like most other land managing agencies, he maintained, the Park Service wanted "parks to be square or rectangular in shape with limited access points for management control."[30] Eastman was not optimistic that the Park Service would ever fulfill its legal obligation to lead acquisition efforts for the Appalachian Trail. As the number of federal agencies devoted to outdoor recreation grew in the 1960s and 1970s, different agencies often had their own styles and approaches to protecting recreation resources. One AT advocate noted that the National Park Service and the

Bureau of Outdoor Recreation had "been at loggerheads on management of the Appalachian Trail" for some time.[31] These types of bureaucratic battles created a major challenge for the cooperative management and acquisition of corridor lands, but they were an inevitable consequence of attaining national status during an era of expanding federal authority.

Despite some encouraging first steps taken in some places like Massachusetts, no state had successfully acquired the entire right-of-way as outlined in the 1971 *Federal Register* during the decade after the 1968 Trails Act. Nor had any state planned to do so within the next five years. A sense of urgency spread among the ATC, and many members felt that "in five years, in some places, there may be nothing left worth acquiring."[32] The diverse reactions of the states demonstrated the weakness of decentralizing the responsibility for a national project among fourteen different states. The failure of this decentralized approach ultimately provided justification for stronger federal control that would occur when Congress amended the National Trails Act in 1978.

HIKERS, HIPPIES, AND HOMEOWNERS

While attempting to sort out the administrative steps necessary to begin acquiring and protecting trail lands in order to complete the AT corridor, bureaucratic delays exacerbated growing tensions among an increasingly diverse set of trail users and landowners. During the early 1970s, the number of new trail users and new landowners continued to rise. Newcomers to the trail project brought with them a range of attitudes toward the federal government as well as a variety of ideas about the control and use of land.

Prior to 1968, volunteers went to great measures to bolster the trail and encourage new users. After the act, they found themselves confronting rapidly changing patterns of use and an urgent need to protect the trail from overuse, particularly from new users.[33] In 1973, the ATC estimated that approximately four million people had hiked on the trail that year. At one checkpoint on the AT in the Great Smoky Mountains National Park, park rangers reported one hiker passing every twenty seconds.[34] In an attempt to quantify these changes in trail use, long-time trail volunteer and hiker Ed Garvey compared detailed notes he had taken during a 140-mile hike from Springer Mountain in Georgia to Wesser, North Carolina, in 1970 with notes from the same stretch of trail in 1976.[35] In a log book he had designed with Lester Holmes, Garvey had recorded the condition of the trail every day, the amount of litter he picked up, and the number of hikers he encountered. In 1976, he used the same set of procedures and covered the same distance at a similar time of the year. In 1970, he met 33 hikers in eleven days—including two weekends. In 1976, he met 214 hikers in nine days—including only one weekend. Of these 214 hikers, 117 were through-hikers on their way from Georgia to Maine.[36] By 1975, the *Washington Post* reported that the trail was "in jeopardy precisely because it has become too popular.... overuse, as well as development pressures, are pushing the trail off private lands on which more than 40 per cent of it is located."[37]

Some attributed the increase in trail use to changes in Americans' access to oil. In the 1950s and 1960s, Americans' love affair with auto-based rec-reation had intensified, and road trips to national parks out West became a popular ritual for many middle-class families east of the Mississippi. In the 1970s, the rising cost of gas and long lines at fuel stations deterred many Americans from taking long cross-country vacations. Limited by the impending energy crisis, eastern Americans replaced their pilgrimages to the western parks with jaunts closer to home. Walter Boardman, a through-hiker, trail maintainer, and executive director of the Nature Conservancy, speculated that the energy crisis might lead to "an enforced restriction on non-essential driving and a swing toward more walking and mass transit."[38] Echoing the ideas of Benton MacKaye, Boardman and other AT advocates argued that the trail could be part of a broader national program to promote alternative means of transportation and could be used to promote local land-use planning initiatives.

Regardless of whether visitors came to the AT out of a desire to conserve fuel or simply to walk in the woods, the number of trail users skyrocketed during the 1970s as the demand for outdoor recreation that surged in the postwar era continued to grow in the 1960s and 1970s. According to one comprehensive survey of Americans' outdoor recreation habits, in 1960, approximately 8 percent of people ages 18–44 enjoyed camping outdoors, and 5 percent enjoyed hiking. These numbers increased by 200 percent by 1980. By 1994, those 1960 percentages increased nearly fivefold for camping, and sevenfold for hiking.[39] Visits to the country's national parks increased from fourteen million in 1955 to forty-six million in 1974.[40] For an increas-ing number of hiking enthusiasts, the Appalachian Trail became a life-changing pilgrimage instead of a relaxing weekend outing as the number of through-hikers, those who walk the trail from end to end, increased from a total of 14 between 1950 and 1959, to 760 between 1970 and 1979.[41]

A new generation of hikers. The 1960s and 1970s brought a new generation of hikers to the trail. Courtesy of the Appalachian Trail Conservancy.

Trash at the Wiggins Spring Shelter, 1974. The growing popularity of the AT in the 1960s and 1970s also brought new problems associated with pollution and overuse. Courtesy of the Appalachian Trail Conservancy.

Not only did the sheer number of trail users increase, but the nature of trail users also changed. Although many hikers upheld the image of the wholesome Boy Scout–leading trailblazer of earlier times, there was also an influx of new users with a range of hiking and camping experience, as well as a range of respect for private property. For many young hikers who identified with the counter-culture revolution of the 1960s and 1970s, the trail provided a place to experiment with anti-establishment lifestyles. At an increasing rate, AT volunteers from Maine to Georgia reported that shelters along the trail were being turned into havens for the homeless, pads for pot parties, and sites for general beer-drinking debauchery. Times had changed, noted the *Washington Evening Star*, "The wilderness has become real estate and the earnest back-packed nature lovers of another day have been followed by hippies making whoopie in the ramshackle and poorly maintained shelters along the trail."[42] During one hiking season in 1975, rangers at Baxter State Park in Maine arrested over 130 people for smoking marijuana. The officers reported that they had begun to spend more time enforcing vandalism and drug laws, leaving less time for maintaining park resources and the AT. To prevent "the return of the undesirable that wishes to camp for free," rangers in Maine and officials in several other locations unsuccessfully advocated for the implementation of fees and licensing programs to regulate trail use.[43]

Not all new hikers were pot-smoking vandals, of course. Most new users were simply inexperienced. Alan Corindia, the assistant executive director of the Appalachian Mountain Club, noted that first-time users were a major source of environmental degradation on trails. At campsites, inexperienced hikers would often chop down green vegetation for fires or leave their trash strewn about. Corindia believed that most new hikers were not intentionally malicious; they simply lacked knowledge of backcountry etiquette. Regardless, he ultimately felt that there just wasn't "any environmental margin left for the Daniel Boone approach, learning by mistakes."[44] Like many others, he advocated for more hiker education programs and the creation of publications to explain the somewhat tacit rules of hiking and camping along the trail. These practices embodied a new approach to outdoor recreation that was based on an ethic known as the Leave No Trace principle.[45]

As the number and diversity of trail users grew, a division emerged between hikers and the trail-maintaining community. Although volunteers typically enjoyed hiking, not all hikers were trail workers. For many new hikers, the trail was simply a place to recreate, to commune with nature, or to test their physical fitness; not all hikers were interested in maintaining the famous footpath. Several officials involved with the project and some long-time members of the ATC regretfully characterized the new generation of hikers as "more action than conservation oriented."[46] By 1976, the hikers' reputation had become so tarnished, and landowners' reactions to hikers so mixed, that in promoting the Appalachian Greenway project, an

Hikers walking through backyards in the mid-Atlantic. Hikers increasingly found them-selves walking though people's backyards and along busy roads in the 1970s. These kinds of problems eventually led Congress to amend the 1968 National Trails Act in 1978 to authorize a more aggressive land acquisition program for the AT. Courtesy of the Appalachian Trail Conservancy.

effort to protect lands adjacent to the AT corridor, leaders argued that that the "hiker image should be avoided."[47]

Overcoming landowners' aversion to this "new breed of hiker" became an obstacle in the campaign to organize and acquire the right-of-way for the trail corridor.[48] State officials in charge of acquiring the right-of-way found that landowners would only sign agreements or easements if they could be assured that there would be no unauthorized use of the trail, such as hunting or use of motorized vehicles. Furthermore, state agents had to ensure that the trail would "receive adequate patrolling and police protection to prevent the types of incidents that everyone is talking about—the younger generation's pot parties and beer gatherings."[49] Regardless of the states' promises, because of the linear shape of the trail, its remote location, and its complex organizational structure, many landowners had little faith that the trail would be adequately policed.

Through-hikers on AT near Roanoke. Courtesy of the Appalachian Trail Conservancy.

The growing number of new landowners—many of whom were second homeowners—also made coordinating the right-of-way for the AT difficult. As soon as problems in one area were addressed, issues in another section arose. For example, as the Potomac Appalachian Trail Club focused on protecting the corridor from housing developments just outside of Charlottesville, Virginia, in the 1970s, the trail was "evicted" from several properties further north between the Shenandoah National Park and the Potomac River. ATC leaders noted that the area had been "stricken by an affliction . . . termed 'Landowneritis'" in which "multiple and sometimes weird reasons" were used to justify the evictions and force the trail onto busy roads.[50] Increasingly tenuous relations with landowners such as those in northern Virginia posed significant challenges to the acquisition program.

Furthermore, as the number of second homes in the mountains increased, so did the value of surrounding land. As a result, advocates found that the "genial farmer willing to grant a voluntary agreement . . . [was] being replaced by a corporation interested in capitalizing upon the development potential of the land."[51] The cost of land for the trail had always varied, but in all locations, the value of mountain land dramatically increased in the years following the 1968 act. According to figures reported by the ATC, in 1966, land values on the AT ranged from just a few dollars per acre in remote areas like southwest Virginia to seven hundred dollars an acre in parts of New Jersey and New York.[52] In 1974, land cost ten thousand dollars per acre in some parts of New Jersey, and up to twenty thousand dollars per acre in New York.[53] In rural areas like Vermont, land was still relatively inexpensive—approximately three hundred dollars per acre in 1974—but values were growing at a rate of ten percent every six months in some parts of the state.[54] Because the 1968 act had based its budget for AT allocations on an average of one hundred dollars per mile, these soaring land values prohibited acquisition. Even when officials sought written agreements and easements to acquire a thin right-of-way—an option that was initially less expensive than outright purchase—second homeowners who had purchased their mountain property for the explicit purpose of seeking solitude in nature were often not interested in opening their land for public use.

For an increasing number of landowners, the government's efforts to buy land to protect this recreational corridor became viewed as an infringement on their constitutional rights. Many landowners along the AT did not understand how easements would affect their rights, and they feared the threat of condemnation. Although the 1968 act authorized the use of condemnation as a last resort if all reasonable efforts and negotiation options failed, the Park Service generally avoided taking land from uncooperative landowners.[55] Not only would eminent domain create unwanted negative media attention and disrupt increasingly tenuous relationships with other landowners, but the act also didn't provide enough funding to use the power effectively. Regardless, the possibility of having their land condemned made many once-cooperative landowners nervous. Rumors began to spread along the trail that the government was taking land for the AT. In response, project leaders in New York emphasized the need to "soft shoe it" in wealthy areas east of the Hudson River and in the northwest corner of Connecticut, where residents were generally "fearful of any sort of public access."[56] Landowners in the area were particularly concerned about the protection of property rights, and later organized citizen groups such as Nail the Trail in New York and the Appalachian Trail Landowners Association in Connecticut to fight against the Park Service's land acquisition program.

Concerns about property rights in the 1970s were part of a growing resistance toward large-scale government projects and the intrusion of the central state into people's private lives. In northern Virginia, landown-ers had removed the trail from their property, and the *Washington Evening Star* reported that the closings resulted because "native Virginians" did not respond favorably to such "federal intrusions." The author went on to say, "What they bestow freely when politely asked they angrily snatch back when it is demanded of them. Now a bewildered National Park Service, without funds for condemnation or even surveys, is left to cope with enraged Con-federate landowners no less highly motivated then [sic] Moseby's raiders who once ranged through this country."[57] Those who protested federal initia-tives, like the National Park Service's acquisition program for the AT, often used symbolic figures from past rebellions against the US government to frame their opposition as part of a broader political movement. This rhetoric became especially powerful in the early 1980s, when the Reagan administra-tion focused its efforts on limiting the authority of the federal government, and resistance to big government became a powerful force in US politics.[58]

Furthermore, the relatively high social status held by technical experts, federal bureaucrats, and scientists that had characterized earlier generations, particularly in the postwar era, eroded in the 1960s and 1970s—a trend that president Jimmy Carter articulated in his infamous "Crisis of Confidence" speech in 1979. By the late 1970s, Americans on both sides of the political spectrum had become increasingly skeptical of the federal government. For liberals, the federal government had not done enough to follow through with legislation it had passed. For free-market-oriented conservatives, the power of the centralized state had retarded economic progress. Among the general public, scandals like Watergate had promoted a distrust of the country's highest executive office. Many Americans came to believe that the expansion of federal bureaucracy—a trend epitomized by new environmen-tal laws and the agencies created to implement them—was not necessarily the most effective way to address the real needs of local communities.

In the case of the AT, local officials complained that the project would take land off the tax rolls and diminish the economic base of the region. This fear was grounded in the experiences of several southern communities, such as Swain County, North Carolina, that endured decades of poverty after the federal government purchased approximately 80 percent of the land base in the 1930s and 1940s.[59] According to Arthur W. Cooper, the assis-tant secretary for North Carolina's Department of Natural and Economic Resources, local business and real estate interests portrayed the AT project as being led by outsiders who wanted "to save the land for themselves" and did not have "the interests of the local people at all in mind."[60] Antagonism toward the AT project was compounded by the fact that it was no longer primarily promoted by a handful of volunteers, but it had become, in the minds of some landowners, a federal land grab that served the interests of untrustworthy vagabonds.

The combination of these issues—bureaucratic buck-passing, changes in trail use and hiker behavior, parcelization of land for second-home development, concerns about protecting private property rights, and changing attitudes toward the federal government—led to profound changes in landowners' relationship to the project. As state and federal agencies struggled to determine who would lead the land-acquisition process, the development of private land proceeded undaunted. Soon, many trail advocates sensed that provisions for the skinny right-of-way outlined by the 1968 act and published in the *Federal Register* would not be sufficient. They felt that more was needed than a "narrow path winding through vacation home developments, through the noise of chain saws and barking dogs, or through the underbrush that hides the panoramic scenery."[61]

These concerns were part of a larger movement of organizations and individuals concerned about humans' effect on the environment. In the decade that followed the 1968 National Trails Act, the environmental awareness and bipartisan support for environmental protection that began in the 1960s continued to grow, and culminated in the single largest day of grassroots action in US history on April 22, 1970—the nation's first Earth Day. Efforts to protect the AT were tied to the broader environmental movement in two key ways: first by the changing organizational nature of the trail's largest advocacy group—the ATC—and second by the expanded vision that several AT leaders began to promote. Instead of merely seeking protection for a thin thread to walk on, some ATC leaders began to promote an ambitious plan to protect the broader landscapes through which the trail passed.

THE PROFESSIONALIZATION OF THE ATC

After the AT legally became a national trail in 1968, ATC chairman Stanley Murray noted two important changes affecting the AT project. One was the unanticipated growth in the popularity of backpacking and of use of the trail. The second was the "proliferation of paperwork, official agreements, guidelines, regulations, and legal definitions," which Murray felt, though necessary, were "decidedly alien to the notion of a simple, wilderness Trail"

Stanley Murray served as the chairman of the ATC from 1961 to 1975, and was a champion of the idea of an Appalachian Greenway. In addition to being a thin federally protected footpath, Murray felt that the AT corridor could be used to achieve broader land-protection goals. Courtesy of the Appalachian Trail Conservancy.

and the volunteers who maintained it.[62] Yet like other grassroots environmental groups during the late 1960s and 1970s, the Appalachian Trail Conference became a more professional organization and an influential player in national politics. The ATC's member list grew from one thousand in 1964 to ten thousand in 1975.[63] No longer was it a small volunteer organization operating on a shoestring budget. Instead, the organization had become "a business with a nationally known 'commodity.'"[64]

Because the ATC had always enjoyed a rather loose structure, with informal relationships between local clubs and official partners, and because of the rapid increase in bureaucratic responsibilities, the professionalization of the organization was a somewhat slow and complicated process. After hiring its first administrative officer, Lester Holmes, the organization quickly realized that it needed to learn how to raise money. Holmes met R. Phillip Hanes, Jr., through his local Rotary Club and asked him to serve on the ATC's Land Acquisition Committee. Hanes was an accomplished businessman and owner of the Hanes Dye and Finishing Company of Winston-Salem.

In his first year on the Land Acquisition Committee, Hanes raised $100,000 in grants, received numerous pledges from relatives, and donated $105,000 from his own company.[65] Although Hanes was an effective fundraiser, some members of the trail community felt that he lacked "appreciation for the modus operandi of the Trail clubs."[66] They were concerned about Hanes's emphasis on a "super-power structure" and his criticism of the ATC's informal approach to trail work. Although they appreciated his dedication, the ATC cordially asked Hanes to leave the project in August 1974.

After he was asked to leave, Hanes was quick to point out several of the organization's deficiencies, and he compared the ATC to other well-known national environmental groups with which he was involved, such as the Audubon Society, the Izaak Walton League, and the National Wildlife Federation. He attributed the group's inability to draw in large donations to their lack of "power of prestige or organization." He felt that the ATC was composed of people "interested in maintaining the Trail" but who were "unknown to all but a very, very few people in the conservation movement." None of Hanes's "associates" had heard of any of the ATC's board members, nor was any board member listed in any of Hanes's copies of *Who's Who*. Perhaps out of resentment about being asked to leave, he concluded that ATC chairman Stanley Murray "might be a superb chemist, but he was not capable of putting together an operation such as this."[67]

Although some leaders of the ATC recognized the validity of Hanes's claims, others took this perceived weakness as a source of pride. Some even viewed it as a source of strength. They argued that the AT had "grown as a popular movement" and noted that

those who dreamed of a trail from Maine to Georgia and made it a reality were not typical of the membership of comparable organizations which have had similar accomplishments.... They were not captains of industry, financial tycoons or political giants. They were average people—white and blue collars—working together on a single dream—bringing man back to nature.[68]

Although they recognized the need for a hired central staff and more effective strategies for organizing and fundraising, ATC members believed that the power of their organization came from its extended network of citizen volunteers—many of whom were unremarkable in their professional aspirations or congressional lobbying ability. Furthermore, the members believed that their folksy reputation—the antithesis of Hanes's "super-power structure" or a heavy-handed centralized government—would be an asset in negotiating easements and written agreements with landowners.

As state and federal agencies struggled to begin the land acquisition program, and development surrounding the trail proceeded undaunted, a group of ATC leaders decided to launch a program that would chart a new course for protecting adjacent lands. Known as the Appalachian Greenway, the initiative was intended to promote regional planning efforts along the AT and it echoed ideas found in Benton MacKaye's 1921 proposal. The greenway program was designed to build upon federal and state efforts to protect the AT, and its purpose was to protect a larger contiguous swath of land through the eastern mountains on either side of the trail. The ATC and other private organizations would be responsible for protecting land next to the trail by working with local governments on zoning regulations, or by purchasing the development rights to land, leaving landowners able to continue acceptable land uses like farming and forestry. The main champion of the Appalachian Greenway, ATC chairman Stanley Murray, argued that, like MacKaye's initial plan for the AT project, the greenway would address the economic needs of local communities while also satisfying the recreational desires of expanding urban populations.

The Appalachian Greenway would include a "primitive" inner zone consisting of the publicly owned trail corridor that state and federal agencies were working to acquire. In addition, the project would include a "rural or countryside" outer zone that would extend up to ten miles on both sides of the AT, depending on local physical, social, and economic characteristics. The outer zone would remain primarily in private ownership and would be primarily controlled through local land-use planning and zoning programs. In this sense, the purpose of the greenway initiative was not only to expand the physical area to be protected by the AT project but also to begin exploring new political mechanisms for protecting land along the AT.[69]

Trail advocates who had begun to question the federal government's commitment to the AT, and who wanted to expand the goals of the AT project from being a simple footpath to being a catalyst for land conservation throughout the Appalachian Mountains, maintained that the greenway program would rely on a slightly different organizational approach. Although like the AT, the Appalachian Greenway would involve the cooperation of state and federal governments, advocates also emphasized the importance of local government, private entrepreneurship, and direct landowner involvement. The ATC would continue to be responsible for maintaining the trail, promoting the project through publications, and lobbying for greater state and federal support, while new organizations such as the Appalachian Highlands Association would function as quasipublic corporations, focusing on raising public and private funds for land acquisition, operating a revolving fund, and undertaking and reviewing plans for development.[70] As interest in land acquisition as a conservation strategy continued to grow during the 1960s and 1970s, the Appalachian Highlands Association worked with leaders from increasingly powerful land trusts like the Nature Conservancy to develop support for the greenway initiative.[71]

Proponents of the Appalachian Greenway discussed two possible leaders for the program: Elvis Stahr and James Watt. At that time, Stahr was the president of the National Audubon Society, and Watt was serving as director of the Bureau of Outdoor Recreation. Before going on to lead the Audubon Society in 1968, Stahr had served as the secretary of the US Army, and he knew his way around Washington. During his presidency of the Audubon Society, from 1968 until 1981, he had helped the organization transform from a devoted group of birders into a major player in federal environmental politics. Under Stahr's leadership, the membership of the Audubon Society grew fourfold, and the organization began to address contemporary environmental issues ranging from the preservation of the Florida Everglades to the regulation of the international whaling industry. Not insignificantly, Stahr also worked with other environmental groups to establish federal rules regarding the rights of charitable organizations to lobby on public policy issues.

James Watt was also in the process of establishing his own legacy—albeit a decidedly more controversial one. After serving as the director of the Bureau of Outdoor Recreation from 1972 to 1975, Watt founded the Mountain States Legal Foundation in 1976. The foundation was created as "a nonprofit, public interest law firm dedicated to individual liberty, the right to own and use property, limited and ethical government and the free enterprise system."[72] Watt served as a vocal leader of the New Right during the 1970s and 1980s, and became a powerful force in environmental politics when President Reagan appointed him to serve as secretary of the Interior in 1981. Watt supported the right of private industries to extract resources on public lands, including extensive mining and drilling in wilderness areas. Environmental groups criticized Watt for attacking federal regulations that were designed to protect natural resources. Greg Wetstone, director of advocacy at the Natural Resources Defense Council, claimed that the country had never seen a "more intensely controversial and blatantly anti-environmental" political appointment.[73] Watt's controversial ideas eventually led to his resignation as secretary of the Interior in 1983.

Prior to the escalation of the environmental community's criticism of his work as secretary of the Interior, however, Watt made several allies in the AT community. When one organizer of the Appalachian Greenway effort met with him to discuss the feasibility of the project in the mid-1970s, she found Watt to be the "most enthusiastic supporter of the Greenway so far in the federal agency world."[74] He thought the greenway was "a great idea" and wanted to organize a meeting with the ATC and state leaders to plan strategies for acquiring additional funds from within the private sector. He pointed to an example in New York where he had solicited funds from IBM and Xerox to restore the Erie Canal, and argued that in a similar way, stronger support from the private sector could be a great asset to the Appalachian Trail project.

Some members of the trail community worried that a large quasipublic corporation such as the one envisioned by Watt might "magnify its powers to the extent possible" and lose the volunteer, not-for-profit spirit embodied in the project since MacKaye's proposal in 1921.[75] The ATC's information director, Sheldon Pollack, feared that if the primary goal of quasipublic corporations such as the Appalachian Highlands Association was to raise money for private land acquisition, to some degree, these groups would have to be profit-oriented—something antithetical to the spirit and purpose of the AT.[76] Using the Port Authority, the Triboro Bridge and Tunnel Authority, and the Metropolitan Transportation Authority as examples, Pollack pointed out that each had "shown their arrogance in their relationship with the public."[77] Pollack emphasized that trail advocates should instead continue to seek stronger federal support and funding. Because the energy crisis of the 1970s placed greater demand on recreation areas close to the eastern seaboard, he argued that the development of the Appalachian Trail and the Appalachian Greenway were both matters of national interest; a couple billion dollars for these projects would be a drop in the bucket compared to the Department of Defense's annual budget of eighty billion dollars and the twenty to thirty billion dollars that the US government spent on the Vietnam War every year.[78]

Like MacKaye's regional planning ideas in the 1920s, the Appalachian Greenway did not materialize as its promoters had envisioned. In the end, neither Stahr nor Watt took on leadership positions for the initiative. But the two men's prominent positions in the environmental arena—and their vastly different approaches to environmental protection—demonstrated that AT advocates were looking to become more serious players in environmental politics, and that they were willing to work with different types of leaders. Moreover, the greenway project did not take off because federal and state leaders who were already struggling to meet the basic provisions of the 1968 National Trails Act were wary of having their partners with the AT community take on new responsibilities. Park Service officials such as Richard Stanton and David Richie were "leery of any possibility of a new and larger area along the Trail."[79] The agency was nervous that a program like the greenway might divert key partners and weaken efforts to acquire the inner AT corridor.

Like Stanton and Richie, some members of the ATC feared mission creep. They worried that expanding the scope of the project beyond the average two-hundred-foot corridor authorized by the 1968 act would ultimately prohibit anything from being accomplished. Other skeptics argued that involving more groups, such as the Nature Conservancy, the Audubon Society, and a variety of private interests, would bring competing agendas to the project, thus complicating an already complex initiative. While some trail advocates felt that the greenway's goals were "highly admirable," they feared that "concentrating our energy, efforts and money in the pursuit of Utopia we may run the risk of losing by default the imperfect but viable Trail that exists today."[80] At a Greenway Task Force meeting in 1974, one ATC volunteer became flustered and claimed, "We have enough to do. We can't even get a Trail . . . you go on with the Greenway project and let us fight for the Trail. We sympathize with each other but we don't want to work at cross purposes or interfere with each other."[81]

Members of the trail community who held different visions for the future of the project overcame their differences when Congress amended the 1968 National Trails Act in 1978. The amended legislation outlined an intense three-year land acquisition program for the AT. At that time greenway promoters from within the ATC agreed to focus their efforts on assisting the National Park Service's program to protect the inner corridor with the caveat that broader land protections would come later.

Although the greenway program was set aside only a few years after it was first proposed, the idea behind the project revealed one way in which trail advocates responded to challenges associated with changes in land use, ownership, and political authority in the 1960s and 1970s. Several ATC leaders argued that the entrenched bureaucratic weight of increased government involvement needed to be balanced by a stronger private presence and local land-use planning. Designed to complement the slow federally led process of acquiring lands for the Appalachian Trail corridor, the Appalachian Greenway offered another approach to conservation that emphasized the protection of property rights, the diffusion of power through local governments and zoning, and the leadership of the private sector. Although the ideas and approaches of the Appalachian Greenway were temporarily put on the wayside during the National Park Service's land acquisition program in the late 1970s and 1980s, they would resurface again in the 1990s, and find particular resonance in the twenty-first century.

THE MUDDIED RUT OF POLITICAL DEMOCRACY

Although many trail volunteers viewed the passage of the 1968 National Trails Act as a great victory in the movement to protect the AT, because of bureaucratic confusion, lack of funds, changes in trail use and land ownership, and growing resistance to big government, little was accomplished in the decade following the national trails legislation. Most of the people affected by the project believed that the Appalachian Trail was nationally significant, yet ideas about the appropriate size, purpose, and means of land protection diverged widely. Despite the promise of the 1968 act, the project became entrenched in a political quagmire that not only prevented the implementation of protections outlined by the legislation but also inhibited the broader goals proposed as part of the greenway program.

During the decade following 1968, protective action for the trail was stalled by both too much governmental bureaucracy and too many competing private interests. Increased participation at all levels of government, the growth and diversification of the trail community, and the rising number of private landowners caused the historically tangled roots of the project—both the dendritic horizontal roots of its grassroots constituency and its central taproot of state support—to become inhibited by the muddied rut of political democracy. As a result of this political quagmire, by 1977, approximately 825 miles of the Appalachian Trail still remained on private lands or roads. Since 1968, only about 61 miles of the trail had been protected. Supportive state governments, such as Massachusetts, were primarily responsible for those few acquisitions.

The debates about how best to protect the AT and the lands that surround it that followed the 1968 act demonstrate the challenges of federalizing grassroots environmental action. As part of a sweep of federal legislation aimed at protecting America's natural resources in the 1960s and 1970s, the Appalachian Trail project joined a host of other initiatives attempting to navigate public and private authority. Nonprofit environmental organizations became influential players in federal politics, promoting new legislation and entrusting greater authority to federal partners to achieve environmental protection goals. At the same time, another grassroots movement was emerging—one that resisted federal intrusion into the rights of states and property owners. As revealed in the efforts to implement the 1968 National Trails Act, the path to achieving large-scale conservation goals often crossed difficult political terrain and did not always lead to its intended destination.

CHAPTER 5

ACQUIRING THE CORRIDOR

THE APPALACHIAN TRAIL OFFERS ENDLESS PHOTO OPPORTUNITIES, BUT perhaps the most popular place for snapping the quintessential shot of a reflective hiker standing high on a mountain, gazing out across whispering forests below, is on top of McAfee's Knob just west of Roanoke, Virginia. Like many other stretches of the AT, the picture-perfect scenery at McAfee's Knob became part of the AT experience as a result of one of the most complex land acquisition programs in US history.[1] In the 1970s, the trail near Roanoke crossed a perpetual mess of roots and mud on North Mountain that, though less inspiring, was safely located within the Jefferson National Forest. Unlike most southern sections of the AT, McAfee's Knob lay just outside of the national forest boundary on privately owned Catawba Mountain. Because the 1968 National Trails Act required that the AT achieve "maximum outdoor recreation potential" by protecting "nationally significant scenic, historic, natural, or cultural qualities" along its path—and because an amendment to the trail legislation in 1978 authorized the funds and political authority necessary to achieve the goals of the National Trails Act—project partners began to assess alternative routes through the area.[2]

In 1978, Bob Proudman, a long-time professional trail builder with the Appalachian Mountain Club (AMC) who was hired by the National Park Service's Appalachian Trail Project Office (ATPO) to help coordinate the land acquisition program in the late 1970s, met with the president of the Roanoke Appalachian Trail Club to investigate opportunities for relocating the AT off of North Mountain. As the two trail enthusiasts hiked the ridge together, the profound beauty of Catawba Mountain, with its lattice of creeks and farms in the valleys below—the same sublime landscape that inspired writer Annie Dillard's environmental treatise *Pilgrim at Tinker*

View from Tinker Cliffs near McAfee's Knob. In the 1970s, the scenic overlook at McAfee's Knob lay on posted private property. AT project partners battled wealthy landowners and apprehensive Forest Service personnel in order to make this scenic stretch across the Tinker Cliffs in Virginia part of the AT experience. Courtesy of the Appalachian Trail Conservancy.

"No Trespassing" signs at McAfee's Knob. Courtesy of the Appalachian Trail Conservancy.

Creek—also moved the two men. Major barriers stood in the way of purchasing this private piece of land, however. According to Proudman, "The question was 'Do we battle our way across Catawba Mountain which was four or five miles of private landowners, all of whom are well-heeled, and it's going take years of negotiations and probably millions of dollars? Or, do we keep the trail on North Mountain?'" After leaving the Roanoke area and returning to ATPO headquarters in Harpers Ferry, Proudman clearly recalled his conversations with project leaders; he reported, "I have bad news. McAfee's is *beautiful*."[3]

Bob Proudman (left) leading a trail-design workshop with a group of eager volunteers. Experienced trail workers such as Bob Proudman played a critical role in training new generations of trail volunteers to help build and maintain the relocated AT. Courtesy of the Appalachian Trail Conservancy.

Relocating the AT across this privately owned section would require taking on local landowners, state legislators, and even regional Forest Service officials who resisted the idea of moving the trail from the agency's jurisdiction to build a new public resource that would be owned by the National Park Service—a long-time administrative rival. But the ATC and the Park Service decided that the view from McAfee's was worth the political battle. In the end, AT project leaders threw down the gauntlet by using a combination of grassroots support and the expanded power of eminent domain—forces that were not always politically compatible—to eventually acquire the land necessary to make the scenic stretch across Catawba Mountain part of the AT experience.[4]

When Congress amended the National Trails Act in 1978, it established the legal groundwork for an aggressive land acquisition program, gave the National Park Service a stronger leadership role in the project, and increased federal appropriations for land acquisition from five million to ninety million dollars. The amendment expanded the power of condemnation from 25 acres per mile to 125 acres per mile, which enlarged the average width of the corridor from two hundred feet to one thousand feet. The purpose of the land acquisition program authorized by the 1978 amendment was to meet the objectives originally outlined by the 1968 National Trails Act. This typically meant relocating the trail from places where the traces of civilization were clear and present—on or near roads and housing developments, in towns, or on land threatened by private development—and placing the footpath onto a protected corridor of federal land where signs of civilization were more subtle—in the woods and around fields. According to the 1978 amendment, land acquisition for the entire Appalachian Trail corridor was to be complete within three years.[5] This meant that within three years, the Park Service was to acquire approximately 825 miles—about 40 percent of the trail—that remained unprotected in private ownership in 1978. In comparison, between 1968 and 1977, only about sixty-one miles had been protected.

The 1978 amendment marked an unprecedented use of federal power in the development of recreational trails.[6] At the same time, however, the National Park Service attempted to maintain the historic grassroots spirit of the project by continuing to involve local volunteers and the Appalachian Trail Conference in virtually all stages of the land acquisition process— from scouting new routes to locating landowner data to initiating contact with landowners and, in many cases, mediating and negotiating land transactions between private owners and federal representatives. In particularly controversial areas, citizen volunteers also helped coordinate community forums and served as local supporters of the project. Long-time trail leaders such as Bob Proudman, who once was described as a "tough, young, bearded, Camel-smoking, monosyllabic backwoodsman-mountaineer," also played a critical role in implementing the Park Service's AT acquisition program.[7]

At no other point in the history of the National Park Service did the agency rely so heavily upon the knowledge and skills of highly motivated citizens to help facilitate such a complex land acquisition program. Even though the 1978 amendment granted greater federal authority, implementing the new legislation relied on the cooperation of local and nonlocal actors, and the negotiation of public and private interests that had been part of the project since its beginning. Because by 1978 most of the AT in the Southern Appalachians lay within the boundaries of national forests, efforts to implement the amended federal land acquisition legislation mostly focused on the mid-Atlantic and New England regions.[8] Stories from different places along the AT—New York, Maine, Connecticut, and Pennsylvania—demonstrate how the AT slowly became a federal footpath, a corridor of public land crafted from a matrix of rapidly developing private land. On a deeper level, however, these examples also show how, in the process of acquiring land for the AT, project participants helped to blaze a new political pathway for environmental decision making—one that relied on the blending of power between public and private agents.

LAND ACQUISITION AND THE NATIONAL PARK SERVICE'S APPALACHIAN TRAIL PROJECT OFFICE

To facilitate the land acquisition process for the Appalachian Trail, the National Park Service established a headquarters for its Appalachian Trail Project Office in Harpers Ferry, West Virginia—just three blocks away from the ATC's headquarters. The Park Service also set up a central Appalachian Trail land acquisition field office just outside Harpers Ferry in Martinsburg, West Virginia, and regional field offices in Pennsylvania and New Hampshire.[9] The agency transferred David Richie, who had been serving as deputy regional director of the AT in Boston, to manage the land acquisition program.

Richie, who was known to many within the trail community as the "anti-bureaucrat," could not have been a more perfect fit for this challenging campaign. Richie worked for the Bureau of Land Management and spent the last two decades of his career with the National Park Service—serving as superintendent for the George Washington Memorial Parkway in the 1960s and later as the project manager for the Appalachian Trail Project Office. Yet AT project partners noted that "with Dave ... there was no aloofness, no hint of inflated self-importance, no protocol-conscious authoritarianism."[10] When conflict inevitably arose during the land acquisition process, former ATC executive director David Startzell recalled that

> Richie set the tone for the often difficult and protracted negotiations. His approach to such controversies was similar to his approach to human relationships in general: He shunned authoritarianism, greeted adversaries with respect, and consistently struggled to achieve a negotiated settlement, but rarely, if ever, compromised important Trail values. His style and his influence in shaping the form and substance of the land-acquisition program during the initial years of that now 25-year-old program is well-evidenced today.[11]

AT project manager Dave Richie (left), along with real estate specialist Chuck Rinaldi (right), led one of the National Park Service's most complex land acquisition programs. Courtesy of the Appalachian Trail Conservancy.

Richie's demeanor was an important asset in the land acquisition program, as was his vision for the trail. He was a "prophet of partnerships long before the concept of partnerships became fashionable."[12] In both his public correspondence and his internal agency memos, Richie firmly maintained that the land acquisition program for the AT would only be successful if the Park Service maintained the historic grassroots spirit of the project. Richie earned his bachelor's degree in political science from Haverford College in 1958, and he often used the creative ideas that he encountered as part of his liberal arts education in his work with the Park Service. He wrote to agency colleagues that "from a political science perspective, perhaps the most interesting aspect of the Appalachian Trail Project is the extent to which both the state and federal governments are relying on private volunteer organizations."[13] Richie hoped that the Appalachian Trail could help to establish a "progressive example" of how agencies such as the National Park Service could use citizen volunteers and nonprofit organizations to help provide outdoor recreation opportunities.[14]

In the 1970s, working with private partners to achieve major agency goals was not a typical practice for the National Park Service. As the national park system grew dramatically during the 1960s and 1970s, both in sheer number and new types of park units, the agency struggled to keep up with the rapid expansion. Between 1960 and 1980, Congress authorized 5,285,265 acres to become part of the national park system as new national parks, national seashores, historic parks, recreation areas, national monuments, national trails, and wild and scenic rivers. The growth of the park system was both a response to and a cause of increases in visitation. The number of visitors to the national park system more than doubled from 79 million visitors in 1960 to 172 million visitors in 1970. Visitation nearly doubled again between 1970 and 1983, when the parks received 331 million visitors.[15] With the combination of widespread public support for the national parks and Democratic majorities in both the House and Senate in 1978, Congress passed the National Parks and Recreation Act. The act established fifteen new units in the national park system—most of which were in or near cities and were concentrated on the East Coast. To build these new park units— and to purchase remaining inholdings within existing parks—the act also increased funding to $1.25 billion. The agency strove for efficiency and expediency in its efforts to keep up with the growth of the national park system and its use. In the process, it developed a national reputation for being a top-down, expert-driven agency with little inclination to relinquish its power to untrained amateurs.[16]

This reputation also grew out of a series of new policies and programs that the National Park Service employed in the 1970s to acquire land. As demand for vacation homes, ski resorts, and other types of private development increased, so too did the price of rural land. The value of agricultural land, particularly in the eastern United States, grew dramatically in the late 1960s and 1970s. In New York, the average per acre value of farmland rose from $177 in 1964 to $670 in 1978. In places such as Dutchess County, where the AT skirts north around New York City, the average per acre farm value rose to $1,173 in 1978.[17] Many conservationists and Park Service officials worried that the rising cost of land would prohibit the agency from achieving its legislatively mandated goals.[18] In response, the Park Service implemented a series of policies to hasten land acquisition programs before the rising costs of land prohibited acquisitions all together.

Commonly referred to by landowners as the Park Service's "get tough" acquisition policies, the new rules and regulations helped to expedite the use of eminent domain in park projects around the country. Most of the new rules applied to inholdings within existing parks. For example, the new policies authorized the National Park Service to condemn a property if an inholder attempted to develop or rehabilitate a structure on an unimproved property. Such action would prevent the agency from having to pay for the increased property value at a later date.[19] In Wilsonia, California, inholders in Kings Canyon National Park claimed that representatives of the Park Service had plowed snow onto their old porches and roofs, which caused the feeble structures to cave in. When the landowners sought permits to rebuild, the agency forced them to leave their properties.[20]

Such stories spread quickly through the national media, and caused Richie and his colleagues with the ATPO to reevaluate the ways in which the agency would approach land acquisition for the Appalachian Trail. Instead of relying on "get tough" strategies, Richie argued that a partnership approach was necessary for several reasons. First, the linear geography of the trail made it unlike traditional park units. Second, the trail's history of citizen involvement meant that, in many cases, private leaders within the ATC knew the political and physical terrain better than Park Service officials. And third, criticism over the expanding power of the federal government was growing—particularly in rural areas—and beginning to have dramatic effects on the country's political landscape. By using citizens—many of whom had well-established relationships with local landowners—as ambassadors of the Park Service's land acquisition program, Richie felt that the project could cultivate positive feelings toward the AT and thus ensure its future.[21]

Another way in which Richie and the Park Service's Appalachian Trail Project Office tried to build local support for the project was by using a variety of tools for the land acquisition process. At that time, the National Park Service typically acquired land using simple fee acquisition. In a simple fee acquisition, the agency would purchase the full deed to a property. This involved a complete transfer of ownership that included all rights associated with that parcel. Instead of relying on simple fee acquisition—the easiest and most desirable way for the agency to acquire land for park projects—AT partners usually presented landowners with an array of acquisition options, including easements, land exchanges, and tax-deductible donations.[22] In the beginning of the acquisition program, Richie emphasized the importance of using easements, which allowed for greater flexibility. Easements allowed the Park Service to purchase certain rights, such as the right to build condominiums, clear-cut timber, or mine coal, and in this way, project leaders could control land use along the trail while allowing the landowner to retain the title.

Project partners primarily used two types of easements. The most basic protection measure was a right-of-way easement in which the National Park Service would purchase the right for hikers to walk along a narrow corridor. Project partners also sought scenic easements that were designed to protect the aesthetic and environmental qualities of a broader area. Both types of easements—right-of-way easements and scenic easements—prohibited the construction of new buildings within the trail corridor. The Park Service also used reserved interest deeds in situations in which the owner reserved certain rights for a given number of years. The purpose of having different kinds of acquisition methods was to allow more options for landowners and to limit expenditures for the project.[23]

At the time, these kinds of less-than-fee acquisitions were a novel approach to protecting park resources, and not all park employees agreed that the potential political and financial benefits were worth the unseen costs.[24] Several legal experts within the National Park Service expressed concern that easements would be difficult to manage and enforce in future years. For example, a report by the National Park Service noted that in or near urban areas, easements cost nearly as much as simple fee acquisition, and the typical cost of an easement did not account for the costs of monitoring compliance with the easement, or the cost of litigation if an easement was violated. In an area where the Park Service had used an easement to protect landscapes along the Blue Ridge Parkway, a landowner had disregarded the easement and had built structures and cut trees. One Park Service official noted, "It takes only one or two violations to destroy a scenic landscape."[25] Despite these concerns within the agency, Richie and his colleagues at the ATPO argued that given the political geography and history of the AT, easements would be a necessary component of the land acquisition program.[26]

Although it would have been simpler for the Park Service to have a standardized easement document for all cases, Richie maintained that easements could be tailored to meet the particular desires of landowners.[27] He emphasized that the agency should seek easements that limited public recreational activity to a narrow right-of-way, and that most of the land in the corridor would still be owned and controlled by the landowner, with only minor restrictions on land use. Richie maintained that the wording of easements was often intentionally vague. He wrote,

Words like "good" and "accepted" are designated to allow for evolution in acceptable practices rather than to fix restrictions according to current practices. In addition, they are intended to avoid red tape which could be involved in alternative approaches, such as requiring advance approval of local forestry officials. Basically, we have tried to devise an easement that is no more restrictive on landowners than is necessary to provide for the Trail and to avoid incompatible development close to it.[28]

Richie clearly understood the power of language. In a memo to the National Park Service real estate specialists assigned to the acquisition of land for the AT, he encouraged officers to be aware of how they spoke about easements. He maintained that when talking with landowners, the emphasis should be that owners were "selling only a few of their rights, in the form of easements, rather than the notion that the government is buying easements, and allowing landowners certain rights."[29] Although the difference was subtle, he felt that landowners would perceive the latter option to be less of an imposition on their property rights.

The most controversial tool that the National Park Service had the authority to use was the power of eminent domain—the ability of government to take private property for public use. Condemnation proceedings rarely occurred, however. When they did, it was usually for the purpose of clearing title or establishing just compensation. The agency and the ATC typically referred to these kinds of transactions as "friendly condemnations." In such cases, landowners were willing to sell land, but they disagreed on the property's value.

The fifth amendment of the US Constitution states that no person can be "deprived of life, liberty, or property, without due process of law; nor shall private property be taken for public use, without just compensation."[30] As in other cases of federal condemnation proceedings, when the National Park Service used the eminent domain power to build the AT, it hired an independent appraiser to determine the property's fair market value. The fair market value was the typical standard of "just compensation." Like most real estate transactions, the fair market value estimate was typically less than what the landowner felt their property was worth. Yet, again, AT project partners tried to avoid condemnation. Only on the rare occasions when people were absolutely unwilling to sell their land or certain land-use rights, when a price could not be agreed upon, or when project partners could not modify the corridor to some other location, would a declaration of takings be filed.[31]

In 1982, the ATPO reported that condemnation had been used for only fifteen of the seven hundred properties acquired during the land acquisition program for the AT.[32] Condemnation was unappealing to the Park Service not only because of the public uproar it created but also because it was expensive, time-consuming, and tedious. In other park acquisition programs, the agency often had the luxury of waiting three to five years to settle condemnation proceedings. According to the 1978 amendment, however, the acquisition of the AT corridor lands was to be completed within three years. Furthermore, while waiting for one condemnation proceeding to settle in court, adjacent tracts would often become unusable as neighboring landowners sold, logged, or developed their land. Preemptive actions on adjacent parcels would lead to missing links along the route and reduce the scenic value of the condemned property. Because of the long, slender shape of the AT, the acquisition of one property was often contingent upon the successful negotiation of a neighbor's property. Condemnation was not good for maintaining landowner relations or for the logistics of time and finance.[33] When it was used, physical, budgetary, social, and political sacrifices were made.

As the national media reported stories of the National Park Service's "strong-arm tactics" in other parts of the country in the late 1970s, leaders of the agency's Appalachian Trail Project Office experimented with new approaches to land acquisition. They understood that maintaining strong community relations was essential to ensuring the long-term sustainability of the trail. Hostile relations between trail supporters and surrounding communities would only create future problems and "weak links" in the great AT chain.[34] By relying on a variety of acquisition tools and the leadership of private partners, the agency hoped to establish the support of local landowners and to nurture cooperative relationships with rural communities en route. Planning efforts received mixed results, however, and initial reactions to the program were often shaped by the ways in which AT coordinators wielded their quasipublic powers.

COOPERATING WITH CITIZEN COORDINATORS

When long-time AT volunteer Elizabeth Levers planned to start mapping the relocated trail though New York on a hot Fourth of July weekend in 1978, members of the New York–New Jersey Trail Conference responded enthusiastically to her call for help. Like many citizen coordinators who worked with the National Park Service to help broker the new federal powers out-lined in the 1978 amendments, Levers had spent over a decade volunteering for local trail clubs before becoming the state AT coordinator for New York. Coordinators' duties typically included finding property suitable for relo-cations, contacting and interviewing landowners in conjunction with Park Service representatives, blazing the new routes after officials acquired land, and eventually helping to manage the new trail in a particular area.[35]

Because the 1978 amendment to the National Trails Act required that land acquisition for the AT was to be completed in three years, the Park Service wanted to move quickly, and coordinators had only one or two months to determine an initial route. To ensure that the program would proceed swiftly and without controversy, and to establish consistency between regional efforts, the Park Service worked with the ATC to create uniform procedures for coordinators to initiate the land acquisition process.[36] In each state, coordinators compared the route published in the 1971 *Federal Register* with other plausible alternatives. They made note of public land, large corporate ownerships, and smaller individual parcels. Once a route was selected, coordinators recorded data on the local terrain, vegetation, topography, scenic features, historic sites, and other significant aspects of the area for every five-mile section. For example, on the July Fourth week-end in 1978, Levers sent teams of six or seven volunteers to different sections across the state to gather this data. Equipped with walkie-talkies, the eager volunteers spread out and explored different routes to determine where they felt the trail should be relocated. Levers insisted that volunteers go over a potential trail at least "six or eight times, back and forth in both direc-tions" to be sure that they collected accurate data.[37] After this reconnais-sance work was complete, Levers supplied the Park Service with the names and addresses of landowners whose property would be affected by the new route, along with corridor width recommendations. The agency's real estate specialists then began the technical, legal aspects of land acquisition.

The Park Service didn't always agree with the routes that coordinators selected. After reviewing the proposed route through New York, the agency expressed some objections and requested that volunteers go back with state officials and scout another route. This process went on for several weeks, with volunteers flagging and reflagging trails as they discussed the advan-tages and disadvantages of possible paths with public officials.

When the Park Service, state agents, local volunteers, and coordinators agreed on a tentative route, the agency paid for professional surveyors to perform a "center-line survey." The center-line survey was a single dotted line drawn across segment maps produced by the Park Service's real estate specialists. These maps contained information about property boundaries and ownership patterns in each small section along the proposed AT route. The entire trail consisted of about five hundred to six hundred segment maps that showed the arrangement of different parcels and how properties were situated in relation to one another. In addition to field notes on the physical terrain of a given area, the ATC and Park Service used the maps to determine which owners would be contacted and where the trail would ultimately go.

Unlike efforts to determine traditional national park boundaries, where a ring drawn on a map designated the outline of property to be acquired and the Park Service's job was to then fill in the circle, the design of the trail corridor was more flexible. This flexibility depended on the ownership patterns of a given area. If one owner didn't want the trail on her property, there were usually neighbors within the center-line survey who were willing to sell land or a right-of-way easement. As a result, the trail would shift to an adjacent property. The flexible design of the corridor was an attempt to adapt to landowners' desires; in doing so, project partners hoped to create a route that was as locally acceptable as possible.

Once a tentative route was established, but before the National Park Service officially notified landowners to express the agency's interest in their property, coordinators were responsible for making contact with landowners. Coordinators typically sent a "very carefully worded" letter that explained the history of the Appalachian Trail project and "gently suggested" that the Park Service was interested in their property.[38] In the most effective cases, this initial letter maintained a respectful tone and encouraged open conversation with the landowner. In these instances, coordinators helped establish a positive environment for future negotiations by emphasizing their interest in landowners' opinions.

In the case of New York, Levers's knowledge of the local political terrain and her warm personality proved invaluable to the project. Levers was a retired school administrator, and those who worked with her recognized that "some of her power came from appearing to be a helpless little old woman," even though she was "far from helpless."[39] In describing his experience with Levers, Bob Proudman smiled and recalled that she drove the professional trail builders and public officials "kind of nuts" because she was so "friendly, talkative, and totally determined. . . . She would work harder than

Citizen coordinators such as Liz Levers (far left) often helped to gain landowners' support for the AT project. As a couple of landowners (center) sign paperwork to sell their property to the National Park Service, T. R. Jacobson (far right), a representative with the agency, looks on approvingly. Courtesy of the Appalachian Trail Conservancy.

Volunteers mapping the AT. The acquisition of land to make a permanent, federally protected AT corridor involved the unprecedented use of citizen power. Never before had private trail enthusiasts been so deeply involved in mapping new routes and working with landowners to help implement the goals of the 1968 National Trails Act. Courtesy of the Appalachian Trail Conservancy.

any of the staff would—sixteen hour days, seven days a week. And she knew every landowner in Dutchess County, New York." During reconnaissance surveys for the land acquisition program, Levers would sweetly ask landowners, "'Do you mind if I go out and look at these back forty [acres]?'" and they would rarely refuse.[40]

Even though Levers had assistance from the National Park Service, New York's Parks and Recreation Department, and trail-building professionals such as Proudman, the project's public partners insisted that their job was to "help Elizabeth."[41] Although some landowners in New York resisted the acquisition program, conversations with Levers often soothed landowners' anxieties about the federal government's involvement. Her style and approach also allowed for productive dialogue with landowners about alternative locations for the trail when initial routes did not meet their satisfaction. For example, Dr. Joyce Brothers, a landowner in Dutchess County, New York, wrote to National Park Service director William Whalen that she had been misled about the agency's authority, threatened with condemnation, and subjected to trespass by trail enthusiasts looking for a route. Whalen tried to assure her that the Park Service planned to work with landowners to find a suitable route, and he told Richie that in his next visit to talk with Brothers, he should bring Elizabeth Levers to help soothe the situation.[42] Even though federal and state agencies provided funding and support for acquiring the trail, it was often Levers's ability to garner public support and navigate rugged political terrain that ultimately established the trail through New York. By 1979, New York was ready to begin acquiring properties for the corridor.

A RANGE OF REACTIONS IN NEW ENGLAND

The Park Service's approach to land acquisition for the AT relied on new ways of involving private citizens in federal land management, and, as the following examples from New England illustrate, the process produced a wide array of reactions. Although the Park Service created a set of guiding procedures to standardize the process of how trail volunteers were to approach landowners, how coordinators initially contacted landowners—and in particular, how they positioned their authority—influenced landowners' reactions to the land acquisition program. In some cases, such as with Levers in New York, the involvement of nongovernmental representatives helped to ease potential hostility to the project. Yet, in other cases, landowners were confused about AT coordinators' authority and their relationship with the federal government. Such confusion caused initial resistance in some areas, and delayed the land acquisition program.

For example, in 1978, twenty-six-year-old Jonathon Coe had been working for the AMC in Connecticut for about half a year when he sparked an "immediate and catastrophic" reaction by writing a "seemingly harmless" letter to sixty-eight landowners.[43] Although volunteers, AMC employees, and the Park Service had been scouting routes in the area for a couple years prior to Coe's notice, his letter was the first time that most landowners had heard about the initiative. In an editorial in the *Lakeville Journal*, one local resident wrote that landowners were "repelled by what they regarded as an inept and needlessly disruptive approach by representatives of the Federal government."[44] Even though many landowners supported the project, confusion about trail advocates' authority and the initial means by which they contacted landowners—not the project itself—became a cause of concern for local residents.

As the land acquisition program progressed, landowners such as James Gollin, who lived in Salisbury, Connecticut, complained about the "intimidation and blockbusting tactics" used by the National Park Service and its partners.[45] Gollin resisted efforts to build a federal footpath through his property, and he helped to organize the Connecticut Appalachian Trail Landowners Organization. Like other landowner groups that formed along the trail, members of the Connecticut group believed that the Park Service and its private partners had disregarded landowners' rights and were trespassing during reconnaissance work. Critics of the land acquisition program in places like Connecticut also argued that the Park Service should have begun the program by holding public meetings and consulting with local governments, not by having quasipublic officials contact individual landowners.[46]

In places where coordinators were able to engage local community members early in the planning process, there were fewer instances of resistance to the AT land acquisition program. In Maine, David Field, a professor of forestry at the University of Maine and president of the Maine Appalachian Trail Club, was particularly adept at communicating with local residents and played a key role in the relocation of the trail from Bell Pond in the town of Monson to Barren Mountain—a relocation that eliminated 3.7 miles of the trail that existed on roads and eventually put the trail back into Maine's boreal forests.

When first making contact with local landowners and officials, Field

Like many others affiliated with the ATC, David Field, president of the Maine Appalachian Trail Club and professor of forestry at the University of Maine, understood the value of protecting not only wilderness along the AT but also working landscapes that surrounded the trail corridor. Courtesy of the Appalachian Trail Conservancy.

was cautious and honest—taking a straightforward approach without being aggressive or threatening. Field's letters typically began by carefully explaining that although he was not an official agent of the National Park Service, as a long-time AT volunteer and citizen coordinator for the acquisition program, he was partly responsible for exploring options for the AT right-of-way.[47] Field's correspondence also emphasized the historically positive relations between the AT and the town of Monson. In a letter to the residents, he maintained that it was "a good thing for folks from Georgia, Tennessee, Pennsylvania, and the many other places from which hikers come ... to meet some of you and enjoy Maine hospitality. We hope that they are interesting enough for you to talk with so that you enjoy the meetings too."[48] Then Field asked for residents' opinions about the trail relocation:

Do you have trouble with the A.T. hikers or are they no bother? Do you enjoy meeting them? Will the owners of small parcels of land over which the A.T. crosses seriously object to giving up a right-of-way easement for the Trail? Would you like to see the A.T. continue along your main street, as it has for over forty years, or would you rather see it back in the woods?[49]

Field's initial work with the local community established a positive environment for dialogue about the location of the trail. He understood that such pre-acquisition groundwork was necessary before the Park Service could determine the trail right-of-way and purchase land for the corridor, which was eventually relocated off of the road and placed in the forest just outside of town. Today, most northbound hikers hitchhike or walk the two miles into Monson to gather provisions before heading into Maine's Hundred-Mile Wilderness or to simply enjoy the town's renowned hospitality and to listen to some bluegrass music at Tim's General Store on a Friday night.

Landowners and local officials were not the only ones concerned about the new federal land acquisition program. Although most trail volunteers were grateful for greater federal support, and they realized that many sections of the trail would have been lost without federal intervention, many long-time trail advocates worried about how the Park Service's aggressive policies and the potential use of eminent domain would influence the project. Also, the formal bureaucratic nature and somewhat paternalistic structure of the National Park Service differed from the loose, informal processes that had historically characterized relationships between the Appalachian Trail Conference, its local club affiliates, and landowners. For example, after Congress passed the 1968 National Trails Act, new laws required that all relocations of the Appalachian Trail had to be reviewed and approved by the Park Service. These regulations tended to delay trail-managing activities and encumbered long-time volunteers who had cultivated strong relationships with local landowners. In 1977, after spending "countless hours" with one disgruntled landowner in Vermont who wanted the trail relocated to a different part of his property, Earl Jette of the Dartmouth Outing Club acknowledged his frustration with the new policies. As a trail-maintaining club, he explained, the Dartmouth group did not have "power to relocate [the trail] without being told by the Park Service to do so (this is what happens when the Federal Government enters the picture!)"[50]

In the following year, Jette received letters from four landowners requesting that the trail be taken off their properties. The landowners maintained that they had been very satisfied with their previous agreement with the

Dartmouth Outing Club. They wrote to Jette that the removal of the trail from their land was "simply a protest against the National Park Service, the Congress, and the federal government for their attempt to destroy a long-standing partnership between the landowner and the hiker." The landowners maintained that if the Park Service would be "flexible and innovative instead of rigid and reactionary in its approach," the forty-year-old partnership that existed between the landowners and the trail community could continue.[51] Such exchanges became increasingly common, as landowners were given no assurances that condemnation would not be used on their land. Looking to avoid confrontation with the federal government altogether, some owners decided to act preemptively and removed the trail from their lands. This pattern only exacerbated the need for protection and added to the complexity of the program.[52]

These examples from New England illustrate the range of responses to the Park Service's land acquisition program, and highlight the significance of nongovernmental representatives in shaping and facilitating the process. When private citizens made contact with landowners and began to implement national policies outlined in the amended 1968 National Trails Act, the categories of *public* and *private* became blurred. This boundary became even fuzzier when the project moved beyond the initial contact with landowners into more protracted negotiations. At that time, correspondence between coordinators, landowners, and the National Park Service became part of a broader public discourse about the role of the federal government in local land-use decision making.

As the National Park Service's land acquisition progressed in the late 1970s, those who opposed the effort found support from new and sometimes surprising sources. Just as the AT had been built through grassroots support, the project's long-time advocates increasingly encountered a growing form of grassroots resistance that was tied to a national movement to protect property rights.[53] To explore the ways in which landowners resisted the federal land acquisition program for the AT, and how trail advocates tried to work through the conflict, we move from the verdant hills of New England to the lush valleys of Pennsylvania.

RESISTANCE IN PENNSYLVANIA'S CUMBERLAND VALLEY

Pennsylvania's Cumberland County became one of the most contentious areas involved in the acquisition program when the National Park Service

Both Ed Garvey (left) and Thurston Griggs (right) worked tirelessly for the AT. Garvey was one of the first through-hikers on the AT, and his careful description of the journey in the book *Appalachian Hiker* inspired many future hikers. Griggs served as the AT coordinator for the land acquisition program in Pennsylvania's Cumberland Valley. Courtesy of the Appalachian Trail Conservancy.

tried to relocate approximately twelve miles of the existing trail off of roads and onto fertile farmland. Although many factors caused the conflict in the valley, several participants involved—landowners, Park Service officials, and ATC representatives alike—acknowledged that tensions were unintentionally precipitated, in part, by one dedicated trail advocate's initial handling of the program.[54] In May 1978, long-time volunteer Thurston Griggs sent out what became a locally infamous letter to landowners, notifying them of the intent of the National Park Service to relocate the trail through the Cumberland Valley. Griggs's letter provided little explanation of the program or of his role as a citizen volunteer. Instead, he simply told landowners, "Within a matter of months, the government will approach you about acquiring an interest in this corridor."[55] The letter was short and somewhat curt, and it seemed to indicate that the federal government had already selected a final route and was going to establish it regardless of local opinion.

Griggs's cavalier approach caused a major upset with the landowners, and local media were quick to sensationalize the story. An article in the *Carlisle Evening Sentinel* characterized Griggs's attitude as being "We don't give a damn what you think or what you have. We're going to take what we want." [56] One landowner recalled that she would never forget Mr. Griggs and the way he presented himself—"It was like, 'here comes Big Brother comin' in to take your property.'"[57] While Griggs, who received no compensation for his efforts in the valley, perceived his work as a benevolent act serving the greater interests of society, landowners who had no history with the project—and who may have mistakenly thought Griggs was an official with the National Park Service—perceived the initiative as a threat to their personal property rights. Although he was not a public agent, as an outsider to the community, Griggs wielded a kind of authority that was perceived as equally threatening to local landowners. Even though thirty-one of the fifty-four landowners who responded to Griggs's letter said that they would be willing to sell land or easements, Griggs's approach—or at least the way it was portrayed in the media and perceived by members of the local community—seemed to create an inhospitable climate for future negotiations.

As tension over trail relocation in Pennsylvania's Cumberland Valley escalated, several residents and farmers in the area organized a group called CANT—Citizens Against New Trail. The purpose of the group was to oppose the relocation of the Appalachian Trail off the existing road route and to defend local residents' property rights. Led by Arlene Byers, the group wrote to the Cumberland County commissioners to explain that landowners had received "unofficial information" that "extensive areas of land" were going to be taken for the expansion and relocation of the AT.[58] Byers told the commissioners that landowners were "being threatened with land taking procedures which would seriously [a]ffect our homes, farms, and businesses."[59]

In response to their constituents' concerns, county commissioners held a public meeting on a steamy July evening in 1978, and invited representatives of the Park Service and the ATC to hear landowners' concerns. There, members of CANT protested the route that Thurston Griggs had marked— a scenic wooded path through private property known as the "ridge route." Local officials echoed landowners' concern about the loss of control over property and critiqued the "high-handed and arrogant" way in which outsiders to the community had initiated the program.[60] After learning about the Park Service's acquisition program from several irate landowners, Jacob Myers, chair of the Cumberland County Commissioners, declared that it was "deplorable . . . to have a representative or apparent representative of the federal government coming into Cumberland County without having notified any local officials."[61] Several state and federal representatives also sympathized with the landowners. After learning about the way Griggs initiated the acquisition program in Cumberland County, an angry US Representative William Goodling declared that he was "incensed about a non-official outsider sending letters to constituents."[62]

To find a new route for the trail that would be acceptable to local landowners while also meeting the provisions outlined by the 1968 National Trails Act, Myers created the Appalachian Trail Location Advisory Committee. The committee was composed of a number of local actors—township and county officials, residents, landowners, and local trail club members—as well as representatives from the National Park Service and the ATC. The group's first meeting in 1978 had a "cordial and constructive tone," and all members seemed determined to work cooperatively to investigate alternative routes.[63] The group spent a year studying maps, walking potential routes, and discussing plausible alternatives in meetings that would often go well into the night. The Park Service tried to demonstrate a willingness to consider other routes and often reiterated its commitment to fair and open procedures in dealing with landowners.[64]

Local advisory committees like the one in Cumberland County were often most effective when they relied on relatively unbiased leaders who were respected members of a given community. For example, Frank Masland, Jr., had lived in the Cumberland Valley for over fifty years and volunteered to serve on the Location Advisory Committee. Masland was an especially adept communicator, and when the relocation process began to lose its cordial and constructive tone, he was able to facilitate the increasingly contentious group. According to Richie, Masland's diplomacy skills were "the essential ingredient in getting people to work together and to look objectively at the issues."[65] Although Masland represented local residents' interests, he also had a deep respect for the National Park Service and argued that the agency was perhaps "the only branch of the Federal Government not concerned with empire building."[66] At one point when negotiations about the trail relocation in the Cumberland Valley began to look intractable, the Park Service started to consider compromises such as an "improved road route." This route consisted of a cinder path along the shoulder of the existing road route, and concessions on the width and scenic nature of the trail. In response to the compromise, Masland argued that the plan "smacked of capitulation" and "violated the intent of Congress."[67] He noted that creating a wide path along the existing road route would limit farmers' ability to sell roadside frontage—some of the most desirable acreages for future develop-ment. As an owner of farmland himself, Masland argued that the roadside alternative was "far less desirable . . . than having the trail along fence rows and tree lines."[68] Not only would the roadside route be less scenic, it was likely to cause just as much local resistance as other alternatives.

Several of the landowners who would be affected by the relocation of the trail in the area were farmers, like Sheldon Brymesser, who argued that the soils in the Cumberland Valley were particularly suited for growing food and should be kept in agricultural production.[69] Although like landowners in other areas, many farmers in the Cumberland Valley found the "concept of a trail rather pleasing," they believed that "a man-made wilderness . . . [was] a conflict in terms" and they opposed the "possible expropriation of farmland by bureaucrats in a $90 million dollar attempt to soothe the aes-thetic sense of the 300 or so individuals who hike the whole trail."[70] Farmers' concerns about the AT project were based on actions they assumed the Park Service would take in order to maintain a wilderness footpath. They feared that increased public use of the trail would restrict the use of farm equip-ment, decrease crop production, and interfere with livestock management. Farmers were also concerned that the Park Service would restrict the use of herbicides along the proposed route. These kinds of restrictions threatened to limit the viability of farms in the area.[71]

In response, park officials explained that farm practices would be allowed to continue, including the use of farm equipment, herbicides, and other activities necessary to keep farms productive and competitive. The trail crossed a variety of landscapes, and in places like the Cumberland Valley, the agency simply aimed to "preserve an attractive setting for the Trail."[72] Trail advocates had long acknowledged the aesthetic and economic value of preserving farmland along the corridor, and the 1981 management plan for the AT specified that agricultural use of corridor lands that conserved "pastoral scenery" was "not only compatible, but desirable," as were certain forms of timber harvesting.[73]

Although the Park Service tried to reassure farmers that the Appala-chian Trail would not significantly infringe on their livelihoods, fears about how the trail would affect existing land uses were more often assuaged when they were addressed through a broader dialogue between public agents, private landowners, and other members of the local community. At a public meeting in the Cumberland Valley, Robert Shannon, a representa-tive of the Central Pennsylvania Conservancy, addressed concerns about farm losses. He emphasized that the AT would not only avoid interfering with farm practices but would actually give farmers a competitive advantage by paying them for development rights to land within the trail corridor. Shannon shared a letter from a New Hampshire farmer that explained how one of Hanover's last remaining farms had been protected through the combined efforts of the National Park Service and concerned local landowners.[74] Instead of having National Park Service officials or Washington-based ATC representatives tell local residents the benefits they would reap by having the trail rerouted through their community, the message was often more powerful when it came from neighbors, fellow residents, or private citizens in similar situations.

At the same time, however, critics of the National Park Service's land acquisition program also increasingly relied on the support of citizens in situations that were similar to their own, and used examples of property rights activism from around the country to justify their opposition. Although widespread concern about property rights and local autonomy was somewhat new to the East, the Park Service's aggressive land acquisition policies in the 1970s added fuel to a political wildfire that began burning in the West as the federal government expanded its control of public lands. In 1976, Congress passed the Federal Land Policy and Management Act, which established new federal regulations for grazing, mining, and ranching on public lands. In 1977, the Bureau of Land Management and the US Forest Service began Roadless Areas Review and Evaluation II to examine possible new wilderness and multiple-use designations. These kinds of new federal initiatives angered many westerners—including a growing posse of conservative western senators such as Orrin Hatch (R-UT) and James McClure (R-ID)—and sparked the Sagebrush Rebellion to resist federal control over public lands in the West, and to advocate for greater state authority.[75]

Although the Sagebrush Rebellion focused on states' rights, the rebels found common ground with another growing movement that resisted large-scale federal land programs—the property rights movement. By 1981, the League of States Equal Rights (LASER), one of the main organizational vehicles of the Sagebrush Rebellion, had a $1.5 million budget and began organizing other like-minded groups. That year, LASER sponsored a conference that included representatives of a range of interests—including the mining, timber, snowmobiling, and oil industries—as well as the recently established National Inholders Association.[76]

Charles Cushman organized the National Park Inholders Association in

1978 in a concerted attempt to defend property rights against the National Park Service's land acquisition programs (the group later became known as the National Inholders Association). Cushman, a landowner within the borders of Yosemite National Park, believed that the agency's land acquisition programs in the late 1970s were no longer subject to "any checks and balances." In his view, the Park Service had "leaned over backwards to accommodate the environmentalists" and had become "arrogant and cavalier" when dealing with inholders.[77] In 1978, Cushman left his home in the West to meet with landowners around the country who had been affected by the National Park Service's land acquisition policies. The purpose of his trip was to bring national media attention to the stories of disaffected property owners. For example, an article in *Newsweek* described the story of Herb Van Deven, a schoolteacher in the Ozark Mountains who was fighting the Park Service's plans to create the Buffalo National River—one of the new types of units within the national park system. Van Deven claimed that the agency's efforts were a violation of individual property rights, and he complained about "annoying telephone calls from park officials . . . late-night visits from government land acquisition officers, and . . . strong-arm tactics."[78] Van Deven's statement reflected a growing concern among many citizens who believed that the Park Service was using unfair and aggressive tactics to implement policies that infringed on private property rights.

Although the politics of park development in the East differed from debates over public land management in the West, stories like Van Deven's indicated that there was a shared fundamental concern about the expanding powers of the federal government. Cushman's work helped to spread the organized antigovernment sentiment of the West to the East. He became so effective at capturing the nation's attention and demonstrating landowners' opposition to the National Park Service that, within conservation circles, he earned the nickname "Rent-A-Riot."[79] Although many eastern conservationists were quick to dismiss his tactics, Cushman played a key role in helping to organize landowners' protests in the late 1970s and 1980s. In the 1990s, his organization went on to become the American Land Rights Association—one of the most powerful players in the property rights movement.

After visiting fifty-five national parks to talk with landowners affected by national park policies, Cushman went to the Cumberland Valley in 1979 to work with landowners along the Appalachian Trail. He claimed that the purpose of his visit was to "promote improved relations" between landowners and the National Park Service, and to ensure that the agency avoided intimidation, condemnation threats, and communication failures—attributes that he claimed had characterized national park acquisition programs in other parts of the country.[80]

Cushman met with a group of about ninety members of CANT and explained that in order to have the Park Service take their interests seriously, they needed to seek support from congressional representatives and powerful lobbying groups such as the American Farm Bureau. He emphasized that the only way they would be successful in postponing the land acquisition program, or thwarting it altogether, would be through organized political resistance. If the group could make "enough of a stink" by telling their stories though a variety of media sources and garnering the support of influential outsiders, Cushman suggested that landowners might be able to "force them [the Park Service] to move that trail or keep it where it is [on the road]."[81] Cushman served as an important resource to landowners and helped them frame their opposition not as a few isolated instances of selfishness and sentimentality but as part of a broader protest against injustice and unchecked federal authority.

Landowners in the Cumberland Valley heeded Cushman's advice and drove a busload of CANT members to Washington, DC, to participate in hearings about federal land acquisition. They met with sympathetic representatives and other landowners who had been affected by National Park Service programs. By 1980, landowner resistance to the AT acquisition program crossed state boundaries. New landowner groups formed, including the Appalachian Trail Landowners Organization in Connecticut and Nail the Trail in Philipstown, New York. Members of these different landowner groups decided to form an interstate organization, and called themselves the Appalachian Trail Interstate Coalition.

The National Park Service recognized the growing political influence of the landowner organizations, and invited the interstate coalition to delegate one representative to serve on the Appalachian National Scenic Trail Advisory Committee, which had been reinstated by the 1978 amendment to the National Trail Act. The amendment also required that the secretary of the Interior consult with the committee on all major trail-related decisions. Members of the coalition were eager to participate in the group, but instead of a single delegate, they wanted nine out of the thirty-five total committee members to represent landowner interests. Without greater representation, members of the coalition argued, the concerns of small landowners would be "overlooked amid the activities of state officials, big corporate landlords,

Warren Doyle, who helped to found the Appalachian Long-Distance Hikers Association in 1983, was particularly concerned with how the Park Service's land acquisition program would affect relations between hikers and landowners along the route. Courtesy of the Appalachian Trail Conservancy.

the Park Service, and of course, the Appalachian Trail Conference."[82] Since the 1968 act limited the size of the group, and because the secretary of the Interior had already designated seats to other interests, the coalition was offered only one position. Appalachian Trail landowners were not satisfied with having only one representative on the advisory committee, but they soon found support from some unanticipated sources.

Although hikers generally supported efforts to protect the corridor, negotiations involved in the AT acquisition program—particularly in the Cumberland Valley—caused the hiking community to splinter. Some hikers were content with existing road walks and with the trail's relatively close proximity to human populations. The land acquisition program often involved relocating the trail away from towns and deeper in the eastern forests. But for many through-hikers, road walks like the twelve-mile stretch through Cumberland County provided a break from the monotony of the woods and added a unique cultural dimension to the trail experience. One outspoken hiker and founder of the Appalachian Long-Distance Hikers Association,

Warren Doyle, claimed that he was "tired of the 'roadaphobics' who feel it is their patriotic mission to remove the trail from all roads regardless of the repercussions. . . . I doubt if Benton MacKaye will roll over in his grave if the trail across the Cumberland Valley remains where it is. . . . Hasn't road walking always been part of the AT experience?"[83] Doyle sent a letter to Russell Dickenson, the director of the National Park Service, to "question the need for certain relocations from a longitudinal, thru-hiker perspective."[84]

As tensions in Cumberland County escalated, one local resident, Bonnie Shipe (known to long-distance travelers as "the Ice Cream Lady" because she gave away free ice cream to hungry hikers), conducted an informal survey of hikers' opinions on the issue. Of the 120 hikers she surveyed in one season, 115 were in favor of keeping the route on the road.[85] Shipe shared some of the hikers' responses at a public meeting in 1985. One hiker, Todd Ingberg of Annadale, Virginia, noted that the Cumberland Valley road walk was similar to sections in Hot Springs, North Carolina, and Damascus, Virginia, where the trail led hikers down small-town streets.[86] Explaining his experience in the Cumberland Valley, Inberg wrote,

> We were greeted by children on bicycles asking us about our trip, families meeting us to talk and people asking us if we needed water. The cars moved slow on this beautiful stretch of road. The folks in the cars were full of smiles and waves. . . . People is what the Appalachian Trail is all about to me. . . . Before the people behind the desks make any decisions regarding altering the Cumberland Valley section, please read and consider what the hikers have to say. It is the hikers that have to live with your decisions. I would like to see the Cumberland Valley remain friendly and avoid another hostile section like the off the road vehicles in Tennessee.[87]

When hikers contacted the Park Service about their concerns, Richie was surprised to learn that long-distance hikers' priorities differed from the Park Service's plans for protecting the trail. Richie noted that for many hikers, the AT was "a social experience in the out-of-doors" as opposed to a "wilderness hiking experience."[88] Although hikers seemed to appreciate the natural environment, Richie felt that it was not "the main reason they hike the whole Trail."[89] Because the AT served a much broader constituency than the through-hiking community, however, Richie felt that the agency had "correctly interpreted Congressional intent and the wishes of the Appalachian Trail community in seeking a protected, essentially natural

Trail route."[90] Even though Park Service representatives were often thankful for the hikers' advice and constructive criticism, they maintained that the agency was legally obligated to uphold the conservation objectives outlined in the 1968 act.[91]

Although hikers were often viewed as outsiders to negotiation processes, they had vested interests in debates about locating the trail. In addition to the aesthetic and ideological questions raised by hikers, they also added other dimensions to public discourse. For example, Warren Doyle, who went on to teach courses in Appalachian studies at Lees-McRae College in North Carolina, expressed his concern that the National Park Service was targeting landowners based on their financial and political ability—or rather, inability—to fight the acquisition efforts. He noted that in other campaigns to acquire national parks, federal agents had sought land from landowners in some of the poorest counties in the nation. In the early 1980s, Doyle sent Richie a copy of Si Kahn's *The Forest Service in Appalachia* that explained how the US Forest Service had historically been insensitive to residents' rights and needs in efforts to implement conservation policies.[92] Doyle was concerned that in a similar manner, the National Park Service was treating wealthy and politically powerful landowners in the Northeast differently than poor farmers in southwestern Virginia or in the Cumberland Valley.[93]

In response to Doyle's concerns about class discrimination, Richie explained that "quite a few safeguards" had been "built into the National Forest planning process and land acquisition" since Kahn's publication in 1974. Yet Richie also acknowledged that

> even though the system may protect people and interests better than it used to, it is still important to be sensitive to those interests. Poor people and inadequately funded local communities are still at a disadvantage in dealing with more powerful elements in our society, agencies of the federal government included.

Richie concluded his letter to Doyle by emphasizing that he would be "grateful . . . if you will remind us of the need to be sensitive to these interests whenever you suspect we may not be."[94] Instead of dismissing Doyle's criticism, Richie emphasized the importance of having private citizens keep federal agents in check when they may be overstepping their authority or employing discriminatory policies.

Although my review of the ATC's and the National Park Service's

ATPO's files did not provide clear evidence of discrimination in the case of purchasing land for the AT, historians have documented examples of how federal land policies—including those of the National Park Service—have affected poor, disadvantaged, and minority communities. To establish the early western national parks, the agency displaced hundreds of Native Americans.[95] To create the Great Smoky Mountains and Shenandoah National Parks in the 1930s, the National Park Service removed many mountain farmers who lacked the resources to organize opposition against the federal agency.[96] In the late twentieth century, a legal representative working pro bono for landowners in Arkansas near the proposed Buffalo National River argued that a "substantial portion" of landowners that the Park Service sought land from fell below the federal poverty guidelines.[97] Like other federal agencies, in order to promote the broader public good, the National Park Service has had some negative effects on minority populations—particularly those situated in rural, resource-dependent areas.

While it would be inaccurate to argue that in the case of the AT, wealth and political clout were not factors in determining the relocation of the trail, the ways in which these sources of power affected location decisions were not as clear-cut as one might expect. Plans to relocate the trail affected large, wealthy landowners' property as well as that of people with more modest incomes. If a landowner did not want to sell their land or rights to access their land, the Park Service would typically talk to willing neighbors to find an alterative route that still met the criteria outlined by the 1968 act. In the rare cases in which no suitable alternatives could be found, condemnation proceedings would begin. In some cases, wealthy landowners may have been able to prolong negotiations longer than landowners who were less financially well-off, but the net result was often the same.

For example, from 1978 until his death in 1992, William Ray fought the National Park Service's efforts to relocate the trail on his property. Ray owned most of Schaghticoke Mountain on the border between New York and Connecticut, but he spent most of his time tending his exclusive yacht club in California and his luxury resort in Florida.[98] According to dairy farmer and long-time AT advocate Norm Sills, who worked on field surveys of the property with Elizabeth Levers and the Dutchess County Relocation Committee, Ray rejected Levers's initial route, as well as a second route scouted by David Richie in 1984. Richie's route involved only the higher elevations and inaccessible reaches of Ray's property. When the Park Service planned condemnation proceedings for May of 1987, Ray contacted the director of the National Park Service, William Penn Mott, and asked him to intervene on his behalf. Mott personally surveyed the property with Ray, and together they came up with an alternative route that involved an exchange of land for a piece of existing National Park Service property nearby.

The incident on Schaghticoke Mountain caused quite a stir within the trail community. The ATC objected to Mott's proposal and claimed that it was "politically motivated and a very poor compromise from the standpoint of trail quality."[99] The trail community viewed the agency's decision as "capitulation to a fellow Californian."[100] When it looked like the Park Service was going to proceed with the subpar route, the ATC notified Mott that unless he reconsidered the route on Ray's property and agreed to find a more acceptable alternative, the ATC was going to file a lawsuit against the National Park Service. Just before Mott resigned from his position, he sent notification to Ray that condemnation proceedings would occur to acquire land for the route planned by Richie and the ATC. This example demonstrated that while wealthy and politically well-connected landowners may have been able to delay the land acquisition program, because of the checks and balances imposed by ATC representatives, local volunteers, and the general public, the end result of negotiations was not determined solely by landowners' political or financial clout. As with lower- and middle- class landowners in Virginia and Pennsylvania, the National Park Service and the ATC tried to find routes that were suitable to all parties involved, but they were also, by law, required to find the best physical and scenic location for the trail.

Less than five percent of transactions involved in the acquisition program went to condemnation. Many of those cases involved landowners who were willing to sell land but could not agree on a price. For those landowners, the end result was the same: the government taking their land for what they often felt was an unfair price. But, unlike the acquisition of land for earlier eastern national parks, the process for acquiring the AT corridor gave landowners more opportunities for working with neighbors, local officials, the Park Service, and citizen intermediaries to try to come up with amenable alternatives. Acquiring land for the AT also relied on a wider array of tools and often less-than-fee acquisitions, which did not require residents to leave their homes.

Unlike some of the infamous stories told about places such as Shenandoah National Park, where poor mountain families were forcibly removed from their homes, the AT project involved a dynamic exchange of power between local and outside agents, and between private and public interests. Instances of land acquisition for the AT were not analogous to the removal of Native Americans, as some landowners claimed they were.[101] Instead, the AT land acquisition program depended upon local conditions and the interaction of a number of different local actors, government agencies, and citizen volunteers. Trail advocates and rural residents responded to the three-year land acquisition campaign that followed the 1978 amendment in a variety of ways—from organized resistance to enthusiastic accommodation. The final location of the trail was determined by a constellation of factors—including wealth and politics, as well as regional culture, economic conditions, patterns of land ownership, and broader changes in the national political landscape.

AN UNPRECEDENTED APPROACH TO FEDERAL LAND ACQUISITION

Although the National Park Service and the ATC failed to complete the land acquisition program for the Appalachian Trail by 1981, as authorized in the 1978 amendment of the National Trails Act, project partners had protected 1,730 miles of the 2,100-mile trail by 1984. Most of this land was acquired during the three-year acquisition program from 1978 to 1980. The remaining 370 unprotected miles primarily lay in Maine, Pennsylvania, and Vermont.[102] Yet perhaps even more impressive than the sheer number of miles protected was the fact that through this unusual land acquisition program, collaborations between public and private partners set in motion a new approach to land conservation and national park protection.

Instead of forcing the trail to go in a particular direction and relying on the use of eminent domain, the National Park Service relied on local volunteers, nongovernmental representatives, and alternative tools such as easements to negotiate routes. The ways in which citizen coordinators and the agency worked with landowners along the Appalachian Trail ranged widely—and generated an equally wide range of reactions. The land acquisition program for the Appalachian Trail lacked historical precedents, and local responses to the project were often shaped by residents' existing beliefs and attitudes toward the federal government and other outsiders to their community. The quasipublic status of AT coordinators helped to maintain positive relationships with landowners in some areas, while in other places, it led to confusion and landowners' suspicion of what they perceived to be a powerful special interest group in cahoots with the federal government. In many instances, conflict was resolved through community-based negotiation processes. In only a few instances where negotiations failed—on less than 5 percent of the trail—condemnation was used and resentment toward the project lingered.

As one of the National Park Service's most complex land acquisition initiatives, the AT project was riddled with disputes. Yet it also demonstrated new possibilities for cooperation between different groups. For better or for worse, the program relied on unexplored forms of public-private partnership and involved new roles for civic engagement in land-use decision making. Although the National Park Service did not complete the acquisition program within the three-year time frame, the agency did succeed in establishing viable channels for working with local landowners and communities. In places like the Cumberland Valley, CANT continued their protests against the project through the 1980s. As in many other locations, the trail eventually ended up not as any one group envisioned it but as a thin thread shaped by the interaction of disparate groups and different ideas about land use. The trail, in effect, became the physical embodiment of negotiations that occurred between local landowners, citizen volunteers, Park Service officials, and a wide range of other public and private interests.

In the process of blazing this relocated path, participants helped to establish a new form of environmental decision making that relied on the partnering of public and private powers. This model of public-private partnership was, in part, grounded by the project's history of citizen leadership. But it also evolved in response to broader political changes and sprouting seeds of both grassroots and corporate resistance to large-scale federal initiatives. These shoots would soon reach fruition when Ronald Reagan was elected president on the promise of ushering in an area of "new federalism" and "creative conservation"—both of which would require reducing the power of centralized government.

CHAPTER 6

THE APPALACHIAN TRAIL AND THE RISE OF THE NEW RIGHT

WHEN APPALACHIAN TRAIL ADVOCATES APPROACHED ARTHUR DELMO-
lino in 1985 with a request to purchase land for a corridor through his cornfields and pastures in Sheffield, Massachusetts, the farmer stated that he was
unwilling to cede his land to the US government and "sacrifice my property
and 60 years of hard work . . . clearing this land to benefit a bunch of hikers
in fancy boots."[1] Delmolino's farm was located at the site of Shays' Rebellion—a famous revolt of local farmers who resisted payment of debts and
taxes to wealthy state officials in the late 1780s. Shays' Rebellion ultimately
inspired national leaders to write the US Constitution and establish a stronger system of centralized government that could protect individuals from
local autocrats and prevent unequal economic policies between the states.
In contrast, when the National Park Service began taking land to create
new parks and trails in the late twentieth century, farmers such as Delmolino argued that a tyrannical centralized government had begun to infringe
on the rights of individuals and state and local governments. As he leaned
against the monument that marked the final battle of Shays' Rebellion, Delmolino told a New York Times reporter that not much had changed since the
1780s. For Delmolino and many other landowners along the Appalachian
Trail, the fundamental question was still the same: how much power should
the government have in controlling the lives of private citizens?

The picture of the twentieth-century farmer standing at the site of
Shays' Rebellion provided a powerful image to support protests against
the National Park Service's land acquisition program for the Appalachian
Trail. By using symbols associated with the Revolutionary War era and the

Massachusetts farmer Arthur Delmolino leans against the monument that marks the final battle of Shays' Rebellion. Delmolino argued that the issue was still the same: the government infringing on the lives of private citizens. Photo by Steve Miller.

founding of the US Constitution, even if the analogies lacked historical precision, the protests of landowners along the Appalachian Trail evoked basic questions about the relationship between private citizens and government power. Moreover, this kind of historical rhetoric helped landowners link their concerns to a political movement that had been stirring since the 1960s.[2] As members of an expanding middle class became alienated by cultural changes in the 1960s and 1970s that were codified through federal legislation such as the Civil Rights Act and the environmental statutes of the 1970s, many engaged in their own form of political organization. Central to this movement was organized resistance to the growing power of the federal government to control the economic and social lives of everyday Americans. As exemplified in the campaign to elect Barry Goldwater in the 1960s, in the Sagebrush Rebellion in the West in the late 1970s, in the "wise use" movement in the late 1980s and 1990s, and, most recently, in the organization of the Tea Party, the New Right rose in status from being a fringe of the conservative movement to becoming a central player in federal politics.[3]

One of the most significant events in this shift from the periphery to center stage was the election of president Ronald Reagan, a self-proclaimed sagebrush rebel. Reagan's appointment of James Watt as the secretary of the Interior in 1981 indicated that president Jimmy Carter's extension of New Deal liberalism was being replaced by New Right conservatism. To limit the power of federal government and to promote private ownership, economic productivity, and local control, the Reagan administration reinvigorated Nixon's plans for "new federalism."[4] New federalism aimed to give more power to the states and to promote local decision making, weakening the power of the federal government that had grown since Roosevelt's New Deal programs in the 1930s. Reagan's call for "creative conservation" essentially applied the tenets of new federalism to the administration's environmental policies and programs. In the case of the Appalachian Trail and many other land conservation projects, this meant promoting local autonomy and private entrepreneurship by keeping land on local tax rolls and slowing the flow of federal funds for land acquisition.

With the advent of the new administration and the economic recession of the early 1980s, leaders from within the AT community recognized that the landscape of national policy had fundamentally changed. Longtime ATC volunteer Maurice Forrester acknowledged that "the federal largess on which the ATC has in part come to rely appears unreliable, and we must seek to become self-supporting as quickly as we can."[5] Although project partners had successfully protected nearly 80 percent of the trail by 1981, they realized that they would have to develop new strategies to complete the remaining twenty percent. ATC executive director Larry Van Meter emphasized that volunteerism had been the "irreplaceable key" in

James Watt gives Ruth Blackburn award for her service as chair of the ATC from 1980 to 1983. As director of the Bureau of Outdoor Recreation and as secretary of the Interior, Watt often praised the leadership of citizen volunteers in helping to build the AT. Courtesy of the Appalachian Trail Conservancy.

protecting the Appalachian Trail for the past five decades, and he argued that the new kinds of public-private partnerships proposed by the AT community would be "fully compatible with the new federalism" promoted by Reagan and Watt.[6] In this way, leaders within the trail community tried to frame the project using the language of the Reagan administration and by adapting to a rising political movement that sought to limit the power of the centralized state. These rhetorical and political acrobatics would prove to be even more essential as the national property rights movement matured in the 1980s and 1990s.

In the 1980s and 1990s, AT project partners responded to new political challenges associated with the growing power of the New Right. Appalachian Trail advocates adapted to these changes by experimenting with new approaches to land conservation. These new approaches included the development of a land trust devoted to the private acquisition of trail lands, and another unprecedented decision by the National Park Service in 1984 to delegate the managerial responsibility of newly acquired AT corridor lands to the ATC. The 1984 delegation and the redistribution of authority for managing the nearly completed federal footpath had important implications not only for the AT project but for other environmental initiatives at the end of the twentieth century.

As the land acquisition program for the AT slowly progressed in the 1980s and 1990s and project partners sought to acquire the remaining four hundred miles of unprotected trail, the seeds of opposition witnessed by trail partners during the first three years of the land acquisition program sprouted roots and shoots. Resistance to the National Park Service's land acquisition program for the AT came from several sources, including all levels of government, landowners, national property rights organizations, and even minority factions within the trail community. As the movement to protect private property matured, AT advocates began to view the voices of those who protested the project no longer as isolated cases but as part of a larger chorus of resistance to centralized state power and federal land acquisition.

One of the most dramatic indicators of the political shift in Washington was the appointment of James A. Watt as secretary of the Interior. More than any other official in the Reagan administration, Watt served as a critical link between the administration and the New Right.[7] Watt, a born-again Christian who became famous for making controversial public statements, viewed his work as secretary of the Interior as part of a broader crusade to save America from the burden of federal bureaucracy. Working with others in the new administration, Watt hoped to push back the "high tide of centralized government" in support of the "creative entrepreneurial spirit" of the private sector.[8]

Before serving as secretary of the Interior, Watt had been the director of the Bureau of Outdoor Recreation, and in public speeches, he had frequently pointed to the leadership of private individuals and organizations involved in the Appalachian Trail as an example of this "creative entrepreneurial spirit." Despite his supportive statements, however, in 1981 Watt called for an immediate moratorium on all funding for federal land acquisition—including all provisions for the AT. Watt argued that federal agencies such as the National Park Service "should seek to become good stewards of the lands and facilities we own before we acquire more."[9] The moratorium occurred just as AT project partners began to settle negotiations with many landowners, and the need for funding was greater than ever before. In places such as Connecticut and Virginia, the ATC's land acquisition coordinators had procured verbal agreements from landowners who anticipated being able to sell their land to the government. Without immediate funding, AT advocates argued that millions of dollars invested in the pre-acquisition stage of land acquisition would be wasted. Karen Wade, a regional coordinator for the ATC, expressed concern that landowners would "have to live with the uncertainty of when we will have funds to complete their transactions."[10] This would add tension to an already complicated process that had started several years earlier. Other trail advocates noted that if the administration delayed the acquisition program, soaring land values would rapidly decrease the likelihood of the trail's completion.[11]

When a group of senators and representatives learned about the potential cessation in funding, they argued that the Appalachian Trail was a unique case and should be considered separately from other national park acquisition initiatives. New Hampshire senators Gordon J. Humphrey and Warren B. Rudman explained that when the National Park Service withdrew offers on 1,400 acres of land in their state, local resentment replaced peaceful and productive relations with landowners.[12] The senators also noted that, unlike acquisition programs out West, the AT was "but a thin corridor of land. . . . additional acquisitions would not lock up significant energy or mineral resources." Furthermore, they noted that because the "maintenance and 'stewardship' of this trail . . . [had] traditionally been the responsibility of those who use it," there would be relatively little additional federal expense once it was established.[13] By framing the AT in this way, the senators hoped to demonstrate that the project was consistent with the goals of the new administration. Their efforts were successful; despite the moratorium on federal acquisitions, Congress allocated $2.7 million to the AT in 1981. Although this was considerably less than what the Park Service's Appalachian Trail Project Office had anticipated, it allowed the agency to work with ATC coordinators to finish land acquisition negotiations that were already in progress.

In addition to these changes at the federal level, town and county governments expressed concerns about the effect of federal land acquisition on the local tax base. In several communities along the AT, local officials feared that a federal corridor would increase the tax burden on local residents, who would be forced to make up the loss in revenue. For example, the 1984 annual report for the town of Tyringham, Massachusetts, stated that the AT

TOWN OF TYRINGHAM
Annual Report
FISCAL 1984
July 1st, 1983 to June 30th, 1984

•

I WANT YOUR
LAND
★ ★ ★ ★ ★

𝔅𝔈𝔚𝔄ℜ𝔈

The U.S. Department of the Interior
seeks to protect our Tyringham Valley
from ourselves.

Town of Tyringham, annual report, 1984. Several towns along the AT resisted the federal government's efforts to acquire land for the trail. Town leaders in Tyringham, Massachusetts, were concerned about the possible erosion of the local tax base and loss of control to outside agencies.

Landowner sign expressing concern. Landowners that resisted the land acquisition program for the AT used a variety of measures to garner support for their cause. This large roadside sign expresses concern about the perceived misuse of public monies. Courtesy of the Appalachian Trail Conservancy.

would eliminate three million square feet of land for each mile of relocated trail. Although the state planned to supplement 100 percent of the tax loss for the first year after the acquisition, 75 percent the second year, 50 percent the third year, and 25 percent the fourth year, in year five and thereafter, the town would receive no compensation. In protest, town officials emblazoned the cover of the annual report with a picture of a fierce Uncle Sam declaring "I want your land" and the message "Beware: The U.S. Department of the Interior seeks to protect our Tyringham Valley from ourselves."[14] These views resonated with Reagan's new federalism and with the administration's desire to protect local tax bases.

Many landowners shared their local representatives' concerns about the additional tax burdens, and argued that private citizens were better stewards of the land than federal bureaucracies. In the 1960s and 1970s, the nation witnessed a great expansion of federal agencies and legislation aimed at protecting the environment, and with that bureaucratic growth came a suite of complex rules and regulations that were implemented with varying degrees of success. Most Americans—Democrats and Republicans alike—supported environmental issues. Yet the way in which environmental problems were increasingly solved in the 1970s, often through large-scale federal programs including land acquisition, became a point of contention in debates about environmental protection. Many Americans maintained that private landowners had a greater incentive to protect their investment and were the real stewards of the country's natural resources—not federal bureaucrats. For example, when officials from the National Park Service asked to purchase one hundred acres for the AT corridor from Eugenie J. Fawcett, she maintained, "The Tyringham Valley has been kept rural by a few families like ours who kept large tracts of land and prevented development. Now our reward is to have part of our land taken away."[15] Fawcett's family had lived in the area for over a century, and like many Americans, she embraced Jeffersonian ideas of individual landownership as the key to conservation and, more fundamentally, to American democracy. This resounded in the rhetoric of the New Right, which frequently evoked Jefferson as an ideological anchor to support efforts to reduce federal authority in favor of the power of states and local citizens.

Like debates about environmental protection during this period, most landowners and local communities did not oppose the Appalachian Trail project outright. Instead, they resented the tactics used by the federal government to build a permanent corridor. In Vermont, landowners emphasized that land stewardship had long been part of their "stoic Yankee ownership traditions," and representatives of the ATC sensed that local resistance to the AT project was rooted in "a fear of the federal steamroller coming through and knocking everybody silly."[16] Although the National Park Service had tried to broker federal power through the use of citizen volunteers associated with the ATC and local clubs, after private partners made initial contact and helped to negotiation the acquisition process, the agency's real estate specialists would finalize the legal aspects of acquisition. If negotiations didn't go well and the project partners could not find suitable alternatives, the National Park Service was still ultimately responsible for implementing the 1968 National Trails Act, and the agency had the power of eminent domain to condemn land to do so. Although the agency tried to avoid using condemnation, the fact that the federal government could take private land to build a recreational footpath was not lost on landowners.

As they had during the first three years of the land acquisition program, landowners used a variety of tactics to build public support for their concerns in the 1980s. In some places, these tactics became more radicalized as landowners sought to link their protests against the AT to a broader discourse about the expansion of the federal government. Local newspapers in several states reported instances of angry landowners sabotaging the trail. These stories of sabotage often came from the Southern Appalachians, where the creation of large federal land holdings in the early twentieth century had cultivated mixed feelings toward the government. For example, in Carter County, Tennessee, hikers encountered fishhooks dangling from monofilament fishing line at eye level. In the same area, arsonists burned the Don Nealand shelter. US Forest Service officials from the Cherokee National Forest believed that the saboteurs were related to the Oaks family, inholders within the national forest boundary who had lived on their property for four or five generations and were extremely resistant to having their land taken for the AT. When three foresters went to discuss the possibility of buying land from the Oaks for the AT corridor, they were greeted by a group of twenty people who verbally abused the officers and smashed their vehicle with rocks and two-by-fours.[17]

Other landowners took a more organized and less violent approach. For example, at a speech at a ribbon-cutting ceremony for a new four-mile section of the trail east of Hanover, New Hampshire, governor Hugh Gallen praised "the spirit and cooperation of the private sector" involved in the Appalachian Trail project since its origins. Yet while the governor sang the praises of private citizens and the power of grassroots organization, another form of social action took place below the podium as angry landowners stood near the jubilant group, wearing signs that read "Stop the Federal Land Grab."

One of the protesters, Dave Cioffi, lived in the nearby town of Etna and owned 135 acres through which the Park Service wanted to blaze a 1,000-foot strip that would include sixty acres and divide his property into two pieces. Cioffi was not opposed to the trail and even enjoyed walking on it, but he wanted the AT to be a much narrower 250-foot corridor that would cross through the back of his property. That way he could maintain a contiguous piece of land for grazing sheep and managing a woodlot and sugar bush. Even more than the logistics of the trail's location, however, Cioffi was opposed to the threat of condemnation and the power of the federal government to interfere with land-use activities on private land. He told local reporters that the government had been using the condemnation power "like a hatchet. . . . They want to railroad this thing through with a 600- to 1,000-foot corridor on farmland."[18]

When leaders from increasingly powerful national property rights organizations heard stories like Cioffi's, they were quick to assist landowners affected by the Park Service's land acquisition campaign. During the first three years of land acquisition for the AT, Charles Cushman, founder of the National Park Inholders Association, became a powerful player in the debates about the trail relocation when he helped landowner groups along the trail such as CANT (Citizens Against New Trail) in Pennsylvania, Nail the Trail in New York, and the Appalachian Trail Landowners Organization in Connecticut link up to form the Appalachian Trail Interstate Coalition. In the 1980s, Cushman continued to help landowners along the AT fight legal battles with the US government. After hearing New Hampshire farmers' complaints that the National Park Service and the Dartmouth Outing Club had teamed up to condemn farmland to build the federal footpath, Cushman arranged a meeting in Washington, DC, between the agency's lawyers, powerful leaders within the emerging property rights movement, and sympathetic representatives as well. After much debate, the agency agreed to move the trail from the middle of farms to the back of fence lines.[19]

In addition to the support of Cushman and the National Park Inholders Association, landowners also worked with leaders from the National Association of Property Owners. When four landowners in Harmony Hollow, an area located just north of the Shenandoah National Park, complained that the Park Service had given a member of the Potomac Appalachian Trail Club preferential treatment in negotiations about land acquisition, the landowners set up a meeting with the ATC's regional coordinator, Karen Wade. Wade was "quite surprised" when she arrived at the meeting and found Ric Davidge, a leader of the National Association of Property Owners, sitting with the landowners. Reagan would later appoint Davidge to serve in several important subcabinet positions within the Department of the Interior, through which he became responsible for managing the Land and Water Conservation Fund. Davidge also went on to work with rising stars within the New Right, including serving as the economic development advisor to Wasilla mayor and 2008 vice presidential candidate Sarah Palin.

Davidge's work with the northern Virginians was one indication of the power that AT landowners found in the growing influence of the property rights movement. Furthermore, the surprise appearance of Davidge at the meeting between Wade and the landowners demonstrated one strategy that landowners used to try to catch AT project partners off guard, and to get them to say or do things that might be used against the land acquisition program in a court of law. Wade noted, "It was obvious to me that Mr. Davidge represents these landowners. . . . it was extremely unprofessional of him to not advise me that that is the case." Wade went to the meeting hoping to work out an amenable solution to the landowners' concerns, but she left feeling as though she had been set up to provide evidence for future legal battles. Just as many landowners were wary of the National Park Service and their citizen representatives, Wade complained about being manipulated by this powerful outsider, and she stated that she would "not meet with Mr. Davidge under the same circumstances again."[20]

In addition to property rights advocates' protests against the AT, resistance also came from other sources, including some members of the trail community. Although long-term AT advocates worked closely with the National Park Service to implement the land acquisition program, and most volunteers defended the agency's policies and tactics, some did empathize with landowners and opposed the use of eminent domain for the trail. At the twenty-fifth meeting of the ATC at Green Mountain College in Poultney, Vermont, in 1985, Roger Brickner, a life member of the ATC from Greenwood Lake, New York, submitted a resolution calling for the termination of the use of condemnation to acquire Appalachian Trail land. He argued that the power of eminent domain had:

greatly offended the sense of decency in the Appalachian Trail Community
and among many citizens living along and near the Appalachian Trail. . . .
Further intensification, now clearly evident, of this extremist policy for
100% "protection" can only result in publicity detrimental to our own
self-esteem as members of the Appalachian Trail Conference, oppression by powerful government powers over ordinary citizens and setting
our organization apart from the very spirit of the society under which our
nation thrives.[21]

Brickner's resolution was met by a resounding "nay" from the leaders of
the ATC, who mostly supported the Park Service's efforts to aggressively
acquire land for the project. Long-term leaders of the ATC had witnessed
the erosion of the trail's integrity and continuity by decades of development
and intensive use of the trail, and most AT advocates felt that strong federal action was necessary to protect land within the corridor. Yet Brickner's
statement indicated that even some members of the trail community ques-
tioned the ethics and political consequences of relying on the National Park
Service and the possible power of eminent domain to build this footpath
through the wilderness.

By 1982, only one year into the new administration, it was clear that relying on federal land acquisition was no longer a sustainable strategy for conserving land along the Appalachian Trail. The rising influence of the New
Right and an increasingly pervasive concern about the power of the federal
government inspired AT project partners to seek new strategies for protecting the trail environment. As federal budgets for land acquisition shrank
and the momentum of the property rights movement grew, AT advocates
sought greater support from the private sector by establishing a land trust
and working closely with local conservation organizations. At the same
time, many trail advocates began to sense that preserving the Appalachian
Trail experience would also require protecting the lands adjacent to the
thin footpath. To finish the land acquisition program and to expand conservation programs along the AT, project partners relied not only on support
from Washington, DC, but also increasingly on private initiative and the
volunteer base that had sustained the project since the 1920s. In response to
the political changes in the 1980s, leaders of the ATC sought strategies that
would "capitalize on the Trail as a symbol of partnership—federal, state,
and local—public and private—landholder and public."[22]

As early as 1980, David Richie, project manager for the National Park Service's Appalachian Trail Project Office, began circulating ideas among leaders of the ATC about "an alternative organizational structure."[23] Richie pointed to examples such as the Housatonic River Commission and the Naromi Land Trust, where local conservation leaders outside of the trail community had overcome conflict along the trail in northwestern Connecticut. Richie wanted to promote local autonomy by encouraging "people who live in an area to take responsibility and to guide decisions that affect the destiny of the area in which they live. From what I've seen in Connecticut, the best people are the ones who live in the area [and] are largely outside of the state-club structure."[24]

In many cases, local conservationists who lived in a particular area but were not necessarily affiliated with the AT played an important role in shaping local opinion toward the project. For example, in Pennsylvania, when Mrs. Laurence Benander learned that the Cumberland County commissioners were resisting plans to relocate the trail through the county, she wrote a letter to the editor of the *Harrisburg Patriot News*. Benander stated, "The federal government seems ready, willing, and able to spend approximately 6.6 million dollars in our county to preserve some green space for us. I cannot believe that my elected county commissioners . . . actually intend to reject this stroke of good luck."[25] She was concerned about the county's rapid development and argued for stronger protection of the area's natural resources, including the county's rich agricultural land. Benander pointed out that farming was much more compatible with the Appalachian Trail than industrial development, and she predicted that in a few years, landowners "who currently claim to be preserving their lands for agricultural use will . . . be seen selling it to developers for large but temporary profits which will eventually cost the rest of us in terms of pollution, higher school taxes, and a lower quality of life."[26]

Carol Witzerman, another Cumberland County resident who shared Benander's concerns, formed the group Pennsylvanians Rallied on a Trail Route Advocating Improved Location (PRO-TRAIL). The group was composed not of long-distance hikers but local green space advocates. PRO-TRAIL proposed a route that made partial use of an old railroad right-of-way in the eastern part of the valley. The involvement of individuals such as Benander and Witzerman demonstrated that negotiations were not solely

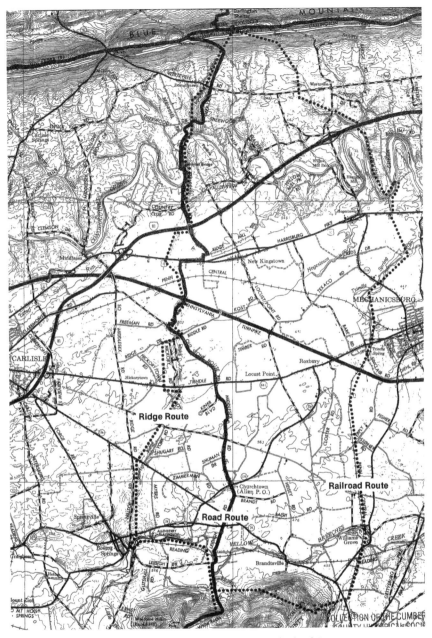

Map 3   Three Potential Routes through Pennsylvania's Cumberland County
In the late 1970s and 1980s, conflict arose over where to locate the trail through Pennsylvania's
Cumberland Valley. One group, Citizens Against New Trail (CANT), wanted the trail to
remain on the existing Road Route. The ATC wanted the trail relocated to a scenic stretch
across a wooded ridge that lay to the west of the existing road walk. Another local group of
open-space advocates, Pennsylvanians Rallied on a Trail Route Advocating Improved Location
(PRO-TRAIL), want the relocated route to go along an old railroad bed in the eastern part of
the valley. The trail was ultimately blazed closest to the Ridge Route, but not exactly where any
of the groups envisioned it. Map courtesy of the Appalachian Trail Conservancy.

between local and outside forces, or between private landowners and the federal government. Instead, public debates also involved a range of private citizens from within particular communities who were able to link their concerns with broader national trends and like-minded organizations.

AT project leaders like David Richie foresaw the important role that organizations such as PRO-TRAIL would play in the future of the Appalachian Trail. As federal leadership of environmental issues and financial support for land conservation waned in the 1980s, the nation witnessed a growing number of local and regional nonprofit organizations devoted to protecting natural resources. Leaders of these private groups, such as George Wislocki, the executive director of the Berkshire Natural Resources Council, noted that diversity was "the strength of the land use movement in our country." Wislocki supported efforts to protect land adjacent to the AT corridor, and he argued that such a project should not be undertaken by an "agency or a commission but rather something like the National Trust for Historic Preservation—a public/private corporation."[27] Although they tended to take different forms and have varying degrees of influence depending on their location and constituency, the growing number of local and regional public-private conservation partnerships played an important role in the AT project as trail leaders began to experiment with private approaches to land conservation.

One of the most significant ways in which AT advocates sought support from the private sector was by forming the Trust for Appalachian Trail Lands in 1982. The purpose of the new land trust was to help the National Park Service acquire the corridor through private mechanisms and to work with local groups to protect adjacent lands. Although the Nature Conservancy and the Trust for Public Lands existed at that time, the Trust for Appalachian Trail Lands was one of the first regional land trusts in the country and the first to specifically protect trails. Leaders of the new land trust emphasized that the organization would supplement the federal land acquisition program; the Trust for Appalachian Trail Lands was in no way trying to take over the agency's congressionally mandated responsibility to purchase and protect land for the AT. Instead, the trust would assist the Park Service's efforts and also help to protect adjoining lands. Members of the trail community responded enthusiastically to the new strategy for land conservation along the trail, and when the ATC sent out a letter to its members to request funds, they received $48,000 by the end of the year.[28]

The Trust for Appalachian Trail Lands allowed for greater flexibility and efficiency in dealing with landowners. If a landowner was unwilling to accept the National Park Service's offer of the appraised fair market value of a property, as was often the case, the agency could turn to the land trust to negotiate with the landowner and pay the difference on the negotiated price. Once a property was acquired by the trust, it would typically be transferred to the National Park Service. For example, in June 1982, the newly formed land trust helped to prevent the Wintergreen resort from obliterating several miles of the trail in Virginia. The trust allowed trail advocates to privately acquire 2,700 acres that had been slated for development in April 1983. The land was then immediately handed over to the National Park Service to officially become part of the AT corridor. According to the ATC,

> It was a good deal all around: Wintergreen got $2 million cash to plow into its development and made money for its owners, ATC got the peace mind of knowing that no one would be building split-levels on the ridgeline or in the visual foreground, and the National Park Service took a big step toward fulfilling its congressional mandate and saving the taxpayer $400,000, because the trust negotiated a better price for the land than the government could have.[29]

Relying on the Trust for Appalachian Trail Lands also allowed AT advocates to pursue a broader program for land conversation that did not rely on federal authority. This became particularly important when Congress approved a series of cuts to the Land and Water Conservation Fund in the late 1980s. By then, the trust had helped ATC representatives to work with local and state authorities as part of a broader movement to help preserve "a fast-disappearing rural lifestyle and heritage unique to eastern America."[30] In places like Woodstock, Vermont, advocates worked with new partners to develop a comprehensive "countryside conservation" program. The program's proponents emphasized that land would remain primarily in private ownership and would support a variety of land uses, including farming, grazing, and logging. The program would also protect historic small towns and unique cultural resources. In this way, instead of managing the trail solely as a wilderness footpath, advocates argued that the corridor should be part of integrated regional land-use plans that would also protect places where people worked and lived.

In a report on the feasibility of the countryside program in his home state of Vermont, AT advocate Preston Bristow, Jr., referred to Benton MacKaye's call for community camps and cooperative systems of food production. Building on ideas sketched in MacKaye's 1921 proposal, Bristow wondered if there was some way in which the Appalachian Trail could "instill in the American people a desire to care for and protect the rural Appalachian countryside."[31]

Bristow was one of several trail volunteers who looked to the British methods of trail protection and land conservation as models of how to organize countryside conservation along the AT. By the 1980s, British conservation leaders had successfully protected over 120,000 miles of public footpaths and byways. These serpentine strips were part of comprehensive land-use plans that also protected working farms and rural villages. The British footpath system served as a model of the kind of integrated land-use planning that countryside conservation advocates in the United States envisioned. To share ideas, Bristow worked with the National Park Service, the Atlantic Center for the Environment, the Center for Rural Massachusetts, and the Vermont Land Trust to organize an international exchange between American and British land conservation planners. A small party of land conservation professionals from the United States and the United Kingdom came to Vermont to investigate ways to guide growth, provide recreational access to land, develop affordable housing opportunities, and preserve open space around the Woodstock area. When the group reviewed resort developments near Killington Peak—an area through which the AT passed—the British planners were astonished. They claimed that the massive ski resort development at Killington and the second home "ghetto" near Queechee Lakes would never have had a chance of being approved in their country. The United Kingdom had passed a National Planning Act in 1947 that had eliminated the right to build without a long and complicated approval process, and had essentially nationalized development in an effort to eliminate uncontrolled growth.[32]

The British planners were critical of Americans' use of large lot sizes as a land conservation tool. They preferred smaller parcels and denser clustered development to promote open common spaces and to protect rural land uses.[33] British laws also allowed public access to large acreages of privately owned rural land, unlike property laws in the United States that favored individual property rights and set limits on the public's right to wander.

In addition to different ideas about property rights and land ownership, British hikers generally had different ideas about the types of landscapes that trails should traverse. Citing a publication by the National Land Trust,

Bristow noted, "Americans hike to get away from culture while the British hike to immerse themselves in culture."[34] Through the exchange program, AT volunteers who were interested in countryside conservation learned that, on a fundamental level, England had preserved its countryside not through complex regulatory mechanisms but because Englanders based their land-use decisions on different ideas about nature, culture, and land ownership. Like the AT Greenway advocates of the 1970s, Bristow hoped that sharing the British experience in America might develop awareness of the need to conserve not only places to escape to but also places to live and labor in.

This trend was becoming more widespread not only in private land conversation circles but also within the National Park Service's programs. As advocates from the private sector sought to conserve land along the AT through programs such as the AT Greenway and countryside conservation initiatives, the National Park Service also began to expand its efforts to protect cultural resources, in addition to its traditional role as steward of the country's natural and scenic beauty. To facilitate this expansion, the agency increasingly relied on local partners. For example, as part of the 1978 National Parks and Recreation Act, Congress established Ebey's Landing National Historic Reserve in Washington State. This new unit of the national park system included historic structures, open space, the small village of Coupeville, and community farms and forests. Although the Park Service had protected these kinds of landscape elements before, Ebey's Landing was the first unit of the national park system that was to remain in private ownership. The Park Service never had the authority of eminent domain to acquire land for the reserve. Also, the area was to be managed by a local unit of government—the Trust Board of Ebey's Landing—that was established by the cooperative efforts of local residents, the National Park Service, and officials from all other levels of government—town, county, and state. These kinds of creative alternatives for national park protection became more popular in the 1980s as political and financial support for large-scale federal land acquisition dramatically declined.

PUBLIC LAND, PRIVATE MANAGEMENT

Although the land acquisition program for the Appalachian Trail had progressed more slowly than Congress had planned, by 1984, approximately

84 percent of the trail had been protected. At that point, many involved in the AT project—both advocates and opponents—wondered what the next phase of the Appalachian Trail would look like. With the economic recession and decline of political support for large federal land managing programs, many wondered who would be responsible for the completed trail. James Gollin of the Connecticut Appalachian Trail Landowners Association wondered, "Who will cut away the blowdowns? Who will help injured people on the Trail that runs through private land?"[35]

The National Park Service responded to these questions with another unprecedented decision. In 1984, the agency delegated the managerial responsibility of the total 70,000 acres of land within the AT corridor—some of which was yet to be acquired—to the Appalachian Trail Conference, a nongovernmental, nonprofit, volunteer-based organization. The delegation of authority included the management responsibility for all corridor lands outside of existing public areas—about 30 percent of the entire trail.[36] Under the new arrangement, the ATC would maintain the trail and shelters, monitor the corridor boundaries, and raise private funds. The Park Service would continue the federal land acquisition program and maintain the legal authority for acquired properties. The agency would also be responsible for the initial boundary survey, structure removal, NEPA compliance, federal budgeting, and coordinating law enforcement efforts.[37]

The 1984 delegation officially recognized the interdependence of grassroots social action and centralized state power embodied in the Appalachian Trail project since its origins in the 1920s. The executive director of the ATC, Larry Van Meter, noted that the Appalachian Trail was the only unit of the national park system that could attribute its origins and development to the efforts of an army of volunteers who received assistance from a number of public agencies. Van Meter maintained that while there was "nothing . . . wrong with the Trail being managed and run by the government . . . the spirit of the Trail—what Benton MacKaye called its 'soul'—is volunteerism. . . . The delegation from NPS to ATC recognizes that, without the private, voluntary sector, the Appalachian Trail would not exist."[38]

Others offered more pragmatic reasons for shifting managerial authority, including the cost of maintaining a 2,070-mile corridor across the eastern mountains and the appropriateness of the decision-making process. David Richie, the project manager of the National Park Service's Appalachian Trail Project Office, pointed out that having the Appalachian Trail managed by a federal agency would be a huge expense to American taxpayers.

Administrators would have to hire new staff and haggle over operating budgets. He insisted that it would be much more cost-effective to use volunteers; he estimated the value of volunteer labor involved in the AT project to be over one million dollars per year.[39] Richie was optimistic about the delegation. He appreciated the way in which the ATC and local trail advocates made decisions and felt it was more appropriate for the AT than how federal bureaucracies made decisions. He said, "People who have expertise are encouraged to share it. And that's not typical [in government]. Most systems try to limit it. There are no hang-ups about professional qualifications . . . and you don't have to go through hurdles. . . . The A.T. offers a way for people to add their own ideas . . . and using the Trail as a basis, they can be experimental, open to innovation."[40]

Not all officials within the Park Service shared Richie's optimism, however. At a meeting of the presidents of all of the local trail clubs affiliated with the ATC, Bob Jacobson, superintendent of Shenandoah National Park, gave a speech explaining why he thought private partners associated with the ATC were bound to fail. Jacobson acknowledged that delegating the responsibility of managing public lands to private organizations seemed to be "both noble and timely." Yet he believed that the 1984 delegation would fail because of (1) a "lack of understanding by the volunteer community of the scope and content of the land management responsibility that is has agreed to undertake, and (2) because of the lack of capability and commitment on the part of some of the individual member clubs to manage the public lands in a satisfactory manner and to do it on a long-term basis."[41] The delegation required navigating uncharted terrain, and many officials were uncomfortable with relinquishing control over their traditional duties. Some members of the trail community suspected that certain government officials were jealous of volunteer accomplishments on the AT and what they may have perceived as "creeping amateurism" in the management of public lands.[42]

When Congress gave the ATC and its local clubs management authority over the new publicly owned lands within the AT corridor in 1984, decisions traditionally made by trained foresters and park officials were handed over to enthusiastic volunteers. The ATC and its affiliates quickly stepped up to the challenge. By 1986 the organization had grown to twenty staff members, with four regional offices and twenty thousand members. The ATC recognized that paid staff and volunteers would both continue to be important, but the ATC, local clubs, and agency partners would all serve different functions. The ATC would be responsible for cultivating politi-cal relationships at the national level, while the affiliated trail clubs would be responsible for developing and maintaining relationships at the local level—including relationships with landowners and local government.[43]

One of the greatest challenges that the ATC and their local affiliates faced in managing land within the new AT corridor was interpreting the legislative intent of the 1968 National Trails Act and translating that intent into management practices. Should herbicides be used to control invasive species along this wildness footpath? What kinds of agricultural and sil-vicultural practices should be allowed to continue in and along the AT corridor? How should the trail clubs deal with adjacent landowners who built pools, barns, and other structures within the AT corridor boundary? Although citizen advocates received technical support and advice from public partners in their attempts to answer these kinds of questions, the transfer of managerial authority marked an unparalleled exchange of power and opened up the arena of decision making to a wide variety of ideas about proper land management.[44]

For many volunteers, the use of chemical herbicides was an acceptable way to control weeds and invasive plants. Yet others felt that it was incon-sistent with the notion of a "wilderness footpath." In a letter to the editor of the ATC's newsletter, Maurice Forrester wrote, "Either we accept nature as it is—unedited—or we acknowledge that hidden all along behind our ideal-ized language has been nothing more than an exurbanized Central Park."[45] Although he agreed that the trail needed to be cleared and maintained, For-rester asked, "How can we argue that the A.T. in the Cumberland Valley must be moved off the roads because the roads are not natural, while at the same time we claim the right to eradicate along the trail *Rhus radicans* [poi-son ivy] which *is* natural?"[46] Volunteers held a wide range of ideas about the appropriate kind of nature that hikers should encounter on the trail, and determining the appropriate level of "naturalness" complicated the ATC's task of managing corridor lands in the 1980s. In the case of herbicides, the ATC and the Park Service ultimately decided that, outside of designated wilderness areas, they could be used to control invasive plants, but the size and scale of herbicide applications would depend on local conditions.

In addition to questions about the use of herbicides to manage veg-etation, as the partnership between the ATC and their public partners matured in the early 1980s, long-time trail workers became more deeply involved in decisions about timber management along the trail corridor and in the viewshed. For many volunteers who did not have forestry training, their ideas about forest management initially focused on preserving the aesthetic qualities of the trail environment. After working with the US Forest Service, and, to a lesser extent, the National Park Service, AT volunteers' ideas often expanded to also consider the ecological and economic dimensions of managing forest land. For example, in Georgia, Whit Benson, the leader of the Georgia Appalachian Trail Club's Conservation Committee, had been studying forest management practices as part of his involvement in a RARE II evaluation in northern Georgia.[47] At the beginning of the process, like many other trail advocates, Benson opposed clear-cutting because it left "ugly scars" on the landscape.[48] After considering other options and working with federal foresters, he began to understand the complexity of the decision.

In a report to his fellow Georgia Appalachian Trail Club members, Benson explained that part of the US Forest Service's mission was to provide a sustained yield of timber. Given that some kind of harvesting had to occur, he asked, "Is it better to do selective cutting of designated trees over extended periods of time with continued low level disruption of the environment, or is the short term massive disruption of a clearcut followed by an extensive period of latency preferable?"[49] He pointed out that selective harvesting would require multiple trips, as well as the creation and maintenance of forest roads. He noted that places that seemed like quintessential wilderness, such as the Smoky and Cohutta Mountains, had been extensively logged at the beginning of the century.

At the same time, however, Benson also pointed out that beyond the aesthetic havoc clear-cutting might wreak on a forest, there was the problem of regeneration. He feared that because pine was well adapted to the southern Appalachians, clear-cutting would ultimately turn the southern forest into one massive pine monoculture. Not only would such homogeneity look bad, but Benson also argued that it was "contrary to the biological axiom that the more complex and diverse a natural community is, the greater its stability."[50] Instead of advocating that the Georgia Appalachian Trail Club oppose clear-cutting altogether, however, Benson maintained that the organization needed to figure out a rational alternative and to consider other silvicultural methods. He suggested that the group focus on protecting hardwood forests at higher elevations, and he also encouraged his trail colleagues to support timber harvesting on private lands so as to limit the pressure to cut on public lands.

Not all members of the trail community supported cutting trees in and near the corridor, however. Representatives of the ATC's Southern Regional Management Committee resolved, "Timber harvesting is incompatible with the goals of a primitive experience and the concepts of 'wild lands' and 'the primeval environment.'"[51] The Southern Committee recommended that the ATC's board of managers prohibit harvesting trees within the corridor unless it was specifically being done to improve the "aesthetic, recreational, and primitive values for which the Trail was established."[52] Although logging was prohibited in national parks, the National Scenic Trails Act of 1968 permitted compatible land uses, and the Appalachian Trail Comprehensive Plan of 1981 acknowledged that timber harvesting had been a traditional land use along the trail. Ultimately, the ATC's board of managers decided that managing forest resources to enhance the corridor was acceptable and should be encouraged. Local clubs could harvest timber if it was done for the purpose of maintaining a particular view. Before harvesting, however, clubs had to check with project partners. In this way, decisions about timber management were to be based on cooperation between public officials, technical experts, ATC representatives, and local volunteers.[53]

Like decisions about forest management, the AT comprehensive plan of 1981 also required that the ATC and its volunteers work with public officials and local residents to determine appropriate agricultural practices along the trail corridor. Although some trail advocates discouraged extensive agricultural operations near the trail, David Field, a professor of forestry at the University of Maine, past president of the Maine Appalachian Trail Club, and chair of the ATC in 1995, argued that in addition to silviculture, farming should also be encouraged along the corridor. He wrote,

If you think that the farmlands of the Cumberland Valley or of northern New Jersey should be managed to revert to their natural (forested) condition, so that the Trail's Greenway will provide a "natural" environment, I suggest that you read "Who Will Feed China?" by Lester Brown of the World Watch Institute. . . . If you think that it would be a good idea to turn much of the land along the Trail in Maine from its current use in timber production to a wilderness park, consider the alternatives for producing paper and construction materials.[54]

Although many long-time trail workers, like Field, had extensive experience in land management and promoted the trail as a project that could help protect working landscapes as well as wild lands, these views were not shared by all members of the increasingly diverse trail community. Many trail advocates wanted the AT to be managed as a resource more like the federally designated wilderness areas—places that were "untrammelled by man" and free from extractive uses. As the ATC and its affiliates took on greater responsibility for managing land in the AT corridor, cooperating partners' ideas about the way the AT should be managed sometimes conflicted. Final decisions about harvesting, farming, and other land uses typically relied on negotiation and dialogue between citizen volunteers and their professional partners.

Just as AT advocates sought advice from their public partners, public land managers increasingly sought ideas from volunteers about the local conditions of the trail. For example, in the early 1990s, Art Rowe of the Pisgah Ranger District wrote to Jim Roddy, president of the Carolina Mountain Club, to explain that the Forest Service was "changing the way we develop our project plans." Rowe emphasized that the agency was going to "involve you, the public, much more than we have in the past." Although the new approach was "somewhat experimental," Rowe maintained that the agency was committed to working more closely with citizen collaborators. In the future, Rowe wrote, "all of our planning will be done in this manner."[55]

Starting with the National Environmental Policy Act of 1970, public land managers were required to involve citizens in management decisions in more meaningful ways. By the 1990s, the federal government had become an active player in the environmental arena, but so, too, had citizen organizations and private interests.[56] Because of the project's history of civic engagement, the AT provided public land managers with the ideal terrain to test new approaches to collaborative decision making.

To support cooperative planning efforts at the local level, the ATC worked closely with the National Park Service to develop a systematic process for land planning along the AT corridor. This process involved four steps: inventorying existing resources, identifying issues of concern, writing a statement of policy, and designing an action plan to address the issue. The process helped to clarify the long-term land management needs for each trail section. The ATC emphasized that members of local clubs would be responsible for writing and implementing local land management plans, with support from representatives of the ATC and government agencies. Through workshops, one-on-one meetings, field excursions, and regular correspondence, the ATC and the Park Service trained local volunteers in how to engage in this kind of long-term land management planning process. As private citizens successfully took on new land management responsibilities, the line between expert and amateur became increasingly fuzzy, and the process revealed that the traditional top-down structure of land-use decision making had been permanently altered.

The form and degree of partnership between AT advocates from the private sector and the National Park Service was unmatched at that time, and the 1984 delegation allowed the Park Service to begin experimenting with new ways to involve private partners and local governments in the management of the nation's park resources. Up until the early 1980s, the primary way in which private organizations partnered with the National Park Service was in helping to acquire land for new national park units. This typically occurred through land trusts and philanthropic foundations. In the 1980s and 1990s, the agency began to work with a wider array of private organizations to help manage the expanding system. At that time, organizations such as Friends of Acadia and Friends of Great Smoky Mountains formed to assist the National Park Service in its efforts to protect and manage park resources and to work on the conservation of land surrounding the parks.[57]

In helping to pioneer this new path to public-private partnerships, AT leaders found local management plans to be "the cornerstones for cooperative management of the Appalachian Trail."[58] The planning process was to encourage dialogue, and to establish channels of communication not only between federal officials, employees of the ATC, and local volunteers but also between trail partners and nearby residents. For example, in Dutchess County, New York, local advocates hosted several meetings with landowners near the trail to "develop a good neighbor feeling, identify potential volunteers, publicize the AT," and to "provide opportunities for people to talk about their concerns with the AT, and make suggestions or ask questions."[59] Volunteers solicited participation in the meetings by hand-delivering to nearby residents a brochure that explained the project's history and future goals. Although the New York volunteers reported that none of the meetings were particularly well attended, they felt that the initiative served an important function by opening the conversation up to future cooperation.

Because of the general desire to maintain the historic voluntary spirit of the project, local planning processes were to avoid "the 'efficient' approach of unilateral planning and plan writing by one or a few individuals."[60] Instead of focusing on "professionalism," officials with the National Park Service's Appalachian Trail Project Office maintained that the project should focus on "adequacy of management."[61] This required that project partners put their trust in volunteers to take charge and establish their own local systems of management. Although the ATC employed a handful of professional trail builders such as Bob Proudman, published user-friendly manuals, and sponsored a variety of training workshops to teach volunteers how to build trails, the organization maintained that the basic skills of trail maintenance did not require esoteric knowledge or extensive technical training. Many volunteers felt that the collaborative approach to management was "a lot more exciting than the old style . . . stamping out complicated plans and then establishing bureaucracies to control them."[62]

The Park Service's delegation of authority to the ATC reflected a shift in decision making about federal land management. Instead of being made predominantly through bureaucracies and professional experts, decisions were increasingly made through partnerships and collaborations that combined the centralized power of the state with the decentralized involvement of nonprofit organizations and citizen volunteers. AT project partners often used the metaphor of a three-legged stool to describe how management decisions were made along the trail. The three legs of the stool were the local clubs, the ATC, and state and federal agencies—especially the National Park Service. Without all three legs involved in decision making, the stool—that is, the AT—would collapse.

Taking this partnership approach was a slow and complicated learning process, as demonstrated by the variety of ways in which local land planning occurred after the 1984 delegation of managerial authority to the ATC. Reflecting on the initial years after the 1984 delegation, Brian King, a long-time employee of the ATC, wrote that the organization's leaders "freely admitted for years that no one in the organization could quite spell out what 'land management' meant for a dispersed, volunteer-based force with more than one hundred active stewardship-partner organizations at the Trail level."[63] Yet, by the 1990s, the ATC was working with its public and private partners to actively manage 100,000 acres of national park land and had assumed responsibility for the longest publicly owned greenway in the world.[64] In the process, trail partners helped to blaze a new organizational path for conserving and managing the country's natural resources.

During the last decade of the twentieth century, the nation witnessed the continuation of political trends that had begun in the 1980s. The number of public-private conservation partnerships expanded as countless numbers of local land trusts and "friends" groups sprouted across the country. At the same time, the property rights movement continued to evolve and gain strength as leaders within the New Right remained in influential positions in Washington—particularly in the 104th Congress, when Newt Gingrich's Contract with America aimed to dismantle the regulatory system on which the nation's environmental laws and policies depended.[65] In the 1990s, several southern states passed legislation to reduce the effects of regulations on property owners. For example, in 1995, Florida legislators passed the Property Rights Protection Act, which outlined courses of action that those who had been "inordinately burdened" by regulations could take to protect their property.[66] That same year, Charles Cushman's National Park Inholders' Association changed its name to the American Land Rights Association, to reflect the expansion of the organization's focus from inholders to US property owners more broadly.[67]

As the nation debated the politics of environmental protection and fought over the constitutionality of environmental laws and federal programs, leaders of the Appalachian Trail held fast to the project's history of volunteerism and adapted to a changed political landscape. The National Park Service sought to complete its land acquisition program, while leaders of the ATC worked to develop the organization's volunteer base and used the Trust for Appalachian Trail Lands to seek financial support for land acquisition from the private sector. In spite of decreased federal support for large-scale conservation and park projects in the 1980s, by relying on the combination of decentralized and centralized power that had characterized the project throughout the early and mid-twentieth century, it appeared as though the entire Appalachian Trail would be protected by the start of the new millennium.

THE APPALACHIAN TRAIL AT

THE END OF THE TWENTIETH CENTURY

Hours before Congress authorized $15.1 million to acquire the remaining 10,800 acres of land for the Appalachian Trail by 2000, president Bill Clinton and vice president Al Gore celebrated Earth Day by working with volunteers from the Potomac Appalachian Trail Club and a representative of the ATC's mid-Atlantic office on a small section of the Appalachian Trail. On April 22, 1998, the country's executive leaders spent forty-five minutes moving large boulders and planting red, white, and blue phlox at a rock wall near Harpers Ferry. Then, with Gore in his Gore-Tex boots and

Clinton in his office oxfords, they moseyed a quarter mile down the trail to give speeches at Jefferson Rock, a precipice visited by Thomas Jefferson in 1785 that offers stunning views of the confluence of the Shenandoah and Potomac Rivers.

Clinton used the Earth Day festivities on the Appalachian Trail to talk about his environmental agenda. In addition to committing one billion dollars to the national parks, including funds for acquiring the final sections of the Appalachian Trail, he spoke about the need to "encourage and support better stewardship on our private lands through voluntary partnerships to help private landowners preserve their own land."[68] He emphasized the important role of civic engagement in environmental affairs and applauded the AT community for setting a powerful example of grassroots environmental action.

Clinton's emphasis on volunteerism and the involvement of the private sector in his Earth Day talk indicated that the downshifting of federal involvement in environmental affairs that occurred under the Reagan and Bush administrations would continue to influence environmental policy in the 1990s. Since the first Earth Day demonstration in 1970, organized citizens had made great advances in getting officials in Washington to support environmental legislation and federal land protection programs. As the environmental movement gained traction, however, other Americans organized to oppose the regulations and restrictions on private activities brought on by new legislation. The economic recession of the 1980s added to people's concerns about federal spending on land acquisition and environmental programs. By the end of the century, it was clear that the era of large-scale federal environmental initiatives that characterized the 1970s was over and had been replaced by a new model that emphasized partnerships between the public and private sectors. Clinton and Gore's Earth Day service on the Appalachian Trail, moving rocks and planting flowers with local volunteers and representatives of the ATC near Jefferson Rock, provided a photogenic symbol of this new partnership model.

Before their helicopter swooped the nation's top executives back to Washington, Gore told the small audience assembled, "We loved helping you on that trail. I look forward to coming back and seeing those flowers take root and grow, seeing how many of them do." Jokingly, he added, "We did the best job we could with those." Like the patriotically colored flowers planted by Clinton and Gore in 1998, over the course of two decades, a new strategy for political action and environmental decision making had taken

President Bill Clinton and vice president Al Gore help AT volunteers in Harpers Ferry build a rock wall near the AT, Earth Day 1998. During their visit, the nation's top executive leaders spoke about the value of civic involvement in environmental initiatives. Courtesy of the Appalachian Trail Conservancy.

root and had grown on the Appalachian Trail. This new approach embodied elements of two major political traditions—New Deal liberalism, with its support for large-scale federal conservation projects, and New Right conservatism, with its support for local control and private enterprise. When put into practice on the Appalachian Trail, these ideological and political roots often led to conflict, and required unprecedented levels of cooperation to overcome a tension that was written into the very fabric of American governance: how does a pluralistic society balance the needs of local people and private citizens with the need to achieve broader national goals?

In 1785, not long after Thomas Jefferson visited the same scenic spot where Clinton and Gore gave their Earth Day addresses, the drafter of the Bills of Rights commented on a farmer rebellion in Massachusetts that had been led by Daniel Shays. Reflecting on Shays' Rebellion, Jefferson made his famous remark, "The tree of liberty must be refreshed from time to time with the blood of patriots and tyrants. It is its natural manure." Although building the Appalachian Trail did not involve the literal "blood of patriots and tyrants," over the course of nearly a century, project partners had to navigate contentious public debates about the role of the federal government in regulating the lives of everyday Americans. They did so by relying on the project's historic volunteer base and by emphasizing the decentralized structure of the project. In this sense, the tangled roots of the Appalachian Trail were nourished by the natural manure of conflict as well the compost of cooperation.

HIKING THROUGH HISTORY

WHEN WALKING THROUGH THE CAREFULLY MANAGED APPALACHIAN TRAIL corridor today, more than 99 percent of which is now protected through public ownership, it is difficult for hikers to see evidence of the hard-fought political battles that created a place so seemingly removed from the world of people and politics. The eastern forests that have regenerated after at least two or three major cutting periods tend to hide the landscape's history and provide a sense of wildness and timelessness. Yet there are places along the trail that lead hikers out of the woods and through small towns, behind suburban developments, and across active farms. In these places, where the effects of human activities are more obvious, travelers on the Appalachian Trail (AT) might begin to wonder about what they are seeing. Why are there corn and soybeans growing along this footpath through the wilderness? Who owns these cows whose pasture I'm walking through? Why are the people in this town so friendly to hikers? Or, in some rare areas, why are they so rude or hostile? Back in the forest, one might wonder why trees in certain areas were cut or burned. Particularly rugged sections might cause a hiker to pause and consider why the trail was routed on what seems to be the most challenging terrain possible. To truly "see what you see" on the AT, as Benton MacKaye instructed, one must look deeply into the surrounding scenic surfaces, and consider the complex human histories contained along the corridor.

From MacKaye's grand plans for transforming America's hinterlands in the 1920s to new initiatives in the twenty-first century, the history of the Appalachian Trail demonstrates the power of collaboration and partnership. It also reveals that in a pluralistic society, conflict is often necessary to achieve large-scale goals, and people from all points along the political spectrum need to be willing to engage in meaningful interaction in order to arrive at pragmatic outcomes. The trail's history also illustrates that the line between public and private efforts to conserve land and protect park resources has never been clear-cut. Since the 1920s, those involved in building the AT—as volunteers, federal agents, and landowners—adapted to broader changes in the national political landscape by relying on the interaction of grassroots action and the power of the centralized state. The project started as a seed in the Progressive Era—one of the first proposals of the recently formed Regional Planning Association of America that combined the growing authority of federal experts with the voluntary spirit of dedicated citizens. This seed took root in the 1930s, first through the efforts of a handful of influential citizens, then with support from the Civilian Conservation Corps (CCC). The involvement of the CCC—one of Roosevelt's most popular New Deal programs—reflected a commitment by Washington to become a more active player in developing the AT as well as other park resources.

This commitment by Washington helped to put into effect many of the Progressive ideas expressed by MacKaye and his contemporaries, and would later blossom in the 1960s and 1970s as the modern environmental movement coevolved along with the growing power of the federal regulatory state. As unchecked economic growth during the postwar era began to cause ineradicable damage to the nation's natural resources, more and more Americans grew concerned about environmental issues. In response to widespread public support for environmental protection, Congress passed a series of environmental laws, including the 1964 Wilderness Act, the 1970 Clean Air and Water Acts, the 1973 Endangered Species Act, and the 1976 National Forest Management Act. At the same time, the number and power of federal agencies began to grow, and federal regulators began experimenting with new rule-making processes to help them achieve congressionally mandated goals. The National Trails Act in 1968 and the National Park Service's land acquisition program for the AT were a small part of this bigger regulatory package that sought to use federal power to achieve large-scale environmental goals. By using the power of the centralized state to counteract the forces of private industry, AT project partners and organized environmental interests navigated complex legislative and executive processes to protect resources for the common good. Like many other federal projects, protecting the AT for the public good sometimes had negative effects on smaller populations within the American public.

As the environmental movement gained strength with broad federal laws and programs in the 1970s, the seeds of a new political movement were also planted: the property rights movement. Although many typically associate the property rights movement with the organized political resistance that occurred in the 1980s and 1990s, as exemplified in the "wise use" movement, the trend began decades earlier. When Congress started to pass key pieces of environmental legislation in the 1960s and 1970s and called for restrictions on individual and corporate rights to land and resources, many Americans resisted new federal laws and policies—particularly in the West, where most of the country's public lands were located. These protests against federal land-use regulations and environmental laws were part of a broader chorus of resistance to centralized state power and its infringement on individual and states' rights. Just as the environmental movement relied on civic engagement and the growing power of nonprofit organizations in the 1960s and 1970s, the property rights movement moved from being a series of isolated cases to becoming a major player in national politics in the 1980s and 1990s. At that time, leaders of the property rights movement, many of who were connected with the New Right, found themselves at center stage in a broader debate about the role of government and the regulation of resources, communities, and individuals. This ongoing debate about the role of the federal government in regulating the everyday lives of private citizens lies at the core of early twenty-first century American politics.

As the political landscape changed in the final decades of the twentieth century, it became apparent that the era of large-scale federal land acquisition was over. It is unlikely that the nation will ever see the expansion of the national park system through federal land acquisition to the extent witnessed during the 1970s. Instead, the National Park Service, like other land managing agencies, has come to rely more heavily on the private nonprofit sector—organizations like the ATC working in partnership with state and federal agencies to achieve land conservation goals. This shift to public-private partnership was, in part, a response to the growing influence of the New Right on the country's political landscape. In the case of the AT, it was also a response to the long-time commitment of volunteers and the growing institutional capacity of nonprofit organizations such as the ATC.

THE APPALACHIAN TRAIL IN THE TWENTY-FIRST CENTURY

As the land acquisition program for the Appalachian Trail neared completion in the early twenty-first century, the ATC launched new initiatives that, in many ways, have brought the AT project full circle back to Benton MacKaye's ideas about regional planning and civic engagement. The National Park Service spent over two decades working with trail partners and landowners to build and protect a final route, and by 2013, only about seven miles of the Appalachian Trail remained unprotected. The sylvan swath that now runs 2,180 miles from Georgia to Maine is one of the largest—and most culturally and biologically diverse—units of the national park system.[1] The ATC continues to work with local clubs to maintain the footpath, but since the turn of the twenty-first century, the organization has expanded its programs to focus on land conservation and community development—elements of the project that were central to MacKaye's original vision. To reflect this shift, the ATC changed its name from the Appalachian Trail Conference to the Appalachian Trail Conservancy in 2005.

One of the twenty-first century programs launched by the ATC that embodies MacKaye's regional planning ideas is the Appalachian Trail Community program. Through this program, members of the ATC and local clubs have worked to build and maintain strong relationships between the trail community and the trail's neighbors. AT advocates have collaborated with rural residents and other conservation groups to promote compatible land uses along the AT corridor, including the conservation of farmland, open space, sustainable development, and recreational opportunities. Although the federal government has provided financial support, local planning initiatives along the AT have been led primarily by the ATC, and have involved a wide range of new partners, including leaders of land trusts, local zoning coordinators, and landowners.[2]

For example, in September 2006, the Cumberland County Cumberland Valley Visitors Bureau, the Pennsylvania Recreation and Parks Society, the Pennsylvania Department of Conservation and Natural Resources, the National Park Service, and the Conservation Fund jointly sponsored the Appalachian Trail Cumberland Valley Gateway Community Forum. Participants in the forum included long-time ATC employees such as Karen Lutz and Bob Proudman, as well as Sheldon Brymesser, a local farmer who was once a vocal member of CANT—Citizens Against New Trail—a landowner group that resisted the National Park Service's land acquisition program through Pennsylvania's Cumberland Valley in the late 1970s and 1980s. After witnessing new housing developments consume his neighbors' farms in the fertile valley, Brymesser agreed to sell ninety-six acres of his family's one-thousand-acre farm to the National Park Service. Today, Brymesser continues his family's farming tradition and leases those ninety-six acres. Through activities like the 2006 Gateway Community Forum, he also works with the ATC and local partners from Cumberland County to plan for the sustainable economic development of the region. As highlighted in the ATC's July–August 2011 magazine, Brymesser and his family are working to "help preserve the A.T. experience, maintain MacKaye's vision of 'food camps,' and uphold the viability and integrity of the foodscape."[3]

As evidenced by the enthusiastic participation of local residents like Brymesser in contemporary regional planning processes, many rural communities have come to embrace the Appalachian Trail and the economic and conservation opportunities that it has helped to foster. As traditional natural resource industries such as farming, logging, and mining declined in the late twentieth century and the United States began importing its natural resources from other countries, a service-based economy became essential to sustain many rural communities. Since 2000, towns along the AT have seen an explosion in the number of hostels and hiker-oriented service businesses. Instead of viewing the AT as a threat to their livelihood or personal property, many local residents now see the AT as a major economic asset for their community and future. Through the Community Partners program, trail-friendly towns such as Hot Springs, North Carolina, and Norwich, Vermont, invite hikers in to learn about the different ways in which the AT has been integrated into local land-use planning processes.

In addition to engaging trail towns in regional planning initiatives, the ATC has worked with new partners to develop programs that revive some of MacKaye's other ideas about the AT. In 1932, MacKaye published an article in *Scientific Monthly* titled "The Appalachian Trail: A Guide to the Study of Nature." In it, he explained that the AT would someday become a resource for helping Americans develop deeper understandings of the natural world.[4] In 2000, the ATC launched the MeGaTransect program to engage "citizen scientists" in long-term ecological studies from Maine to Georgia ("MeGa"). Through this program, trail leaders have coordinated partnerships with a variety of nontrail-related organizations, such as the American Chestnut Foundation, the Vermont Center for Ecostudies, and the National Geographic Society, to study the effects of climate change, and to monitor rare and invasive species along the corridor.[5] Through the MeGaTransect program, AT leaders hope to use the 250,000 acres of protected land within the AT corridor to study changes in earth's systems, and to help people understand the causes of those changes.

The ATC has also used the now-protected trail for educational purposes through its Trail to Every Classroom program. This program provides professional development for K–12 teachers who want to use the AT as a teaching tool. Teachers participate in a series of place-based workshops, and develop their own curriculum that uses the AT to teach lessons in civics and environmental education. Like the MeGaTransect program, the Trail to Every Classroom program has helped to shift the focus of the AT project from protecting the corridor through land acquisition to a new era that emphasizes education and long-term stewardship through creative partnerships.

As with all stages of the project's past, initiatives launched in the twenty-first century, such as the Appalachian Trail Community, MeGaTransect, and Trail to Every Classroom programs, have relied on a number of organizations and individuals. New programs have combined elements of previous initiatives in which private citizens provide the bulk of the labor, the ATC provides organizational support, and state and federal governments offer funding, training, and technological assistance. In this sense, recent programs have not only broadened the physical scope of lands to be protected but also widened the project's political arena and expanded opportunities for learning and collaboration.

THE TRAIL AHEAD

Although the Appalachian Trail was unlike most federal land projects in the twentieth century, and it differed from other grassroots environmental initiatives in many ways, the history of the project reveals five important lessons about the politics of environmental protection and the evolution of land conservation in the United States. These lessons have important implications for environmental initiatives in the twenty-first century. First, the history of the AT reveals the importance of coordinated grassroots action that can operate on multiple scales—from the local level to the national political arena. Second, the trail's history demonstrates that bipartisan federal leadership is often necessary to achieve large-scale conservation goals. Representatives of all political persuasions must be willing to engage in productive dialogue to seek practical solutions to environmental problems. Efforts to protect land along the AT corridor showed that conservation is compatible with conservative principles, and that while preserving wild land is important, so, too, is protecting working landscapes—a third and fourth lesson contained in the history of this famous footpath. A final lesson embodied in the AT's history is that our political institutions must remain flexible and able to adapt to new cultural and economic realities. This kind of pragmatic evolution will involve conflict, compromise, and cooperation—all processes that are necessary to address the broad and often daunting environmental challenges of the twenty-first century.

One of the most important lessons contained in the trail's history is the importance of civic engagement in environmental protection. More specifically, the trail's history speaks to the need to coordinate decentralized private efforts on multiple levels. While trail volunteers associated with the local clubs provided the bulk of the labor for on-the-ground maintenance and upkeep of the AT in the last half of the twentieth century, the ATC focused on lobbying efforts in Washington, DC, and coordinated new trail-wide programs to protect the corridor. The nested structure of the ATC and its affiliated clubs began in the 1920s, when project leaders realized that because of the long, linear shape of the trail and the vast geography that it covered, a single grassroots group would be insufficient for building a two-thousand-mile footpath. By organizing an informal federated structure, the ATC and its affiliated local trail clubs were able to operate on multiple fronts. This distributed system allowed members of the trail community to perform different functions—from clearing up blowdowns to testifying in congressional hearings—that were all necessary to maintain and protect the AT.

Throughout the project's past, the distributed system of trail clubs also served as a conduit for developing social capital among like-minded outdoor enthusiasts—many of whom had important political connections in Washington. Like other grassroots environmental groups such as the Audubon Society, the Sierra Club, and the Wilderness Society, by the 1960s and 1970s, the ATC had grown from a handful of nature lovers who liked to hike into a powerful player in federal politics.[6] Part of the organization's influence came from its members' professional networks and relationships with like-minded groups. The number and types of regional environmental organizations exploded in the 1990s, and the ATC discovered new partners interested in assisting state and federal agencies in efforts to manage public lands.[7] By the end of the twentieth century, the ATC had proven its ability to operate on many levels and to protect a national resource that was not beholden to traditional political jurisdictions.

Another lesson contained in the AT's history is that, just as the private sector was engaged in protecting the corridor on multiple fronts, so, too, were public leaders—no matter what political party or philosophy they represented. Although the ATC maintains that the heart and soul of the AT—what MacKaye often referred to as the "spirit" of the project—has been the thousands of citizen volunteers who have worked to create and manage the trail, the role of federal and state agencies in creating the AT cannot be underestimated. Nor can the power and influence of congressional representatives who were historically able to overcome deep political and ideological differences to achieve workable compromises. The recent gridlock in Congress has contributed to the decades-long decline in Americans' faith in one of our core political institutions. Yet the history of the Appalachian Trail reminds us that in order to make progress on environmental issues, we have needed supportive leaders in Washington—Republicans, Democrats, and Independents alike.

Without the power of federal government, we would likely never have had an Appalachian Trail in the twenty-first century. Unlike the AT, other national scenic trails never received the same level of financial or administrative support from Congress or the National Park Service. As a result, many miles of other trails remain unprotected. For example, Wisconsin's Ice Age Trail is one thousand miles long on paper, but only about half of the trail has been physically established. In a similar way, without federal leadership in the twentieth century, the quality of our air, water, and other natural resources would likely be much worse in the twenty-first century. Our rivers today may not be pristine, but at least they do not catch on fire with any regularity. This is largely due to federal legislation such as the Clean Water and Clean Air Acts—and the suite of environmental laws passed in the 1960s and 1970s that more recent Congresses have not been able to improve upon, and, in some cases, have even tried to weaken.[8] Although it may not take the same form as it has in previous eras, confronting environmental problems of the future will require a renewed commitment from all branches—and all levels—of government. Much like in the past, reminding representatives and agency leaders of the importance of environmental protection will likely be, in large part, the responsibility of private citizens and environmental organizations.

A third and related lesson revealed in the history of the Appalachian Trail is that conservation is compatible with conservatism, and acknowledging common values may be an important way to overcome entrenched and polarized debates about environmental protection. Historically, liberals and moderates—mostly Democrats—have been primarily responsible for leading environmental initiatives in Washington, and the partisan divide on environmental issues in Congress has grown deeper in recent decades. Although the Republican Party has been increasingly viewed as antienvironmental, among the general public, conservative Americans seem to have a much more nuanced view of the environment.[9] Often, it is not the idea of protecting the environment that divides liberals and conservatives; rather, it is the means by which decision makers propose to do it. Public-private conservation partnerships such as the AT project embody several conservative principles, and may provide a possible middle ground for future collaboration and leadership on environmental initiatives.[10]

There are at least three conservative principles embodied in the AT project that indicate the possibility of common ground and challenge the idea that the relationship between environmentalism and conservatism is an antagonistic one. First, conservative political philosophers tend to emphasize the decentralization of social institutions. With its nested system of trail clubs and local volunteers, the ATC provides an excellent example of community-based decision making. Second, conservative thinkers often advocate for limited government and the leadership of the private sector. These characteristics have been central to the AT project and were widely lauded by James Watt, who fought to limit federal power in favor of greater private authority as secretary of the Interior under President Reagan. Third, the trail's history of volunteerism is a powerful expression of conservatives' belief in duty, patriotism, and civic responsibility. As MacKaye wrote in 1922, the process of building the AT and conserving surrounding lands would help to cultivate a "particular kind of patriotism." According to MacKaye, this kind of patriotism was the best possible kind—the "love of our own country."[11] Nearly a century later, this idea still resonates. By viewing the care of the countryside and the protection of resources for future generations as a literal act of patriotism, as MacKaye advocated, we can begin to see the potential for values shared by liberals and conservatives alike.

Although, in theory, conservation and conservatism share common ground, ideology and politics tend to obscure our understanding of that relationship. Too often, conservatives are portrayed as being against environmental protection. As the history of the AT suggests, however, the relationship between modern conservatism and modern environmentalism is much more complex than the narratives offered by the media or by the relatively thin academic literature on the history of conservative views of the environment. One of the purposes of this book has been to begin to illustrate the intricate contours of that relationship.

One of the ways of more clearly seeing the contours of the historic relationship between conservation and conservatism, particularly in rural areas, is by examining efforts to conserve working land as well as initiatives to protect wild land. Several scholars have pointed out that in opposing extractive land uses in favor of preserving wilderness, a large part of the environmental movement made itself vulnerable to critiques of elitism, and alienated many miners, loggers, ranchers, and other members of rural resource-dependent communities.[12] Perhaps just as problematic, preserving land in the United States from industrial use has resulted in our getting energy, toilet paper, and hamburgers from someplace else—a place where we are not likely to encounter the consequences of our consumption.[13] In a 1995 essay titled "The Trouble with Wilderness," historian William Cronon argued, "Idealizing a distant wilderness too often means not idealizing the environment in which we actually live, the landscape for better or worse we call home."[14] Instead of just focusing on wild, remote areas, Cronon suggested that environmentalists and conservationists should also consider the value of protecting more familiar landscapes. The essay was part of a rich dialogue in the 1990s about the purpose of wilderness preservation and the future of the conservation movement. These debates had important implications for public land management and the protection of resources like the AT.

Although the Appalachian Trail is known as a "footpath through the wilderness," it lies in the backyards of major eastern cities on land that has had a long history of use and ownership. As such, its history offers a kind of response to critiques of wilderness preservation. Appalachian Trail advocates have debated the appropriate scale and location of land uses in proximity to the trail since the project's origins in the 1920s. Throughout the project's history, the ATC has maintained that traditional land-use practices are compatible with the project. Today, members of the ATC continue to fight to protect the corridor from incompatible uses such as roads, buildings, and communication towers, but new initiatives such as the MeGaTransect and the AT Community program also reflect the trail community's desire to work with new partners on broader land-use initiatives. Through these new programs, the ATC seeks to not only protect the aesthetic experience of hiking the AT as a footpath through the wilderness but also preserve the ecological, economic, and cultural systems that sustain that experience.

The ATC's emphasis on both wild land protection and sustainable development reflects broader trends and debates in twenty-first-century environmentalism. As the demand for local food and renewable energy has grown in recent decades, the environmental movement has continued to grow and diversify. Although traditional environmental organizations such as the Sierra Club and the Wilderness Society continue their work to protect wild lands, often by using the defensive strategies of the past—relying on legislative and regulatory pathways to block exploitative land uses—there is a growing number of organizations dedicated to seeking the sustainable use of land and resources. Participants in these kinds of initiatives are working to shift the debate about environmental activism away from the framework of NIMBY—not-in-my-backyard—to WHIMBY—what's in my backyard?[15] How can people work and live in a landscape and still protect the ecological stability and beauty of the earth's resources? These questions have become central to twenty-first-century environmentalism and yet, in some ways, they harken back to the earlier conservation movement of the Progressive Era. This may be why many of MacKaye's ideas seem so appropriate for the challenges we face today.

When MacKaye first proposed to create a footpath across the eastern mountains in 1921, he argued that the project would address fundamental economic and social problems of his era. In an unpublished essay in 1922 titled "Why an Appalachian Trail?" MacKaye asked,

> How can an Appalachian Trail conserve natural resources and human labor? Resources and labor are bottom social questions of the day. How can hiking affect *them*? We live in tough times. Nations are starving and new wars brewing, class antagonisms are tightening. We approach a cross-roads in history. Why plan "trails" in days like these? Why fiddle when Rome burns?[16]

The reason, MacKaye argued, was that trail building provided a relatively politically neutral ground for forming alliances for future problem solving. The footpath would serve as an entry point into broader land-use planning initiatives, as its creators established lasting collaborations dedicated to the care of the countryside.

In the twenty-first century, our country is again at a crossroads and experiencing "tough times" not unlike the ones described by MacKaye in 1922. Nations continue to starve. Wars are brewing in the Middle East. There is an expanding gap between rich and poor. Ecosystems are being altered at unprecedented rates. State governments are threatening to shut down and liberal back-to-the-landers and conservative right-wingers alike have given up on government. Within this context, making progress on environmental policy has been difficult. Yet, over the course of nearly a century, the development of the Appalachian Trail, with its search for common ground—and occasional crossing of contested terrain—has demonstrated the need for flexibility in our institutions, and the importance of pragmatism in our approaches to environmental problem solving. This is the final lesson contained in the tangled historical roots of the AT: just as the movement to protect the AT responded to economic and political changes throughout the twentieth century—with the balance of public and private powers tipping toward one side or the other at different times—future institutional models must adapt to new political and cultural contexts.

In the twentieth century, the Appalachian Trail pioneered a path for public-private conservation partnerships that have come to dominate twenty-first-century environmental policy and politics. In blazing this trail, the AT project blurred boundaries between local citizen and state power. Although we tend to think of the ideas of "public" and "private" as distinct categories, the AT shows that, as two sources of power and authority, they have frequently overlapped in surprising and complex ways. In acquiring land for the corridor, private volunteers often performed functions typically associated with public land managers. As the status of government experts declined during the late twentieth century, and citizens became more involved in environmental decision making, the border between amateur and expert—and the power associated with these categories—became less clear-cut. The history of the Appalachian Trail reveals the fluidity of the categories "public" and "private," "expert" and "amateur," and demonstrates the paradox of what it means to be a *national grassroots* initiative.

In seeing the Appalachian Trail in historic context, from its origins to today, it becomes clear that the corridor is as much a human landscape as it is a wild one. As northbound through-hikers "walk with spring," starting their journeys with the budding rhododendron in the south and then walking north as spring unfolds, they leave the humble southern terminus on Springer Mountain, cross over the long and often misty walk across Fontana Dam, drink the rejuvenating waters of Hot Springs, take a photo perched on a ledge overlooking southern hardwood forests at McAfee's Knob, dodge cows in the rolling hills of Virginia, skirt corn fields in Cumberland

County, brave the backyards of New Jersey suburbs, stroll by an old nuclear plutonium plant in New York, circumnavigate ski resorts in Vermont, take a majestic tour through the alpine vegetation on top of the White Mountains, and eventually summit otherworldly Katahdin. Each of these places along the trail—and every step of the way in between—was built on tangled roots. The AT project combined several branching strands of grassroots social action with the strong, centralized power of the state. Navigating these entwined political roots posed unforeseen challenges, and, like the trail itself, led to some surprising destinations. Although this simple footpath through the wilderness tends to hide a complex history, unveiling that tangled history helps us to see the often-necessary role of conflict, and the power and possibilities of creative partnerships. As we look up from our muddied boots and see the Appalachian Trail project in this way—with all of its political ruts and entanglements—we can view possible steps forward for protecting the places that we live and love.

Notes

NOTES TO INTRODUCTION

1   As quoted in Megan Gambino, "Tales from the Appalachian Trail," http://www.
    smithsonianmag.com/history-archaeology/Tales-From-the-Appalachian-Trail.
    html (accessed March 14, 2013). The original quote comes from Benton MacKaye's
    interview with Philip W. Bourne, in Hugh B. Johnson, "The Appalachian Trail
    and Beyond," *American Institute of Architects Journal*, 1971.

2   Although early scholarship on US conservation during the Progressive Era
    focused on federal efforts to protect resources, more recent scholarship has also
    explored the role of private citizens and nongovernmental organizations. Classic
    texts on early US conservation efforts include Samuel P. Hays, *Conservation and
    the Gospel of Efficiency: The Progressive Conservation Movement, 1890–1920* (Cam-
    bridge, MA: Harvard University Press, 1959); J. Leonard Bates, "Fulfilling Ameri-
    can Democracy: The Conservation Movement, 1907 to 1921," *Mississippi Valley
    Historical Review* 44 (1957): 29–57. More recent work that has examined the role of
    private citizens and nonprofit organizations in promoting public land conserva-
    tion during the early twentieth century include Susan Schrepfer, *Nature's Altars:
    Mountains, Gender, and American Environmentalism* (Lawrence: University Press of
    Kansas, 2005); Richard Judd, *Common Lands, Common People: The Origins of Con-
    servation in Northern New England* (Cambridge, MA: Harvard University Press,
    1997); John F. Reiger, *American Sportsmen and the Origins of Conservation*. 3rd ed.
    (Corvallis: Oregon State University Press, 2001). For an impressive nonacademic
    history of private hiking clubs, see Laura and Guy Waterman, *Forest and Crag: A
    History of Hiking, Trail Blazing, and Adventure in the Northeast Mountains* (Boston:
    Appalachian Mountain Club, 1989).

3   For histories of the removals of mountain families in Shenandoah National Park,
    see Charles M. and Nancy Martin Perdue, "Appalachian Fables and Facts: A Case
    Study of the Shenandoah National Park Removals," *Appalachian Journal* 7, nos.
    1–2 (Autumn/Winter 1979–1980): 84–104; Charles M. and Nancy Martin Perdue,
    "'To Build a Wall Around These Mountains': The Displaced People of Shenan-
    doah," *The Magazine of Albemarle County History* 49 (1991): 48–71; Tom Floyd,
    Lost Trails and Forgotten People: The Story of Jones Mountain (Vienna, VA: Potomac
    Appalachian Trail Club, 1981); Darwin Lambert, *The Undying Past of Shenandoah
    National Park* (Boulder, CO: Robert Rinehart, Inc., 1989); Carolyn Reeder and
    Jack Reeder, *Shenandoah Secrets: The Story of the Park's Hidden Past* (Vienna, VA:

Potomac Appalachian Trail Club, 1998); Dennis E. Simmons, "Conservation, Cooperation, and Controversy: The Establishment of Shenandoah National Park, 1924–1936," *Virginia Magazine of History* 89, no. 4 (Oct. 1981): 387–404. For the history of the creation of Great Smoky Mountains National Park, see Durwood Dunn, *Cades Cove: The Life and Death of a Southern Appalachian Community, 1818–1937* (Knoxville: University of Tennessee Press, 1988). Margaret Lynn Brown also discusses the effects of the Tennessee Valley Authority (TVA) and the Fontana Dam in *The Wild East: A Biography of the Great Smoky Mountains* (Gainesville: University of Florida Press, 2000). For more on how the Blue Ridge Parkway affected local communities, see Anne Mitchell Whisnant, *Super-Scenic Motorway: A Blue Ridge Parkway History* (Chapel Hill: University of North Carolina Press, 2006). In *The New South's New Frontier*, Stephen W. Taylor explains the complexity of local residents' relationships with TVA projects, see Taylor, *The New South's New Frontier: A Social History of Economic Development in Southwestern North Carolina* (Gainesville: University Press of Florida, 2001). Also see Kathryn Newfont, *Blue Ridge Commons: Environmental Activism and Forest History in Western North Carolina* (Athens: University of Georgia Press, 2012).

4   For more on how postwar changes in America's hinterlands affected environmental politics in the United States, see Adam Rome, *Bulldozer in the Countryside: Suburban Sprawl and the Rise of American Environmentalism* (Cambridge: Cambridge University Press, 2001); Hal K. Rothman, *The Greening of a Nation? Environmentalism in the United States since 1945* (New York: Harcourt Brace, 1998); Thomas Wellock, *Preserving the Nation: The Conservation and Environmental Movements, 1870–2000* (Wheeling, IL: Harlan Davidson, 2007); Samuel P. Hays, *Beauty, Health, and Permanence: Environmental Politics in the United States, 1955–1985* (New York: Cambridge University Press, 1987).

5   This characterization of "old" conservation issues versus "new" environmental problems was presented by Samuel Hays in *Beauty, Health, and Permanence*. Also see Hays, *A History of Environmental Politics since 1945* (Pittsburgh: University of Pittsburgh Press, 2000). Hays's distinction between the early conservation movement and the modern environmental movement has been challenged by historians such as Robert Gottlieb who argue that Progressive reformers such as Benton MacKaye were interested not only in the conservation of natural resources and preservation of wild lands but were also concerned about issues such as public health and urban planning—the stuff of the modern environmental movement. Gottlieb, *Forcing the Spring: The Transformation of the American Environmental Movement* (Washington, DC: Island Press, 2005). Historian James Morton Turner also argues that, as new environmental issues arose in the late twentieth century, older conservation issues—specifically wilderness and the protection of public lands—did not fade away. Although public debates about these older issues had shifted, conservationists used the legislative and scientific tools of modern environmentalism to continue their work in a changed political and cultural landscape. See Turner, *The Promise of Wilderness: A History of American Environmental Politics, 1964–2004* (Seattle: University of Washington Press, 2012). Also

see Kirkpatrick Sale, *The Green Revolution* (New York: Hill and Wang, 1993); and Robert Cameron Mitchell, Angela A. Mertig, and Rilet E. Dunlap, "Twenty Years of Environmental Mobilization: Trends among National Environmental Organizations," in *American Environmentalism: The Environmental Movement, 1970–1990* (Washington, DC: Taylor & Francis, 1992), 11–25.

6   For more on the bipartisan nature of environmental legislation in the late 1960s and early 1970s, see Riley E. Dunlap and Angela G. Mertig, *American Environmentalism: The U.S. Environmental Movement, 1970–1990* (Philadelphia: Taylor & Francis, 1992); William Cronon, "When the G.O.P Was Green," *New York Times*, January 8, 2001, A17.

7   Lisa McGirr explains the grassroots emergence of the New Right in *Suburban Warriors: The Origins of the New American Right* (Princeton: Princeton University Press, 2001). For more on how this growing conservative movement affected the politics of managing wilderness and federal lands in the West, see James Morton Turner, "'The Specter of Environmentalism': Wilderness, Environmental Politics, and the Evolution of the New Right," *Journal of American History* 96, no. 1 (June 2009): 123–49; Turner, *Promise of Wilderness*, 225–66.

8   For more on the relationship between property rights groups and the "antienvironmental" or "wise use" movement in the United States, see Harvey Jacobs, *Who Owns America? Social Conflict over Property Rights* (Madison: University of Wisconsin Press, 1998); C. Brant Short, *Ronald Reagan and the Public Lands: America's Conservation Debate, 1979–1984* (College Station: Texas A&M University Press, 1989); R. McGreggor Cawley, *Federal Land, Western Anger: The Sagebrush Rebellion and Environmental Politics* (Lawrence: University Press of Kansas, 1993); Christopher McGrory Klyza, *Who Controls Public Lands? Mining, Forestry, and Grazing Policies, 1870–1990* (Chapel Hill: University of North Carolina Press, 1996); Howard E. McCurdy, "Environmental Protection and the New Federalism," in Sheldon Kamieniecki, ed., *Controversies in Environmental Policy* (Albany: SUNY Press, 1986).

9   Many scholars have written about American conservationists' fascination with wilderness. One of the classic texts is Roderick Nash· *Wilderness and the American Mind·* 4th ed. (New Haven, CT: Yale University Press, 2001). More recently, scholars have critiqued the idea of wilderness and have reexamined the goals and objectives of the wilderness movement. Some critiques of the idea of wilderness and the wilderness movement include Ramachandra Guha, "Radical American Environmentalism and Wilderness Preservation: A Third-World Critique." *Environmental Ethics* 11 (Spring 1989): 71–83; William Cronon, "The Trouble with Wilderness; or, Getting Back to the Wrong Nature," in *Uncommon Ground: Rethinking the Human Place in Nature*, edited by William Cronon, 69–90 (New York: W. W. Norton & Co., 1996), 69–90; Richard White, "'Are You an Environmentalist, or Do You Work for a Living?': Work and Nature" in Cronon, *Uncommon Ground*, 171–85; Mark Spence, *Dispossessing the Wilderness: Indian Removal and the Making of the National Parks* (New York: Oxford University Press, 1999). For a variety of other perspective on wilderness, see J. Baird Callicot and Michael P. Nelson, eds., *The Great New Wilderness Debate* (Athens: University of Georgia Press, 1998).

10　With several notable exceptions, environmental historians have done little to examine the conservative forces that came to characterize an "antienvironmental" movement in the late twentieth century. Some historians who have begun to explore the effects of the New Right on environmental politics include Turner, *The Promise of Wilderness*, and Brian Drake, "The Skeptical Environmentalist: Senator Barry Goldwater and the Environmental Management State," *Environmental History* 15, no. 4 (Oct. 2010): 587–611; Drake, *The Unnatural State: Conservatives, Libertarians, and the Postwar American Environmental Movement* (PhD diss., University of Kansas, 2006); Thomas G. Smith, *Green Republican: John Saylor and the Preservation of America's Wilderness* (Pittsburgh: University of Pittsburgh Press, 2006). Also see Rome, *Bulldozer in the Countryside*, 11.

11　Karl Jacoby, *Crimes against Nature: Squatters, Poachers, Thieves, and the Hidden History of Conservation* (Berkeley: University of California Press, 2001); Sara Gregg, *Managing the Mountains: Land Use Planning, the New Deal, and the Creation of a Federal Landscape in Appalachia* (New Haven: Yale University Press, 2010). Also see Louis Warren, *The Hunter's Game: Poachers and Conservationists in Twentieth-Century America* (New Haven: Yale University Press, 1997); James C. Scott, *Seeing Like a State: How Certain Schemes to Improve the Human Condition Have Failed* (New Haven: Yale University Press, 1998); Benjamin Heber Johnson, "Conservation, Subsistence, and Class at the Birth of Superior National Forest," *Environmental History* 4, no.1 (1999): 80–99; Spence, *Dispossessing the Wilderness* (1999).

12　For research on the hiking experience, see Jamie MacLeannan, "Solitude and Sociability: Social Processes among Appalachian Trail Long-Distance Hikers" (PhD diss., Rutgers–State University of New Jersey, 2005). Also see Clark T. W. Zealand, "Decolonizing Experiences: An Ecophenomenological Investigation of the Lived Experience of Appalachian Trail Thru-Hikers" (PhD diss., University of Waterloo, Canada, 2007). For an analysis of the effect of technology on the trail, see Jason E. Freed, "Creating the Appalachian Trail: Technological Influences on Symbol Production" (PhD diss., Clemson University, 2004); also see Stephen K. Spyker, "Spirituality and Technology on the Appalachian Trail: A Study in Frontiers" (PhD diss., Ball State University, 2004). For examinations of the AT as an educational resource, see Warren E. Doyle, Jr., "An Outdoor-Challenge Experience and the Affective Development of College Students" (PhD diss., University of Connecticut, 1981); Michael L. Bentley, "The Role of Backcountry Experience in Middle School Environmental Education" (PhD diss., University of Virginia, 1985), and James L. Reeves, "A Qualitative Study of Walk with Nature: An Outdoor, Environmental, Experiential Education Program" (PhD diss., University of Georgia, 1993).

13　For a study of the AT as a cultural symbol, see Gerald Lowery, "Benton MacKaye's Appalachian Trail as a Cultural Symbol" (PhD diss., Emory University, 1981). For analysis of wilderness ideals and the AT, see Paul Sutter, "'A Retreat from Profit': Colonization, the Appalachian Trail, and the Social Roots of Benton MacKaye's Wilderness Advocacy," *Environmental History* 4, no. 4 (1999): 553–484; Sutter, *Driven Wild: How the Fight against Automobiles Launched the Modern*

Wilderness Movement (Seattle: University of Washington Press, 2002), 142–93; and Larry Anderson, *Benton MacKaye: Conservationist, Planner, and Creator of the Appalachian Trail* (Baltimore: Johns Hopkins University Press, 2002), 143–68. For an analysis of state and federal cooperation in implementing the 1968 act, see Sally Fairfax, "Federal-State Cooperation in Outdoor Recreation Policy Formation: The Case of the Appalachian Trail" (PhD diss., Duke University, 1973). Although this book looks at the role of the states at different points in the history of the AT project, my analysis focuses more on interaction between federal agents and a variety of private actors.

NOTES TO CHAPTER I

1   D. K. Young, "The History of Stratton, Vermont: To the End of the Twentieth Century," Town of Stratton, Vermont, 2001, http://townofstrattonvt.com/uploads/History_of_Stratton_VT.PDF (accessed March 14, 2013).

2   Benton MacKaye, "An Appalachian Trail: A Project in Regional Planning," *Journal of the American Institute of Architects* 9 (Oct. 1921): 325.

3   MacKaye, "Appalachian Trail," 327.

4   Ibid.

5   Ibid., 329.

6   Ibid., 326.

7   Ibid., 328. For more on MacKaye's ideas about the project's nonprofit and non-industrial status, see Sutter, "Retreat from Profit," 553–484; Sutter, *Driven Wild*, 142–93.

8   MacKaye, "Appalachian Trail," 328.

9   Ibid., 327.

10   MacKaye, "Progress on the Appalachian Trail," *Appalachia* 15, no. 3 (December 1922): 244–52.

11   MacKaye, "Great Appalachian Trail from New Hampshire to the Carolinas: Proposed Plan Favored by America Institute of Architects Includes Correlation of Existing Routes, Fire Prevention, and Forestry Development—Paradise for Hikers," *New York Times*, February 18, 1923.

12   MacKaye, "Address to Chairman and Members of the Conference," 1925, box 183, Benton MacKaye Papers, Special Collections, Dartmouth College Library, Hanover, New Hampshire (hereafter cited as BMP).

13   MacKaye to Clarence Stein, January 19, 1923, box 166, BMP.

14   According to early works in conservation history, the foundations of American environmental thought were based upon two different ethical relationships between humans and nature. On one hand were the ecocentric values that prioritized wild and pristine lands over human use (i.e., "preservation"). On the other hand were the anthropocentric values that prioritized the "wise use" of resources (i.e., "conservation"). Some of the traditional narratives of American conservation history that helped set up the famous preservation vs. conservation debate include Bates, "Fulfilling American Democracy," 29–57; Hays, *Conservation*

and the Gospel of Efficiency, 192–93; and Nash, Wilderness and the American Mind, 129–30, 135–39. For examples of how Gottlieb, Sutter, and Minteer have used MacKaye's ideas and experience to challenge the dichotomy between preservation and conservation, see Gottlieb, Forcing the Spring, 106–20; Sutter, "A Retreat from Profit," 553–77; Sutter, Driven Wild (2002), 142–93; Minteer, The Landscape of Reform: Civic Pragmatism and Environmental Thought in America (Cambridge, MA: The MIT Press, 2006), 81–113. For more on MacKaye's multifaceted life and career, see Larry Anderson's biography Benton MacKaye.

15   For more on the history of Americans' ideas about wilderness, see Nash, Wilderness and the American Mind, 44.

16   Waterman and Waterman, Forest and Crag, 145–50.

17   See Roger Sidaway, "Long-Distance Routes in England and Wales—Their History and Pointers for Future Research," in Long-Distance Trails: The Appalachian Trail as a Guide to Future Research and Management Needs (New Haven, CT: Yale University Press, 1979), 13.

18   The Watermans claim that the reason professional trail crews still manage trails in areas such as the White Mountains "date[s] from the AMC's inability to find any other workable solutions to the maintenance problem during the first forty years of modern trails history." See Waterman and Waterman, Forest and Crag, 283.

19   For more on how the automobile changed Americans' relationship with the country's forested hinterlands and the boom in outdoor recreation, see Sutter, Driven Wild, and David Louter, Windshield Wilderness: Cars, Roads, and Nature in Washington's National Parks (Seattle: University of Washington Press, 2006).

20   Waterman and Waterman, Forest and Crag. Also see Laura Waterman and Guy Waterman, "Early Founders of the Appalachian Trail," Appalachian Trailway News (Sept.–Oct. 1985): 7–11.

21   Richard Brewer, Conservancy: The Land Trust Movement in America (Lebanon, NH: University Press of New England, 2003), 13–21; Sally Fairfax et al. Buying Nature: The Limits of Land Acquisition as a Conservation Strategy, 1780–2004 (Cambridge, MA: The MIT Press, 2005), 50.

22   Alfred Runte, National Parks: The American Experience, 2nd ed. (Lincoln: University of Nebraska Press, 1979, 1987), 114–15.

23   David A. Adams, Renewable Resource Policy: The Legal-Institutional Foundations (Washington, DC: Island Press, 1993),128. Also see Brown, Wild East, 81–82; Newfont, Blue Ridge Commons, 61–69.

24   Prior to the Weeks Act, the president had the power to establish national forest reserves out of public domain lands located out West, as outlined in the 1891 Forest Reserve Act. The national forest system expanded dramatically under president Theodore Roosevelt's administration, and in 1905 Roosevelt transferred the forest reserves from the Department of Interior to the Department of Agriculture and hired Gifford Pinchot to serve as the first chief of the US Forest Service.

25   Until the Clarke-McNary Act of 1924, the federal government could acquire land for federal forest reserves only if they could prove that they needed the area to protect navigable streams. Specific laws that outlined the responsibility of

managing lands for a broader range of uses did not occur until the 1960 Multiple-Use Sustained Yield Act. For more history on forest conservation, see Michael Williams, *Americans and their Forests: A Historical Geography* (New York: Cambridge University Press, 1992). Also see Thomas Cox, *This Well-Wooded Land: Americans and Their Forests from Colonial Times to the Present* (Lincoln: University of Nebraska Press, 1985); Char Miller, *American Forests: Nature, Culture, and Politics* (Lawrence: University of Kansas Press, 1997); Adams, *Renewable Resource Policy.*

26   Paul Sutter provides an excellent analysis of the development of MacKaye's relationship with wilderness, and his role as a social planner and thinker. See Sutter, *Driven Wild*, 150.

27   MacKaye, "Some Social Aspects of Forest Management," *Journal of Forestry* 16, no. 2 (February 1918): 210.

28   See Robert Gough, *Farming the Cutover: A Social History of Northern Wisconsin 1900–1940* (Lawrence: University of Kansas Press, 1997).

29   For a description of the dispute in Everett, see Anderson, *Benton MacKaye*, 103–6. Also see Norman Clark, *Mill Town* (Seattle: University of Washington Press, 1970).

30   Benton MacKaye, "After-the-War Colonization: A Suggested Plan for Land Settlement and Forest Employment of Returned Soldiers and Workers" unpublished manuscript, May 1918, p. 10, BMP. Emphasis in original.

31   See Anderson, *Benton MacKaye*, 85.

32   Benton MacKaye, *Employment and Natural Resources: Possibilities of Making New Opportunities for Employment through the Settlement and Development of Agricultural and Forest Lands and Other Resources*, US Department of Labor (Washington, DC: General Printing Office, 1919), 29.

33   Ibid.

34   Ibid.

35   Benton MacKaye, "Outdoor Culture: The Philosophy of Through Trails," paper delivered before the New England Trail Conference, January 21, 1927, New England Trail Conference, pub. no. 16, Boston, 1927.

36   For more on MacKaye's role in the Regional Planning Association of America (RPAA), see Ben Minteer, *Landscape of Reform*. For more on the RPAA and its relationship with conservation policy, see Sarah Phillips, *This Land, This Nation: Conservation, Rural America, and the New Deal* (Cambridge: Cambridge University Press, 2007), 30–32. Also see Roy Lubove, *Community Planning in the 1920s: The Contribution of the Regional Planning Association of America* (Pittsburgh: Pittsburgh University Press, 1964); and Edward K. Spann, *Designing Modern America: The Regional Planning Association of America* (Columbus: Ohio State University Press, 1996).

37   Robert Foresta has argued that in the late 1920s and early 1930s, the urban hiking elite embraced the recreational aspect of MacKaye's plan and left plans for social and economic reform by the wayside. Initial reactions to MacKaye's proposal are explored further in chapter 2. See Foresta, "Transformation of the Appalachian Trail," *Geographical Review* 77, no. 1 (1987): 76–85.

38   Benton MacKaye, "Regional Planning and Social Readjustment," [c. 1919], p. 12, BMP.

39   Benton MacKaye, "Memo on Suggested Article On: A Project for an Appalachian Trail (A New Approach to Industrial Problems)," n.d., box 182, BMP.

40   Benton MacKaye, "Wilderness Ways: A Plan for the Distribution of Open Spaces in Massachusetts" unpublished draft, August 27, 1928, box 183, BMP.

41   Charles V. Willie, *Theories of Human Social Action* (New York: General Hall, 1994), 99.

42   MacKaye, "Great Appalachian Trail," *New York Times*, February 18, 1923.

43   Benton MacKaye, "What Is the A.T.?" unpublished screenplay, 1924, p. 8, box 183, BMP.

NOTES TO CHAPTER 2

1   Duane Oliver, *Hazel Creek: From Then til Now* (Maryville, TN: Stinnett Printing Company, 1989), 93.

2   For more on the effects of New Deal and national park policy on Appalachian communities, see Gregg, *Managing the Mountains*; Newfont, *Blue Ridge Commons*; and Brown, *Wild East*.

3   "Blue Mountain Club Celebrates Completion of 40 Miles of Trail," November 21, 1932, Natural Bridge Appalachian Trail Club Papers, Jones Memorial Library, Lynchburg, Virginia (hereafter cited as NBATCP).

4   The desire to balance local and national goals was reflected in the choice of speakers at the 1925 conference. Speakers included local Boy Scout leaders such as Fred F. Schuetz of Newark, New Jersey, as well as influential leaders from the National Park Service, such as director Stephen Mather. Schuetz spoke about the importance of building "tributary trails" to connect adjacent communities with the main route, and Mather mentioned the possibility of one day developing a "trail service" to build trails throughout the country. Mather's support for the project foreshadowed the role that the National Park Service would eventually play during post–World War II trail developments, and indicated that the ATC had powerful allies within national land management agencies. "Brief Proceedings of the Appalachian Trail Conference Called by the Federate Societies on Planning and Parks," Washington, DC, March 2–3, 1925, box 203, BMP.

5   Gregg, *Managing the Mountains*; Neil Maher, *Nature's New Deal: The Roots of the American Environmental Movement* (New York: Oxford University Press, 2008); Phillips, *This Land, This Nation*.

6   New York–New Jersey Trail Conference, *Vistas and Visions: A History of the New York–New Jersey Trail Conference* (New York: New York–New Jersey Trail Conference, 1995), 2.

7   Ibid., 9.

8   Historian Paulena Bren argues that the tramping movement in Czechoslovakia was a way that citizens resisted a dominant political paradigm. As different groups of social outcasts met in the Czech countryside in the post–World War II era, tramping became viewed as a political action aimed to "normalize" socialist life after the Prague Spring and the communist reform movement of the 1960s.

See Paulena Bren, "Weekend Getaways: The Chata, the Tramp, and the Politics of Private Life in Post-1968 Czechoslovakia," chapter 7 of *Socialist Spaces: Sites of Everyday Life in the Eastern Bloc* (Oxford: Berg Publishers, 2002), 123–40.

9   Like the rest of American society at the time, this growth often occurred in a segregated manner, and interest in hiking and trail building remained largely a recreational pursuit of upper-middle-class whites. Recent scholarship has begun to explore the important question of why parks, forests, and trails have traditionally been dominated by middle-class whites. For example, see Kimberly K. Smith, *African-American Environmental Thought: Foundations* (Lawrence: University of Kansas, 2007); Erin Krutko, "Lewis Mountain: Segregation in Shenandoah National Park," paper delivered at Designing the Parks Conference, Charlottesville, Virginia, May 21, 2008.

10 In addition to his work leading the NYNJTC, and later with the ATC, Torrey held office in several noteworthy conservation and outdoor recreation organizations, including the New York State Council of Parks, the National Council of State Parks, the American Scenic and Historic Preservation Society, and the Association for the Protection of the Adirondacks.

11 In public parks or forests, blazing the Appalachian Trail often meant marking existing trail systems with AT insignia or adding small linkages to form a "skyline" path that was generally oriented in a north-south direction along predominant ridges. On private land, existing trail networks were less common. Raymond H. Torrey, "2,000-Mile Trail on Appalachian Ridges Planned; Benton MacKaye's Idea Supported by Institute of Architects," *New York Evening Post*, April 7, 1922.

12 In a report to MacKaye in 1924, Torrey wrote that, although the Interstate Park section of the AT had been completed, they were still negotiating links beyond the park boundaries with a few landowners. Torrey to Benton MacKaye, January 31, 1924, box 166, BMP.

13 Waterman and Waterman, *Forest and Crag*, 494.

14 Joseph Bartha to Torrey, February 9, 1938, New York–New Jersey Trail Conference Archive, New York–New Jersey Trail Conference Office, Mahwah, New Jersey (hereafter cited as NYNJTCA).

15 Ibid.

16 Torrey to Franklin D. Roosevelt, February 14, 1926, NYNJTCA; New York Chapter of Appalachian Mountain Club to Vanderbilt Webb, Esq., April 1929, box "Arthur Perkins, 1922–32, 3-2-1," Appalachian Trail Conference Archives, Appalachian Trail Conference, Charlestown, West Virginia (hereafter cited as ATCA).

17 Torrey to Bartha, April 16, 1928, NYNJTCA.

18 Arthur Perkins, "Memoranda as to Opportunity of Appalachian Trail," c. 1928, folder "1918–1928 (30)," box "Arthur Perkins, 1922–32, 3-2-1," ATCA.

19 Torrey, "Appalachian Trail: Atlantic States Trail Conference Planned: Federation of Volunteer Workers Suggested to Co-ordinate Effort on Maine-Georgia Appalachian Trail, at Meeting of the New York–New Jersey Trail Conference," *New York Evening Post*, February 16, 1923.

20 "Brief Proceedings of the Appalachian Trail Conference Called by the Federated Societies on Planning and Parks," Washington, DC, March 2–3, 1925, box 203, BMP.

21 Although Benton MacKaye was elected to be the AT project's first field organizer in 1925, the position was unpaid and MacKaye did not have the financial security to do the extensive scouting that such a position entailed. Welch continued to collaborate with members of the NYNJTC to develop trails in the area, but, like MacKaye, he had other commitments, such as working for the National Council of State Parks, that took precedence over his leadership on the AT. See Torrey to MacKaye, August 8, 1931, box 167, BMP.

22 Appalachian Trail Conference, "The Appalachian Trail," pub. no. 5, Appalachian Trail Conference, Harpers Ferry, West Virginia, 12.

23 Lee J. Alston, "Farm Foreclosures in the United States during the Interwar Period," *The Journal of Economic History* 43, no. 4 (Dec. 1983): 885–903. Also see Michael E. Parrish, *The Anxious Decades: America in Prosperity and Depression, 1920–1941* (New York: W. W. Norton & Company, 1994); and William Leuchtenburg, *The Perils of Prosperity, 1914–1932*, 2nd ed. (Chicago: University of Chicago Press, 1993).

24 As cited in Gregg, *Managing the Mountains*, 18.

25 Philips, *This Land, This Nation*, 87.

26 "Appalachian Trail Conference Record of Annual Meeting," May 10–11, 1929, Easton, Pennsylvania, box "Arthur Perkins, 1922–32," ATCA. Also see Perkins to Myron H. Avery, October 19, 1927, box "Arthur Perkins, 1922–32, 3-2-1," ATCA.

27 "Asheville Fast Becoming Home of Many Hikers," *Asheville Times*, July 17, 1923; "The Appalachian Trail," *Gainesville Eagle*, n.d., article found in folder o-2, box 8, Georgia Appalachian Trail Club Records, Manuscript Collection, Georgia Archives, Morrow, Georgia (hereafter cited as GATC MSS); "Trail Club to Hold Meet Monday for Adoption of Rules," *Lynchburg News*, n.d., October 1930, NBATCP; "Trail Club Will Hold First Meet," *Lynchburg News*, October 26, 1930.

28 Myron Avery, "Appalachian Trail Conference Record of Annual Meeting," 10–11 May 1929, Easton, Pennsylvania, box "Arthur Perkins, 1922–32," ATCA.

29 In a letter to a scoutmaster in Reading, Pennsylvania MacKaye wrote, "Daniel Boone was a pioneer because he did something never done before. He and his kind opened the American wilderness to the blessings of civilization. That was the need of that day. Today's need is the reverse—to open American civilization to the blessings of the wilderness. The period for this new opening is now; and he who does it is a pioneer." MacKaye to H. E. Wright, June 24, 1932, box 167, BMP. Many volunteers picked up on this pioneer metaphor in relation to the campaign to bring the trail to the Southern Appalachians.

30 In a history of the PATC, David Bates explains that the group had "always been a working club. The fact that there was a scouting trip . . . to discover whether their hopes were feasible, before there was an actual meeting of the PATC, is indicative of the kind of organization the PATC would be." David Bates, *Breaking Trail in the Central Appalachians: A Narrative* (Washington, DC: Potomac Appalachian Trail Club, 1987), 2.

31 "Appalachian Trail Conference Record of Annual Meeting," May 10–11, 1929, Easton, Pennsylvania, box "Arthur Perkins, 1922–32," ATCA.

32 Fred Davis to Members of the Lynchburg Lions Club, September 30, 1930, NBATCP.

33 Ruskin S. Freer, "The Rambler," *Lynchburg News*, September 28, 1930; "Appalachian Trail Club Meeting Here," *Lynchburg News*, October 1, 1930. In 1932, the PATC worked with the Roanoke Chamber of Commerce to establish an AT club there and to lead trail development in southwestern Virginia.

34 Avery to Perkins, July 24, 1929, folder "1929 Correspondence," box "Arthur Perkins, 1922–32," ATCA.

35 Natural Bridge Appalachian Trail Club, "Bulletin No. 1," October 28, 1930, NBATCP.

36 Kephart spent time near Hazel Creek and published his account in the famous *Our Southern Highlanders: A Narrative of Adventure in the Southern Appalachians and a Study of Life among the Mountaineers* (Knoxville: University of Tennessee Press, 1976). Appalachian historians have critiqued this book as playing up cultural stereotypes of the era; see for example, Dunn, *Cades Cove*, 200. Also see Brown, *Wild East*, 83; and Oliver, *Hazel Creek*, 84.

37 Robert Lindsey Mason to Avery, April 23, 1930, folder "The Appalachian Trail Conference Correspondence File of Arthur Perkins, 1922–32," box "Arthur Perkins, 3-2-1," ATCA.

38 Ibid.

39 "Historical Sketch of N. Georgia," *Gainesville Eagle*, September 1931, folder 0-2, box 8, GATC MSS. Also see R. M. Sears, "The Natural Bridge National Forest," map issued by USFS, Eastern Region, 1930, MF-20 B.7, General Printing Office, 1929, NBATCP.

40 Ozmer to E. B. Stone, January 16, 1930, folder "1-1-3: Correspondence, Jan–May 1930," box 2, GATC MSS.

41 As recalled by Avery in a letter to Judge Perkins, July 24, 1929, folder "1929 Correspondence," box "Arthur Perkins, 1922–32," ATCA.

42 Ibid.

43 Avery to Ozmer, October 28, 1929, folder "1929 Correspondence," box "Arthur Perkins, 1922–32," ATCA.

44 Paul Fink to Avery, November 8, 1929, folder "1929 Correspondence," box "Arthur Perkins, 1922–32," ATCA.

45 Claud C. Boynton to Avery, October 21, 1929, folder "1929 Correspondence," box "Arthur Perkins, 1922–32," ATCA.

46 Ibid.

47 After the 1931 ATC meeting in Skyland, Virginia, S. L. Cole, president of the newly formed Southern Virginia Appalachian Trail Association, took over trail development in southwestern Virginia. Through his work as a county agent, Cole was extremely effective in developing local support in the communities of Galax, Floyd, Stuart, Hillsville, and Pinnacles of the Dan. Myron Avery, "The Appalachian Trail, Southern Virginia: Peaks of Otter to New River," reprinted from

Appalachia, vol. 19, no. 1, June 1932, folder C #64, Myron H. Avery Collection, Maine State Library, Augusta (hereafter cited as MHAC).

48 Ozmer to Avery, November 1, 1929, folder "1929 Correspondence," box "Arthur Perkins, 1922–32," ATCA.

49 Fink to Avery, November 8, 1929, folder "1929 Correspondence," box "Arthur Perkins, 1922–32," ATCA.

50 Literature on the history of attitudes toward and perceptions of Appalachia is extensive. For more background, see Dwight B. Billings, Gurney Norman, and Katherine Ledford, eds., *Confronting Appalachian Stereotypes: Back Talk from an American Region* (Lexington: University Press of Kentucky, 1999); Mary Beth Pudup, *Appalachia in the Making: The Mountain South in the Nineteenth Century* (Chapel Hill: University of North Carolina Press, 1995); Allen Batteau, *The Invention of Appalachia* (Tucson: University of Arizona Press, 1990); Ron Eller, *Miners, Millhands, and Mountaineers: Industrialization of the Appalachian South, 1880–1930* (Knoxville: University of Tennessee Press, 1982); Dwight B. Billings, *The Road to Poverty: The Making of Wealth and Hardship in Appalachia* (Cambridge, NY: Cambridge University Press, 2000); Dunn, *Cades Cove*, 1988.

51 Ozmer, "Hiking Over the Sawteeth," *Atlanta Journal*, n.d., folder 10-4, box 8, GATC MSS.

52 Gough, *Farming the Cutover*, 150–77.

53 Charlie N. Elliott, *Gainesville Eagle*, n.d., folder 0-2, box 8, GATC MSS.

54 Ibid.

55 Ibid. For more on the creation of Appalachian folk culture and the nostalgia it evoked for outsiders, see Jane S. Becker, *Selling Tradition: Appalachia and the Construction of an American Folk, 1930–1940* (Chapel Hill: University of North Carolina Press, 1998).

56 David Bates, *Breaking Trail*, 7.

57 In 1930, a severe drought devastated many mountain families. At that time, approximately 90 percent of the people living in the mountains depended on farming, grazing, and other land-based activities for subsistence. Many of the families that Schairer befriended were eventually removed by the Park Service to create Shenandoah National Park; trail efforts described here preceded the park. For more on the removal of mountain families in northern Virginia, see Reeder and Reeder, *Shenandoah Secrets*; and Perdue, "Appalachian Fables and Facts," 84–104.

58 Brown, *Wild East*, 97. For more on the history of public land acquisition program in Cades Cove, see Dunn, *Cades Cove*, 241–54.

59 For more on legal actions surrounding land acquisition for Shenandoah National Park, see Simmons, "Conservation, Cooperation, and Controversy," 387–92; Lambert, *Undying Past*; Justin Reich, "Re-Creating the Wilderness: Shaping Narratives and Landscapes in Shenandoah National Park," *Environmental History* 6, no. 1 (Jan. 2001): 101. For more on the political dynamic surrounding the Blue Ridge Parkway, see Whisnant, *Super-Scenic Motorway*.

60 Richard David Hawkins, interview by author, April 17, 2012. Also see Newfont, *Blue Ridge Commons*, 104.

61 Unlike private lands, public lands such as national parks do not provide tax revenue. In making the eastern national parks, Congress established that states or private donors would be responsible for the financial and legal costs of purchasing the early eastern parks, but owners were often not compensated at rates they found acceptable. For an overview of the creation of the first eastern national parks, see Runte, *National Parks*, 116. For more on local concerns in western North Carolina about the loss of a private tax base to federal ownership, see Newfont, *Blue Ridge Commons*, 101–4. Also see Oliver, *Hazel Creek*, 95; and Payson Kennedy, interview with author, March 15, 2007.

62 Bates, *Breaking Trail*, 49.

63 Ibid.

64 Ibid., 50.

65 David C. Smith, *A History of Lumbering in Maine, 1861–1960* (Orono: University of Maine Press, 1972). Also see Gordon G. Whitney, *From Coastal Wilderness to Fruited Plain: A History of Environmental Change in Temperate North America from 1500 to the Present* (Cambridge: Cambridge University Press, 1994), 183–85.

66 Arthur M. Fogg to Avery, September 14, 1932, series 2, folder 19, part 8b & 8c, 1/8/32–1/22/33, MHAC.

67 Harry Davis to Avery, January 10, 1933, series 2, folder 19, part 8b & 8c, 1/8/32–1/22/33, MHAC.

68 Ibid. Davis's son Lyman was one of these local woodsmen. Lyman was a young man with college debts. Lyman had previously done work on the trail with the expectation that he would be compensated.

69 Avery to Leon E. Potter, May 8, 1932, series 2, folder 19, part 8a, 6/20/29–7/31/32, MHAC; Avery to Mrs. Robert McDougall, June 15, 1932, series 2, folder 19, part 8a, 6/20/29–7/31/32, MHAC.

70 Walter Greene to "Dear Sir," series 2, folder 19, part 18, 4/10/35–7/24/35 and 4/10/35–10/3/35, MHAC. Before the shelter system was developed, most areas along the AT lacked accommodations. In the southern regions, hikers often stayed in private residences or in abandoned buildings. Early ATC guidebooks listed a number of private houses where hikers could stay and stores where they could buy provisions. As the economy unraveled in the 1930s, rural people welcomed the additional income. Communities from Georgia to Maine hoped that the project would "bring hosts of visitors" and boost the local economy. "The Appalachian Trail," *Gainesville Eagle*, n.d., folder 0-2, box 8, GATC MSS.

71 Greene to Avery, July 24, 1935, series 2, folder 19, part 20, 7/27/35–10/1/35 and 10/2/35–1/20/36, MHAC.

72 ATC volunteers got around this issue because both Avery and Greene were registered guides in the state of Maine.

73 Avery to Greene, July 29, 1935, series 2, folder 19, part 20, 7/27/35–10/1/35 and 10/2/35–1/20/36, MHAC.

74 "Actor and Adopted Son of Maine Start to Work on Maine Portion Long Trail," *Lewiston Journal*, n.d., series 2, folder 19, part 8d, 1/23/33–9/26/33, MHAC.

75 Avery to Greene, July 29, 1935.

76 Historian Edwin G. Hill describes the popularity the CCC program in *In the Shadow of the Mountain: The Spirit of the CCC* (Pullman: Washington State University Press, 1990). Also see Neil Maher's explanation of the CCC's indelible mark on American environmental politics in *Nature's New Deal*. For more on the role of the CCC in Maine, see Jeff W. Neff, *Katahdin: An Historic Journey* (Boston: Appalachian Mountain Club Books, 2006), 305–6.

77 Avery to Sewall, February 20, 1935, series 2, folder 19, part 13, File 7, 7/1/34–10/1/34, and part 15, 10/2/34–4/6/35, MHAC. Also see Avery to R. M. Evans, March 18, 1935, series 2, folder 19, part 13, File 7, 7/1/34–10/1/34, and part 15, 10/2/34–4/6/35, MHAC.

78 Sewall to Avery, December 24, 1934, series 2, folder 19, part 13, File 7, 7/1/34–10/1/34, and part 15, 10/2/34–4/6/35, MHAC.

79 Ibid.

80 Avery to Sewall, April 10, 1935, series 2, folder 19, part 18, 4/10/35–7/24/35 and 4/10/35–10/3/35, MHAC.

81 Avery, "Report of Chairman to the Board of Managers of the Appalachian Trail Conference," April 1, 1935, Washington, DC, series 1, folder C#222, MHAC.

82 Avery to Everett F. Groaton, 11 November 1935, series 2, folder 19, part 20, 7/27/35–10/1/35 and 10/2/35–1/20/36, MHAC.

83 Avery, "Katahdin National Park Plan Is Separate Issue from Baxter State Area," *Portland Sunday Telegram*, July 31, 1938; Avery to Baxter, May 5, 1937, series 1, vol. 8, May–June 1937, MHAC.

84 Baxter to Avery, May 12, 1937, series 1, vol. 8, May–June 1937, MHAC.

85 Ibid.

86 MacKaye to E. B. Stone, Jr., June 7, 1934, folder "1-5-2 Correspondence, April–June 1934," box 2, GATC MSS.

87 Ibid.

88 Ibid. Emphasis in original.

89 Avery, "Report of Chairman of the Board of Managers, Proceedings of the Eighth Appalachian Trail Conference," Gatlinburg, Tennessee, June 26–28, 1937, pub. no. 9, Washington, DC, ATC (August 1937), folder c#219, MHAC.

90 "Report by Edward B. Ballard, Proceedings of the Eighth Appalachian Trail Conference," Gatlinburg, Tennessee, June 26–28, 1937, pub. no. 9, Washington, ATC (August 1937), folder c#219, p. 31, MHAC. Emphasis in original.

91 Ibid.

92 US Congress, "Act to Authorize a Study of the Park, Parkway, and Recreational-Area Programs in the United States, and for Other Purposes," June 23, 1936 (49 Stat. 1894).

93 "Blue Mountain Club Celebrates Completion of 40 Miles of Trail," November 21, 1932, "newsclippings" file, NBATCP.

94 Robert Foresta, "Transformation of the Appalachian Trail," 81.

95 For example, see Newfont, *Blue Ridge Commons*; Gregg, *Managing the Mountains*; Scott, *Seeing Like a State*; Jacoby, *Crimes against Nature*; Warren, *Hunter's Game*; Johnson, "Conservation, Subsistence, and Class"; Spence, *Dispossessing the Wilderness*.

NOTES TO CHAPTER 3

1   Mrs. Leon F. Cross to ATC, April 18, 1955, folder 1-15, box 3, GATC MSS.

2   Ibid.

3   GATC, *The Georgia Mountaineer: Bulletin of the Georgia Appalachian Trail Club* 22, no. 19 (October 22, 1949), box 7, GATC MSS. Also see GATC *The Georgia Mountaineer: Bulletin of the Georgia Appalachian Trail Club*, vol. 27, no. 5, May 4, 1954, box 7, GATC MSS.

4   GATC, *The Georgia Mountaineer: Bulletin of the Georgia Appalachian Trail Club* 22, no. 18 (October 1, 1949), box 7, GATC MSS.

5   Trail leaders decided to locate the southern terminus on Springer Mountain because the other options—Frosty Mountain and Amicolola Lake—were both easy to access and susceptible to development. Springer Mountain was not only more remote, it also represented the geological endpoint of the Appalachian Mountain range, where the chain split and branched south to Oglethorpe and north to Fort Mountain. GATC, *The Georgia Mountaineer: Bulletin of the Georgia Appalachian Trail Club* 29, no. 11 (November 8, 1956), box 7, GATC MSS.

6   Searcy B. Slack, Jr., to A. B. Walker, April 12, 1950, folder 1-15-1, box 3, GATC MSS.

7   Foster R. Dulles, *A History of Recreation: America Learns to Play* (Englewood Cliffs, NJ: Prentice-Hall, 1965).

8   For more on the effects of postwar changes on America's hinterlands and their influence on environmental politics in the United States, see Adam Rome, *Bulldozer in the Countryside*.

9   The first attempt to create a national system of footpaths was sponsored by representative Daniel Hoch from Pennsylvania. Committee on Roads, House of Representatives, *Hearings on H.R. 2142, a Bill to Amend the Federal-Aid Highway Act of 1944 and Authorize a National System of Foot Trails*, 79th Cong., 1st Sess. October 24, 1945, folder 1, box 3-5-6, "Correspondence re. National System of Foot Trails, 1944–49," ATCA.

10 Stanley Murray, "Report of the Vice President," Report of the Chairman to the ATC, 1961, Murray Stevens Papers, box 3-2-4, ATCA.

11 Ibid.

12 Myron Avery, "Reconversion," n.d., folder "Jean Stephenson Correspondence, 1945," box 3-2-5 "General Correspondence 1934–1947," ATCA.

13 Tom Wessels wrote an excellent guidebook explaining how to use clues in the forest to understand the landscape's history. In it, Wessels describes how disturbance events such as the 1938 hurricane have shaped contemporary forest dynamics. See Wessels, *Reading the Forested Landscape: A Natural History of New England* (Woodstock, VT: The Countryman Press, 2005).

14 "Pine Island Camp Boys on the Appalachian Trail near Piece Pond, Maine," photograph from Myron Avery Collection, vol.1., Maine State Library, MHAC. Trail maintenance had always been difficult in Maine because of its remote

NOTES TO PAGES 68–72   211

location and dense forests, and the hurricane damage greatly increased the challenge of maintaining the trail in this section.

15   Charles C. Hardy to Robert Hutton, July 4, 1949, vol. 25, July 1949, MHAC.

16   Avery to B. A. Eger, December 9, 1946, folder "Avery Correspondence on Relocations," NBATCP. Also see Florence B. Adams to Robert B. Sosman, September 9, 1948, folder "Avery Correspondence on Relocations," NBATCP.

17   Robert L. Anderson, "Changing Forests and Forest Management Policy in Relation to Dealing with Forest Diseases," *Phytopathology* 93 (2003): 1041–43.

18   Avery to John Sieker, May 5, 1947, folder "Avery Correspondence on Relocations," NBATCP.

19   NYNJTC general meeting minutes, October 7, 1964, folder "Trail Club Minutes, 1959–1965," NYNJTCA.

20   George F. Blackburn, letter to the editor, *Washington Post*, March 25, 1957, box 206, BMP.

21   George Riley, "Hikers and Conservationists Discuss Problems and Glories of Appalachian Trail," *Philadelphia Sunday Bulletin*, June 4, 1961, box 206, BMP; "U.S. Takes Step to Save Trail," *Washington Post*, February 14, 1971, box ML 5 (206), BMP.

22   Not the author Pearl S. Buck.

23   Stanley Murray to Hon. Roy A. Taylor, March 22, 1966, folder "Murray-Legis.-HR 4865-S.827-NSTA 1964–67," box 5-2-1 "Correspondence re. NSTA 1968, 1966–69, 1964–66," Stanley Murray Papers, ATCA.

24   As cited in NBATC trip report, North Prong of Buffalo River, November 29, 1959, folder "Trail Reports," NBATCP.

25   Robert C. Scott to Henry B. Morris, May 15, 1958, folder 1-18-1, box B, GATC MSS.

26   Lewis R. Writh to Dorothy Crandall, August 9, 1954, folder "Avery Correspondence on Relocations," NBATCP. The radar station on top of Apple Orchard Mountain operated for two decades. It included not only the FAA tower that remains today but also a gymnasium, a dormitory, a mess hall, a bowling alley, and a bomb shelter with eighteen-inch-thick walls for the 150 men who were stationed at the summit. After the complex was dismantled, the AT was eventually routed back onto Apple Orchard Mountain—the highest point in both Bedford and Botetourt Counties. See "Impasse on Apple Orchard Mountain," *The Register: A Newsletter of the Appalachian Trail* 6, no. 10 (October 1983), 6.

27   Avery to B. A. Eger, December 9, 1946, folder "Avery Correspondence on Relocations," NBATCP.

28   Myron Avery, "Conservation: What of the Future?" *Appalachian Trailway News* 6, no. 2 (May 1945), 15–17.

29   Avery, "Reconversion, " folder "Stephenson Correspondence, 1946," box "Jean Stephenson Correspondence," ATCA.

30   According to the Sierra Club's website, the organization grew from 10,000 members in 1956 to 114,000 members by 1970. See http://sierraclub.org/history/timeline.aspx.

31 Although trail organizations such as the ATC and its affiliates often shared fundamental goals for land conservation with these national environmental organizations, they did not always agree on the types of land uses to be protected or on strategies for protecting land. Debates about how to best protect wild lands in the East occasionally led to disagreement among these groups. See Waterman and Waterman, *Forest and Crag*, 632.

32 The Nature Conservancy originally formed as an offshoot of the Ecological Society of America known as the Ecologists Union. For more on the development of national and local land trusts in the United States, see Brewer, *Conservancy*, 31–40, 186–215; Phyllis Myers, "Direct Funding of Nonprofit Land Protection: A New Genre of State Land Conservation Programs," chapter 11 of *Land Conservation through Public/Private Partnerships* (Washington, DC: Island Press, 1993), 289–302. Also see Fairfax et al., *Buying Nature*, 178–202.

33 Committee on Roads, House of Representatives, *Hearings on H.R. 2142, a Bill to Amend the Federal-Aid Highway Act of 1944 and Authorize a National System of Foot Trails*, 79th Cong., 1st Sess. October 24, 1945, folder 1, box 3-5-6 "Correspondence re. National System of Foot Trails, 1944–49," ATCA. The legislation was designed to develop a system of trails that would complement the growing interstate highway system.

34 Ibid., 11.

35 *The Wilderness Act of 1964*, Public Law 88-577, 88th Cong., 2d Sess., September 3, 1964.

36 Anthony Wayne Smith, "A Statement on Proposed Legislation to Establish a Nationwide System of Trails," submitted by invitation to hearings before the Subcommittee on National Parks and Recreation of the Committee on Interior and Insular Affairs, March 7, 1967, folder "Murray-Legis.-HR 4865-S.827-NSTA 1966–67," box 5-2-1 "Correspondence re. NSTA 1968, 1966–69," Stanley Murray Papers, ATCA.

37 US Department of the Interior, National Park Service, *Parks for America: A Survey of Park and Related Resources in the Fifty States, and a Preliminary Plan* (Washington, DC: Government Printing Office, 1964), 4.

38 US Department of the Interior, Bureau of Outdoor Recreation, *Trails for America* (Washington, DC: Government Printing Office, September 16, 1966), 49.

39 See, for example, Samuel Dana and Sally K. Fairfax, *Forest and Range Policy: Its Development in the United States* (New York: McGraw Hill Book Company, 1980); David A. Adams, *Renewable Resource Policy*, 136–37.

40 Historian Paul Hirt provides a summary of the challenges of implementing multiple use management in *A Conspiracy of Optimism: Management of the National Forests since World War Two* (Lincoln: University of Nebraska Press, 1994).

41 Paul Y. Vincent to "Dear Friend," March 22, 1962, folder 1-22-3, box 3, GATC MSS. In a letter accompanying the annual report of the work of the southern region of the Forest Service in 1962, Vincent explained that the next fifty years would continue to pose a host of challenges. He claimed, "We are not likely to discover forest lands on the moon or some other planet. We are going to have to

make the most of what we have on our own troubled planet." Multiple-use practice helped land managers such as Vincent improve recreational opportunities on public lands while simultaneously increasing the production of traditional land uses such as logging, mining, and grazing.

42 Frank Place, "Trails in the Metropolitan Region," (1945), 216. Reprinted from unknown book, copy located in folder "History," NYNJTCA.

43 Reich, "Re-Creating the Wilderness," 95–118; Oliver, *Hazel Creek*, 93–96; Brown, *Wild East*, 98; Dunn, *Cades Cove*; 38; David Hawkins, interview by author, April 17, 2012.

44 Also, in May 1962, several southern clubs affiliated with the ATC, including the Smoky Mountain Hiking Club (SMHC), the Carolina Mountain Club (CMC), and the Georgia Appalachian Trail Club (GATC), submitted a joint statement to Congress in support of a National Wilderness Preservation System. In their testimony, they argued, "Wilderness is multiple use" in that it provides for the "conservation of water resources . . . habitat for wildlife . . . scientific study . . . educational purposes and recreation." According to this definition of wilderness, preserved areas might include a variety of land uses as well as undeveloped, untrammeled areas. See "Statement in Favor of a National Wilderness Preservation System," submitted jointly by the SMHC, the CMC, and the GATC to the Public Lands Sub-Committee on the House Interior and Insular Affairs Committee, May 7, 1962, box 3, folder 1-22-3, GATC MSS.

45 Alfred Percey, "Shelter Sites Named for Trail Sections," n.d., *Lynchburg News*, folder "Minutes," NBATCP.

46 Jean Stephenson, "A National System of Trails," *The Nature Friend: Monthly Organ of the Nature Friends of America* 24, no. 3 (March 1946), folder 2, box 3-5-6 "Correspondence re. National System of Foot Trails, 1944–49," ATCA.

47 Hearings before the Committee on Roads, House of Representatives, First Session on H.R. 2142, October 24, 1945, p. 7, folder 1, box 3-5-6 "Correspondence re. National System of Foot Trails, 1944–49," ATCA.

48 Ibid. After Hoch's bill failed, the Wilderness Society sponsored a bill for Congress to authorize a national system of wildland belts. When ATC chairman Myron Avery heard about the competing legislation, he wrote to its author, Howard Zahniser, to explain that he had not been aware of the Wilderness Society's bill and that he was "somewhat chagrined. . . . Since your organization, as well as ours, seeks legislation, it would seem expedient to put our heads together to see if we cannot develop a project which would meet both needs. Progress, with the election results and economy wave, will be difficult enough for one proposal. Two competing projects may only tend to a competition precluding either from attainment." See Avery to Zahniser, November 21, 1946, Avery Papers, vol. 21, May–December 1946, MHAC.

49 Lyndon B. Johnson, "Natural Beauty of Our County," February 8, 1965, 89th Cong., 1st Sess., House of Representatives, Doc. No. 78, p. 2. folder "Murray-Correspondence + Materials re. President Johnson Message, 1965," box 5-2-2 "Stanley Murray Materials re. Legislation—AT Bills, 1964–66," Stanley Murray Papers, ATCA.

50 Aldo Leopold, *A Sand County Almanac, and Sketches Here and There* (1949; repr.,

London: Oxford University Press, 1970), 204. Although *A Sand County Almanac* was published in 1949, the book gained widespread attention in the 1960s and 1970s.

51 Trail leaders were quick to respond to President Johnson's call. In 1965, Stanley Murray wrote to the proceedings editor of the White House Conference on Natural Beauty, "Trails offer a most intimate means for the observance and appreciation of natural beauty, and a well-developed and -maintained trail system provides justification for the preservation of specific areas in a forested or otherwise natural state." Murray to proceedings editor, White House Conference on Natural Beauty, May 25, 1965, folder "Murray-Correspondence + Materials re. President Johnson Message, 1965," box 5-2-2 "Stanley Murray Materials re. Legislation—AT Bills, 1964–66," Stanley Murray Papers, ATCA.

52 Senator Gaylord Nelson, "Statement in Support of a Bill to Facilitate the Management, Use, and Public Benefits from the Appalachian Trail," box 114, Gaylord Nelson Papers, Wisconsin Historical Society, Madison, Wisconsin (hereafter cited as GNP). Also see also Gaylord Nelson, "Hiking Trails Statement," draft, n.d., box 114, GNP.

53 "Statement of Franklin Wallick, Legislative Representative, United Automobile, Aerospace, and Agricultural Implement Workers of America, AFL-CIO," before the Subcommittee on National Parks and Recreation of the Committee on Interior and Insular Affairs, March 7, 1967, folder "Murray-Legis.-HR 4865-S.827-NSTA 1966–67," box 5-2-1 "Correspondence re. NSTA 1968, 1966–69," Stanley Murray Papers, ATCA.

54 According to historian Robert Gottlieb, when activists such as Ralph Nader started to document the effects of workplace hazards on worker health and safety in the mid-1960s, and Congress began developing occupational and safety legislation, Wallick was "one of the few union officials then exploring both environmental and occupational hazard issues." See Gottlieb, *Forcing the Spring*, 360–64. In the late twentieth century, the gap between the labor and environmental movements grew. By the 1990s, the rhetoric of jobs-versus-the-environment dominated public discourse over natural resource management. In the Pacific Northwest, debates about the spotted owl pitted loggers against wildlife biologists. In Appalachia, controversies over coal mining positioned miners against environmentalists. Those who have critiqued modern environmentalism have argued that one of the movement's greatest limitations was its lack of attention to the relationship between work and nature. See for example, Richard White, "Are You an Environmentalist?" 171–85.

55 In response to these concerns, Myron Avery wrote to Lawrence Dean, a member of the Green Mountain Club's Board of Trustees, "When Vermont's Governor and myself, from the Maine Coast, see this as the only possible solution, any anti-Federal aspect of the situation must be of minor consequence!" Avery pointed out that national trails legislation would provide legal fodder for those against the proposed Green Mountain Parkway that could potentially obliterate both the Long Trail and the AT. Eventually, the Green Mountain Club did support the 1945

legislation, and the parkway was never built. Avery to Lawrence W. Dean, April 27, 1945, folder 5, box 3-5-6 "Correspondence re. National System of Foot Trails, 1944–49," ATCA.

56 NYNJTC meeting minutes, March 7, 1945, folder "Trail Club Minutes, 1935–1950," NYNJTCA.

57 For more on Mission 66, see Ethan Carr, *Mission 66: Modernism and the National Park Dilemma* (Amherst: University of Massachusetts Press, 2007).

58 In the 1960s, scientifically oriented organizations such as the Audubon Society and the Nature Conservancy became increasingly critical of the National Park Service's lack of scientific research to inform its management practices and its focus on development within the parks. Park historian Richard West Sellars argues that, up until the 1960s, the Park Service had focused its management goals on protecting scenery and promoting visitation, rather than on protecting natural resources and ecological integrity. Sellars, *Preserving Nature in the National Parks: A History* (New Haven: Yale University Press, 1997). Also see Rothman, *Greening of a Nation*; and Hays, *Beauty, Health, and Permanence.*

59 Jean Stephenson to Henry Morris, February 7, 1962, folder 1-22-1, box 3, GATC MSS.

60 Gannon Coffey to GATC members, July 14, 1963, folder 1-23-3, box 3, GATC MSS. Also see Carolina Mountain Club, "Open Supper Meeting Minutes," May 11, 1960, box 1, Carolina Mountain Club Archive, Special Collections, D. H. Ramsey Library, University of North Carolina, Asheville, North Carolina (hereafter cited as CMCA). Emphasis in original.

61 George Blackburn to Hester Hastings, March 3, 1957, folder "Crabtree Meadow," NBATCP.

62 Two years later, however, the Forest Service decided to build a "small public camp ground" near the area at the head of Crabtree Creek. The project was supported by the Nelson County Chamber of Commerce and involved a hundred-car parking lot, a blue-blazed trail down Pinnacle Ridge to the top of the falls, and a new paved road one thousand feet from the falls. In addition, the Forest Service planned to build a large lake for swimming and a concession stand. In another letter to Blackburn, Hastings claimed that the project was "not in harmony" with the AT. The alternative, however, seemed to be the "danger that private exploiters will get this land and make an unpleasant use of it." Sarcastically, she exclaimed, "If this is to be another Niagara Falls, how wonderful!" Hastings to George Blackburn, January 26, 1959, folder "Crabtree Meadow," NBATCP.

63 Stephenson to Gannon Coffey, April 25, 1962, folder 1-22-2, box 3, GATC MSS.

64 Hal K. Rothman, "'A Regular Ding-Dong Fight': The Dynamics of the Park Service–Forest Service Controversy during the 1920s and 1930s," in *American Forests: Nature, Culture, and Politics* (Lawrence: University Press of Kansas, 1997), 114. In this essay, historian Hal Rothman traces historical tensions between the National Park Service and the US Forest Service back to the 1920s and 1930s. He argues that the agencies were based on two different value systems: the Forest Service was based on an ethos of "wise use" of natural resources that included outdoor recreation but

focused on maintaining a sustained yield of timber and watershed protection. The National Park Service, on the other hand, "hungrily sought a national constituency" by promoting the parks and catering to the rise in auto-based tourism in the 1920s. Conflict between these different approaches to land protection arose during debates about how to protect and manage the AT. Also see Robert A. Foresta, *America's National Parks and Their Keepers* (Washington, DC: Resources for the Future, 1984), 31.

65   *Appalachian Trailway News* 8, no.1 (Jan. 1947): 15.

66   Ibid. The National Park Service, however, had previously gained jurisdiction over strips in the national forests for the creation of the Blue Ridge Parkway. This had exacerbated administrative tensions between the two agencies. Several trail advocates speculated that at the heart of the Park Service's concern about the AT was a fear about the retaliation of the Forest Service.

67   When Drury resigned in 1950 after a controversy involving dam projects in Dinosaur National Park, Demaray served as director of the National Park Service for a short period before he, too, resigned. See Susan Rhoades Neel, "Newton Drury and the Echo Park Dam Controversy," *Forest and Conservation History* 38, no. 2 (April 1994): 56–66.

68   Avery to Harlean James, January 25, 1946, folder 3, box 3-5-6 "Correspondence re. National System of Foot Trails, 1944–49," ATCA.

69   *Appalachian Trailway News* 8, no.1 (January 1947), 15.

70   Runte, *National Parks*, 173.

71   Although Congress established the first two eastern national parks in 1926—Great Smoky Mountains and Shenandoah National Parks—it did not authorize federal funds to help build them. Early park enthusiasts and the states worked tirelessly to raise money from private sources to acquire land for the new parks. In 1937, Congress also authorized Cape Hatteras National Seashore in North Carolina, but because of limited funds and lack of political momentum to support federal land acquisition, proposed park units such as Cape Hatteras remained as "paper parks"—parks that primarily existed as lines drawn on maps without any actual territorial jurisdiction. As a result, most national parks in the early twentieth century existed in the western states, where there were fewer hurdles to acquiring land. Cameron Binkley, "The Creation and Establishment of Cape Hatteras National Seashore: The Great Depression through Mission 66," special report prepared for Southeast Regional Office, Cultural Resource Division, National Park Service, August 2007. Also see Conrad L. Wirth, *Parks, Politics, and the People* (Norman: University of Oklahoma Press, 1980). Congress eventually designated Cape Hatteras as national seashore in 1953 after state and local entities had acquired enough land to legally establish this new unit of the national park system.

72   *National Scenic Trails System Act*, Public Law 90-543, 90th Cong., October 2, 1968.

73   See Sen. Gaylord Nelson, "The Appalachian Trail . . . the Need to Save a Unique Resource," testimony, n.d., box 1-10 "Misc. Correspondence," NBATCP.

74   Murray to Edward C. Crafts, BOR director, February 22, 1964, folder

"Murray-Legis.-S.622-Bill to Protect AT-1964–65-part1," box 5-2-2 "Stanley Murray Materials re. Legislation—AT Bills, 1964–66," Stanley Murray Papers, ATCA.

75   In 1987, Charles H. W. Foster published a detailed account of his experience with ANSTAC. He noted that, because of its complex mix of state and federal officials, trail club representatives, and array of landowners, ANSTAC's role in the project had always been "problematical." Yet he argued that such a mix was necessary to achieve the goals for establishing and protecting the AT. See Charles H. W. Foster, *The Appalachian National Scenic Trail: A Time to Be Bold* (Needham, MA: Charles Foster, 1987).

76   Statement of Edward B. Garvey, Hearing of Committee on Interior and Insular Affairs, US Senate on S. 827, March 15, 1967, p. 3, folder "Murray-Legis.-HR 4865-NSTA 1967," box 5-2-1 "Correspondence re. NSTA 1968, 1966–69," Stanley Murray Papers, ATCA.

77   For example, see Gaylord Nelson to Stewart Udall, January 6, 1964, box 144, GNP. Throughout the 1960s, Senator Nelson was the strongest advocate in Congress for the National Trail System. He spent several years investigating possibilities for trail development throughout the country and introduced different forms of trails legislation during his congressional tenure.

NOTES TO CHAPTER 4

1   As quoted in "Field Report, Vermont AT, Landowner Problem, June 14, 1974," box DO 1 (65), Dartmouth Outing Club Records, Rauner Special Collections Library, Dartmouth College, Hanover, New Hampshire (hereafter cited as DOCR).

2   Marjorie K. Anderson to Ben Hoffman, July 19, 1974, box DO 1 (65), DOCR.

3   ATC, "Appalachian Greenway," 1975, folder "Appalachian Greenway Task Force Meeting, October 1974-Transcript," box 5-3-5 "Stanley Murray Materials re. Appalachian Greenway 1974," Stanley Murray Papers, ATCA.

4   Ann Satterthwaite, "An Appalachian Greenway: Purposes, Prospects, and Programs, October 1974," p. 73, folder "Satterthwaite Greenway Report and Related Materials," box 5-3-5 "Stanley Murray Materials re. Appalachian Greenway 1974," Stanley Murray Papers, ATCA.

5   ATC, "Appalachian Greenway," 1975.

6   National Scenic Trails System Act, Public Law 90-543, 90th Cong., Sess. 827, October 2, 1968.

7   Howard Brackney to Benton MacKaye, July 5, 1975, p. 3, folder "Loose Materials," box 6-1-5 "Conference Meetings, 20th Meeting, 1975," ATCA.

8   Howard Brackney to ATC board of managers, September 4, 1972, folder "19th Meeting, Plymouth, 1972, Misc.," box 6-1-4 "Conference Meetings, 19th Meeting, 1972," Plymouth, NH, ATCA.

9   ATC, "Appalachian Greenway," 1975.

10   Lester L. Holmes, "Report of the Executive Director," eighteenth meeting of the ATC, Shippensburg, PA, May 29–31, 1970, box 6-1-3 "Conference Meetings 16th–18th, 1964–1970," ATCA.

11 Stanley Murray, "Report of the Chairman," eighteenth meeting of the ATC, Shippensburg, PA, May 29–31, 1970, box 6-1-3 "Conference Meetings 16th–18th, 1964–1970," ATCA.

12 Holmes, "Report of the Executive Director." By 1975, the ATC had a professional staff of six; by the late 1980s, it had grown to about twenty.

13 Fairfax, "Federal-State Cooperation," 87. In her dissertation, Fairfax analyzed the effectiveness of the federal government's attempt to coordinate and stimulate state involvement in the AT project. As stated, she found varying degrees of effectiveness.

14 Massachusetts House, "Special Report of the Department of Natural Resources Relative to the Protection of the Appalachian Trail," House Report No. 4609, Boston, 1968.

15 These attributes—a sense of state pride, political support for the project, and financial wealth—typically determined the extent to which states pursued an acquisition program for the trail or whether they left it up to the federal government. For example, state activity in Virginia was inspired, in part, by the encouragement of and cooperation with the Potomac Appalachian Trail Club—one of the most active and powerful clubs associated with the ATC. The club helped rally public support for the project and also contributed to the campaign financially. Ben Bolen, the commissioner of the Division of Parks for the state Department of Conservation and Economic Development, worked with the PATC and the National Park Service to establish the corridor, and in 1972, the Virginia legislature allocated $80,000 for acquiring the right-of-way. Thomas H. Campbell, "Report of the Vice Chairman," folder "19th Meeting, Plymouth, 1972, Photos, PR," box 6-1-4 "Conference Meetings, 19th Meeting, 1972," Plymouth, NH, ATCA.

16 As quoted in Fairfax, "Federal-State Cooperation," 105.

17 Interviews with Benjamin Hoffman, head of the Land Acquisition Unit, Ed Xoenemann, director of planning, and Ellen Reis, recreation planner, n.d., folder "Satterthwaite Greenway Report and Related Materials," box 5-3-5 "Stanley Murray Materials re. Appalachian Greenway 1974," Stanley Murray Papers, ATCA.

18 Ibid. Satterthwaite noted that the Vermont meeting was the "most unenthusiastic session" she had had concerning the greenway program.

19 Interview with Fairfax, "Federal-State Cooperation," 86.

20 Fairfax, "Federal-State Cooperation," 83. The actual mileage of trails in states such as West Virginia and Maryland was relatively small; this probably contributed to the challenge that advocates faced in getting widespread public support and funding for the project.

21 Satterthwaite, "An Appalachian Greenway," 15.

22 Transcript of Greenway Task Force meeting, October 5, 1974, p. 4, folder "Appalachian Greenway Task Force Meeting, October 1974-Transcript," box 5-3-5 "Stanley Murray Materials re. Appalachian Greenway 1974," Stanley Murray Papers, ATCA.

23 Foster, *Appalachian National Scenic Trail*, 107.

24 Edgar L. Gray to Stanley A. Murray, November 26, 1973, folder "NPS

Implementation-1972-75," box 5-2-6 "Stanley Murray Materials re Legislation Trail Bill Implementation," Stanley Murray Papers, ATCA.

25 Walter L. Criley to Rogers C. B. Morton, December 11, 1973, folder "NPS Implementation-1972–75," box 5-2-6 "Stanley Murray Materials re Legislation Trail Bill Implementation," Stanley Murray Papers, ATCA.

26 Ibid.

27 Although congressional funding specifically devoted to the AT was not renewed in future years, in 1975, the director of the Bureau of Outdoor Recreation, James Watt, told trail advocates that in administering the Land and Water Conservation Fund, he would "give the highest priority to any State request aimed at acquiring right-of-way for the Appalachian Trail"—thus the pressure on states to apply for matching grants. Russell E. Dickenson to Grant Conway, May 10, 1974, folder "Murray Correspondence re. Appalachian Greenway," 1974, box 5-3-5 "Stanley Murray Materials re. Appalachian Greenway 1974," Stanley Murray Papers, ATCA.

28 Interview with Richard Stanton, n.d., folder "Satterthwaite Greenway Report and Related Materials," box 5-3-5 "Stanley Murray Materials re. Appalachian Greenway 1974," Stanley Murray Papers, ATCA.

29 Interview with E. U. Curtis Bohlen, n.d., folder "Satterthwaite Greenway Report and Related Materials," box 5-3-5 "Stanley Murray Materials re. Appalachian Greenway 1974," Stanley Murray Papers, ATCA. An "inholding" is a privately owned parcel of land located within the boundaries of a larger unit of publicly owned land.

30 Interview with Robert Eastman, n.d., folder "Satterthwaite Greenway Report and Related Materials," box 5-3-5 "Stanley Murray Materials re. Appalachian Greenway 1974," Stanley Murray Papers, ATCA.

31 Ibid.

32 ATC, "Appalachian Greenway," 1975.

33 Murray, "Report of the Chairman," folder "19th Meeting, Plymouth, 1972, Photos, PR," box 6-1-4 "Conference Meetings, 19th Meeting, 1972," Plymouth, New Hampshire, ATCA.

34 This survey was conducted in an area of particularly high use. Such use was causing erosion and public safety problems that officials believed could be prevented only "through the cooperation of the new generation of hikers." Jeff McLaughlin, "Hikers Torture Appalachians," Boston Globe, June 12, 1972.

35 Earl Schaffer completed the first official through-hike in 1945, and the numbers generally continued to grow, peaking in 1998 after the publication of Bill Bryson's book A Walk in the Woods (New York: Broadway Books, 1998). The number of through-hikers peaked again at the turn of millennium, when many were inspired to walk two thousand miles for the year 2000.

36 Ed Garvey, "Appalachian Hiker, Revisited," Backpacking Journal (Fall 1977): 28–29, 92, box 10-2-6 "Miscellaneous Magazines with Articles about the AT or ATC," ATCA. Garvey published information about his 1970 hike in the book Appalachian Hiker (Oakton, VA: Appalachian Books, 1971).

37   "Appalachian Greenway," *Washington Post*, August 18, 1975.

38   Walter Boardman, "Statement Concerning H.R. 4865, A Nationwide System of Trails," before the Subcommittee on National Parks and Recreation of the Committee on Interior and Insular Affairs, March 6–7, 1967, p. 2, folder "Murray-Legis.-HR 4865-S.827-NSTA 1966–67," box 5-2-1 "Correspondence re. NSTA 1968, 1966–69," Stanley Murray Papers, ATCA.

39   Ken Cordell, Carter Betz, J. M. Bowker, et al., *Outdoor Recreation in American Life: A National Assessment of Demand and Supply Trends* (Champaign, IL: Sagamore Publishing, 1999), 263.

40   Runte, *National Parks*, 173.

41   For more statistics on trail use, see the Appalachian Trail Conservancy's website, http://www.appalachiantrail.org/about-the-trail/2000-milers (accessed March 11, 2013).

42   Richard Wilson, "City Feet Tread on Feelings in the Blue Ridge," *Washington Evening Star*, September 9, 1971.

43   "Summation: Second Executive Committee Meeting, Appalachian National Scenic Trail Advisory Council," Harpers Ferry, WV, 1976, p. 7–8, folder "NPS Implementation-1976," box 5-2-6 "Stanley Murray Materials re Legislation Trail Bill Implementation," Stanley Murray Papers, ATCA. Efforts to curb illegal and irresponsible behavior through the use of fees and permit systems surfaced at several points in the trail's history but never reached fruition. Today, anyone can hike the AT for free.

44   As quoted in McLaughlin, "Hikers Torture Appalachians."

45   For more on the historical development of the leave-no-trace ethic, see James Morton Turner, "From Woodcraft to 'Leave No Trace': Wilderness, Consumerism, and Environmentalism in Twentieth-Century America," *Environmental History* 7, no. 3 (July 2002): 462–84. Popular books published in the 1970s that taught the principle include Paul Petzoldt, *The Wilderness Handbook* (New York: W. W. Norton & Company, 1974); John Hart, *Walking Softly in the Wilderness* (San Francisco, CA: Sierra Club Books, 1977); and Laura Waterman and Guy Waterman, *Backwoods Ethics: Environmental Concerns for Hikers and Campers* (Boston, MA: Stone Wall Press, 1979).

46   Charles Foster to Ann Satterthwaite, August 19, 1974, 2, folder "Satterthwaite Greenway Report and Related Materials," box 5-3-5 "Stanley Murray Materials re. Appalachian Greenway 1974," Stanley Murray Papers, ATCA. Although they represented only a tiny fraction of the total number of users, the number of through-hikers increased during the 1970s. Several through-hikers, such as Walter Boardman, Ed Garvey, Karen Lutz, and Todd Ramaley, became active workers in the project after their hike, but many others were more interested in simply hiking the trail than in working for its protection.

47   Satterthwaite, "Progress on the Appalachian Greenway: A Report of a Workshop on the Appalachian Greenway," June 1976, 22, folder "Satterthwaite Greenway Report and Related Materials," box 5-3-5 "Stanley Murray Materials re. Appalachian Greenway 1974," Stanley Murray Papers, ATCA.

48 "ANSTAC, Anniversary Report, 1973," folder "NPS Implementation-1976," box 5-2-6 "Stanley Murray Materials re Legislation Trail Bill Implementation," Stanley Murray Papers, ATCA.

49 Theodore Bampton, the deputy commissioner of the Division of Preservation and Conservation for the Connecticut Department of Environmental Protection, tried to reassure landowners that the state would do its best to mitigate problems associated with inappropriate use of the trail. Interview with Brampton, folder "Satterthwaite Greenway Report and Related Materials," box 5-3-5 "Stanley Murray Materials re. Appalachian Greenway 1974," Stanley Murray Papers, ATCA.

50 Thomas H. Campbell, "Report of the Vice Chairman," folder "19th Meeting, Plymouth, 1972, Photos, PR," box 6-1-4 "Conference Meetings, 19th Meeting, 1972, Plymouth, NH," ATCA.

51 Satterthwaite, "An Appalachian Greenway," 10.

52 Murray to Boardman and Garvey, July 29, 1966, folder "Murray-Legis.-S.827/H.R.4865-NSTA 1966–67," box 5-2-1 "Correspondence re. NSTA 1968, 1966–69," Stanley Murray Papers, ATCA.

53 Satterthwaite, "An Appalachian Greenway," 10.

54 ATC, "Appalachian Greenway," 1975.

55 Condemnation was to be used only as a last resort to prevent major breaks in the trail. It could be used only to acquire a maximum of twenty-five acres in any single mile. The following chapter will explain in greater detail the variety of acquisition tools and techniques used to acquire land for the AT corridor.

56 Interviews with Harold Dyer, assistant Commissioner of the Environmental Department for the State of New York, and Douglas Costle, commissioner of Environmental Protection, State of Connecticut folder "Satterthwaite Greenway Report and Related Materials," box 5-3-5 "Stanley Murray Materials re. Appalachian Greenway 1974," Stanley Murray Papers, ATCA. Funding for AT acquisitions in the area eventually came in the mid-1970s through bond issues in New York and the Green Acres fund in New Jersey. Samuel Wilkinson, "Report of the Vice Chairman," folder "19th Meeting, Plymouth, 1972, Photos, PR," box 6-1-4 "Conference Meetings, 19th Meeting, 1972, Plymouth, NH," ATCA.

57 Wilson, "City Feet Tread," *Washington Evening Star*, September 9, 1971.

58 See, for example, Short, *Ronald Reagan*, 17.

59 Newfont, *Blue Ridge Commons*, 101–4. Also see Oliver, *Hazel Creek*, 95; and Payson Kennedy, interview with author, March 15, 2007.

60 Arthur W. Cooper, "Land Use Planning and the Appalachian Greenway," June 22, 1975, p. 9, folder "Speeches-Boone Mtg., 1975," box 6-1-5 "Conference Meetings, 20th Meeting, 1975," ATCA.

61 "Appalachian Greenway," *Washington Post*, August 18, 1975.

62 Stanley Murray, "Report of the Chairman," June 1975, folder "Speeches-Boone Mtg., 1975," box 6-1-5 "Conference Meetings, 20th Meeting, 1975," ATCA.

63 Ibid.

64 "Reports of Officers," p. 17, eighteenth meeting of the ATC, Shippensburg, PA, May 29–31, 1970, box 6-1-3 "Conference Meetings 16th–18th, 1964–1970," ATCA.

65   "The Phil Hanes Story," November 6, 1974, folder "Murray Correspondence re.
     Appalachian Greenway, 1974," box 5-3-5 "Stanley Murray Materials re. Appala-
     chian Greenway 1974," Stanley Murray Papers, ATCA.

66   Ibid.

67   Quotes from this paragraph come from a letter from R. Philip Hanes, Jr., to
     George Zoebelein, October 15, 1974, box 5-3-6 "Appalachian Highlands Associa-
     tion, George Zoebelein-Stan Murray Correspondence re. Appalachian Green-
     way," ATCA.

68   "Remarks to the Executive Committee on the Appalachian Trail Conference and
     Greenway," box 5-3-6 "Appalachian Highlands Association, George Zoebelein-
     Stan Murray Correspondence re. Appalachian Greenway," ATCA.

69   Murray, "Trail Corridor Width—Considerations for Advisory Council Meet-
     ing, June 20, 1975," p. 3, folder "NPS Implementation-1975–March 1976," box 5-2-6
     "Stanley Murray Materials re Legislation Trail Bill Implementation," Stanley
     Murray Papers, ATCA.

70   "An Appalachian Greenway Proposal," n.d., folder "Murray Correspondence re.
     Appalachian Greenway, 1974," box 5-3-5 "Stanley Murray Materials re. Appala-
     chian Greenway 1974," Stanley Murray Papers, ATCA.

71   For more on the emergence and growth of land trusts in this era, see Fairfax et
     al., *Buying Nature*, 151–54. For more on the history of the Nature Conservancy, see
     Brewer, *Conservancy*, 186–215.

72   As of August 2011, the Mountain States Legal Foundation was still one of the
     country's most active legal organizations devoted to the protection of property
     rights. See the organization's website at http://www.mountainstateslegal.org/
     index.cfm (accessed August 3, 2011).

73   As quoted in Amanda Griscom, "How Green Was the Gipper?: A Look Back
     at Reagan's Environmental Record," *Grist Magazine*, June 10, 2004, http://www.
     grist.org/news/muck/2004/06/10/griscom-reagan/ (accessed July 29, 2010).

74   The US Forest Service seemed to be particularly receptive to the Appalachian
     Greenway Project, particularly because of the multiple-use philosophy it embod-
     ied. The agency was also interested in the research aspect of the project, and
     in the prospect of working cooperatively with the states. Folder "Satterthwaite
     Greenway Report and Related Materials," box 5-3-5 "Stanley Murray Materials re.
     Appalachian Greenway 1974," Stanley Murray Papers, ATCA.

75   Sheldon Pollack to Ann Satterthwaite, October 22, 1974, folder "Murray Corre-
     spondence re. Appalachian Greenway, 1974," box 5-3-5 "Stanley Murray Materials
     re. Appalachian Greenway 1974," Stanley Murray Papers, ATCA.

76   Sutter, "Retreat from Profit," 553–77.

77   Ibid.

78   Ibid.

79   Interviews with Richard Stanton and David Richie, n.d., folder "Satterthwaite
     Greenway Report and Related Materials," box 5-3-5 "Stanley Murray Materials re.
     Appalachian Greenway 1974," Stanley Murray Papers, ATCA.

80   Maurice J. Forrester, Jr., to Murray, August 11, 1974, folder "Murray

Correspondence re. Appalachian Greenway, 1974," box 5-3-5 "Stanley Murray Materials re. Appalachian Greenway 1974," Stanley Murray Papers, ATCA.

81 Harry Nees, transcript of Greenway Task Force meeting, October 5, 1974, folder "Appalachian Greenway Task Force Meeting, October 1974-Transcript," box 5-3-5 "Stanley Murray Materials re. Appalachian Greenway 1974," Stanley Murray Papers, ATCA.

NOTES TO CHAPTER 5

1   William Ecenbarger, "Nature Finally Wins One," *Philadelphia Inquirer Magazine*, July 15, 1984; Appalachian Trail Conference, "The Evolution of the Appalachian Trail Protection Program and 'Countryside' Conservation," December 6, 1985, p. 5.

2   National Scenic Trails System Act, Public Law 90-543, 90th Cong., Sess. 827, October 2, 1968. *An Act to Amend the National Trails System Act*, Public Law 95-248, 95th Cong., March 21, 1978.

3   Bob Proudman, interview by author, May 3, 2007. Also see David Richie to Chuck Rinaldi, June 15, 1978, box 2-5-1 "Correspondence, USDOI, ATPO, 1.78–12.79," ATCA.

4   Richie to Rinaldi, June 15, 1978.

5   *Act to Amend the National Trails System Act* (1978). The 1978 amendment also reinstated the Appalachian National Scenic Trail Advisory Committee to help plan and manage the acquisition program.

6   None of the other ten national scenic trails have ever received the same amount of funding or political authority to pursue a land acquisition program similar to the Appalachian Trail's. This is why large sections of other national scenic trails—like the North Country Trail that runs from New York to North Dakota, or Wisconsin's Ice Age Trail, which hugs the path of the terminal lobe of the last glacier that covered North America—exist as "paper trails." Paper trails are trails that have been congressionally designated on paper but do not yet exist in reality.

7   Hiking historians Laura Waterman and Guy Waterman attributed Proudman's trail-building successes to his "antiestablishment image," which was "just right for providing leadership in the rebellious years of the early 1970s." Waterman and Waterman, *Forest and Crag*, 620. Today, Proudman continues his work to protect trails and has written several books on trail maintenance and design, including William Birchard and Robert (Bob) Proudman, *Appalachian Trail Design, Construction, and Maintenance*, 2nd ed. (Harpers Ferry, WV: Appalachian Trail Conference, 2000); and Robert Proudman and Rueben Rajala, *AMC's Field Guide to Trail Building and Maintenance*, 2nd ed. (Boston: Appalachian Mountain Club, 1981). When I met Proudman in his office at the ATC's headquarters in Harpers Ferry in 2007, I found a grizzled man tucked between mountains of filing cabinets, piles of papers, and precariously perched stacks of binders—all of which revealed a decidedly bureaucratic and establishment existence. Yet his passion for the trail was still clearly apparent, and his eyes contained the spark of a young backwoodsman-mountaineer.

8   Between 1969 and 1977, the Forest Service acquired sixty-one parcels that covered
     110 miles from inholders within the national forests of the Southern Appalachian
     Mountains. By 1981, there were only fourteen miles left to acquire. For more on
     the US Forest Service's acquisition of the AT, see Shelley Smith Mastran and
     Nan Lowerre, *Mountaineers and Rangers: A History of Federal Forest Management
     in the Southern Appalachians, 1900–1981,* US Department of Agriculture, Forest
     Service, April 1983.

9   At that time, the main AT acquisition field office had the authority to acquire
     land valued up to $250,000. Properties that cost more than that went through the
     Park Service's regional chief of lands and regional director, who had unlimited
     authority to approve land acquisition, provided the amount was within what
     was budgeted by Congress for the project. See US House of Representatives,
     Committee on Interior and Insular Affairs, *Land Acquisition Policy and Program
     of the National Park Service: A Report,* June 4, 1984, reprinted by the University of
     Michigan Library, 8–9.

10   David Startzell, "The Antibureaucrat," *Appalachian Trailway News* (Mar.–Apr.
     2003), 10.

11   David Startzell, "The Long Journey of Dave Richie, 1932–2002," *Appalachian
     Trailway News* (Mar.—Apr. 2003), 11.

12   Ibid., 35.

13   Richie to Donald S. MacDonald, May 23, 1978, box 2-5-1 "Correspondence,
     USDOI, ATPO, 1.78–12.79," ATCA.

14   Richie to Policy Group, WASO, July 28, 1978, box 2-5-1 "Correspondence,
     USDOI, ATPO, 1.78–12.79," ATCA.

15   House Committee on Interior and Insular Affairs, *Land Acquisition Policy,* 26.

16   Up until the 1960s, Congress created the national parks primarily out of the
     public domain lands in the West. In some cases, land was transferred to the Park
     Service from other federal or state agencies, or donated by philanthropists such
     as John D. Rockfeller, Jr. In the 1960s, Congress began authorizing more eastern
     parks, starting with the Minuteman National Historic Park in 1959 and the Cape
     Cod National Seashore in 1961. In 1968, the National Park Service developed
     formal policies to guide the acquisition of private land. These policies relied on
     agency personnel and real estate experts. Provisions for public participation in
     the Park Service's land acquisition programs began in 1979, when these acquisi-
     tion policies were revised. For more on the Park Service's land acquisition policies
     in the 1970s and 1980s, see House Committee on Interior and Insular Affairs,
     Land Acquisition Policy, 3–5.

17   Between 1964 and 1978, the price of rural land increased in every state through
     which the AT passed. In certain locations, these increases were particularly dra-
     matic. For example, in Connecticut, the average per-acre farm value rose from in
     $561 in 1964 to $2,227 in 1978. In Cumberland County, Pennsylvania, the per-acre
     value of farmland nearly doubled between 1974 and 1978, increasing from $866
     in 1974 to $1,533 in 1978. US Census Bureau, 1978 Census of Agriculture, USDA
     Census of Agriculture Historical Archive, http://agcensus.mannlib.cornell.edu/

AgCensus/censusParts.do?year=1978 (accessed July 5, 2012).

18 Joseph L. Sax, "Buying Scenery: Land Acquisition for the National Park Service," *Duke Law Journal* 4 (Sept. 1980): 709–40; Joseph L. Sax, "Helpless Giants: The National Parks and the Regulation of Private Lands," *Michigan Law Review 75* (Dec. 1976): 239–74. Also see Steven A. Hemmet, "Parks, People, and Private Property: The National Park Service and Eminent Domain," *Environmental Law* 16 (1986): 935–61.

19 House Committee on Appropriations, Department of the Interior and Related Agencies Appropriation Bill, 1979, report prepared by Sidney Yates, 95th Cong., 2d. Sess., (1978), House Report 95.

20 Jim Foley, "Ire in Wilsonia: Property Owners Seek Relief from NPS 'Harassment'" *The Fresno Bee*, April 5, 1978. Also see Robert Jones, "Policy Shift Angers U.S. Park Residents," *Los Angeles Times,* June 11, 1978.

21 Richie to associate director, management and operations, April 30, 1979, box 2-5-1 "Correspondence, USDOI, ATPO, 1.78–12.79," ATCA; National Park Service, ATPO, "Comprehensive Management Plan for the Protection, Management, and Use of the Appalachian National Scenic Trail," September 1981, NPS, Harpers Ferry, WV.

22 Proudman, interview by author, May 3, 2007. Also see Richie to associate director, August 31, 1978, box 2-5-1 "Correspondence, USDOI, ATPO, 1.78–12.79," ATCA; Richie to Charles S. Cushman, October 31, 1978, box 2-5-1 "Correspondence, USDOI, ATPO, 1.78–12.79," ATCA.

23 "NPS Prepares New Easement Policy," *The Register: A Newsletter of the Appalachian Trail* 1, no. 9 (December 1978), 1.

24 Foresta, *America's National Parks,* 240–44.

25 R. Coughlin, T. Plant, and A. Strong, *The Use of Land Acquisition Methods in the Preservation of Urban Open Space,* National Urban Recreation Technical Report Number 4, 1977, as quoted in US House of Representatives, *Land Acquisition Policy,* 30.

26 Richie, "Special A.T. Report," May 22, 1979, box 2-5-1 "Correspondence, USDOI, ATPO, 1.78–12.79," ATCA.

27 Richie to associate director, August 31, 1978. Also see Appalachian Trail Route Alternatives, Cumberland Valley, Pennsylvania, draft discussion paper, p. 108, April 21, 1983, Cumberland County Archives, Cumberland County Courthouse, Carlisle, Pennsylvania (hereafter cited as CCA). "NPS Prepares New Easement Policy," *The Register: A Newsletter of the Appalachian Trail,* vol. 1, no. 9, December 1978, Warren Doyle Collection. Lees McRae College, Banner Elk, North Carolina (hereafter cited as WDC).

28 Richie to Edward J. Koenemann, December 19, 1978, box 2-5-1 "Correspondence, USDOI, ATPO, 1.78–12.79," ATCA. Richie also noted that they were making an effort to keep "legal jargon" to a minimum and to keep easements as user-friendly as possible.

29 Richie to Chuck Rinaldi, Joe Sprinkle, et al., March 12, 1979, box 2-5-1 "Correspondence, USDOI, ATPO, 1.78–12.79," ATCA.

30 US Constitution, amendment 5.

31 In a letter to members of the Conservation Law Foundation, Richie explained

that because the Park Service was "limited in its authority to negotiate price, condemnation proceedings serve[d] as a procedure for establishing just compensation." Richie to Douglas Foy, January 23, 1979, box 2-5-1 "Correspondence, USDOI, ATPO, 1.78–12.79," ATCA.

32 As described in Foster, *Appalachian National Scenic Trail*, 85.

33 Richie to editor of *The Lakeville Journal*, October 12, 1979, box 2-5-1 "Correspondence, USDOI, ATPO, 1.78–12.79," ATCA.

34 Richie noted that it was "not unusual for one ownership to block several miles of Trail involving many other landowners." One antagonistic owner could not only cause a temporary gap in the trail, but could also made it difficult to justify the project to adjacent landowners who sold their land "with the impressions that a permanent location was a high priority." Richie to the files, November 8, 1978, box 2-5-1 "Correspondence, USDOI, ATPO, 1.78–12.79," ATCA.

35 For many volunteers, working with landowners was the most rewarding part of their experience with the trail project. Elizabeth Levers, interview by Glenn Scherer, 1992, transcript, NYNJTCA. Also see Jette to John Tamulynas, November 5, 1981, box DO 1 (65), DOCR.

36 "Preliminary Pre-Acquisition Planning Project," ATPO, June 15, 1977, box DO 1 (65), DOCR. Although the agency's attempts to standardize the process didn't work out exactly in the way it was intended, it gave coordinators a guiding framework from which to work.

37 Elizabeth Levers, interview by Glenn Scherer, 1992, transcript, NYNJTCA.

38 Ibid.

39 Gary Haugland, "Memories of Elizabeth Levers," email to nynjtc@aol.com, November 6, 1998. Also see Dave Sherman, fax to NJNJTC, November 5, 1998.

40 Robert Proudman, interview by author, May 3, 2007.

41 Ibid.

42 Richie to the files, October 20, 1978, box 2-5-1 "Correspondence, USDOI, ATPO, 1.78–12.79," ATCA.

43 In Norm Sills's estimation, "This one letter came closer to destroying the Trail project right then and there than any other one incident." Norman Sills, "A History of the Appalachian Trail in Connecticut," Salisbury, Connecticut, unpublished manuscript, 19. Copy located at the ATCA. This history was Sills's recollection of the acquisition program in Connecticut. Sills was a retired dairy farmer and coordinator for the land acquisition program in Connecticut after Coe. He served in that position from 1979 to 1984.

44 Ibid.

45 Harold Faber, "Hiking Trail's Relocation Hits Obstacle," *New York Times*, March 24, 1980.

46 Richie to Dave Sherman, January 16, 1979, box 2-5-1 "Correspondence, USDOI, ATPO, 1.78–12.79," ATCA; Bill Weary, "Commissioners Rap Trail 'Handling,'" *Carlisle Evening Sentinel*, July 5, 1978.

47 For examples, see Field to Robert E. Mathews, January 2, 1983, WDC.

48 Field to the Residents of Monson, December 1, 1979, WDC.

49 Ibid.

50 Earl Jette to Anna Bingham, September 9, 1977, box DO 1 (65), DOCR.

51 Sylvia and John Doten, and Susan and Hugh Hermann to Jette, January 19, 1978, box DO1 (65), DOCR.

52 Although Jette and his colleagues within the northeastern trail community were eventually able to build the trust and respect of local landowners, in areas that lacked a robust tradition of volunteer trailblazing, relying on coordinators to make contact with landowners proved to be more difficult. For example, in 1979, Karen Wade, the ATC's regional representative for southwest Virginia, noted that local clubs had not been very involved in the land acquisition process. She maintained that the absence of local club leadership had led to "insufficiently established relationships and channels of communication with local officials, landowners, state and fed agencies, congress . . . local media, local/regional organizations." The dearth of local trail advocates also led to deficiencies in trail maintenance, planning, and development, as well as problems with the land acquisition program. Wade to management, ATC, ATPO, August 28, 1979, box 2-5-1 "Correspondence, USDOI, ATPO, 1.78–12.79," ATCA.

53 For more on the relationship between property rights groups and the "antienvironmental" or "wise use" movement in the United States, see Harvey Jacobs, *Who Owns America?*; Short, *Ronald Reagan*. Also see Nancie G. Marzulla, "The Property Rights Movement: How It Began and Where It Is Headed," chapter 1 of *Land Rights*, ed. Bruce Yandle (Lanham, MD: Rowman & Littlefield, 1995), 1–30.

54 Richie to Don Fenicle, October 30, 1978, box 2-5-1 "Correspondence, USDOI, ATPO, 1.78–12.79," ATCA.

55 Griggs to "Dear . . . ," May 10, 1978, CCA; Maurice J. Forrester, Jr., president of Keystone Trails Association, to landowners, May 10, 1978, CCA.

56 Karen Lynch, "Angry Citizens Take Trail Fight to Silver Springs," *Carlisle Evening Sentinel*, June 29, 1978.

57 Pamela Fenicle, interview by author, May 15, 2007.

58 Arlene Byers to Cumberland County Commissioners, June 30, 1978, CCA.

59 Ibid.

60 Bill Weary, "Commissioners Rap Trail 'Handling,'" *Carlisle Evening Sentinel*, July 5, 1978.

61 Ibid.

62 As quoted in Deb Cline, "Group Protesting New Trail Gets Lawmakers' Advice," *Carlisle Evening Sentinel*, June 29, 1978.

63 Richie to associate director, August 31, 1978.

64 Richie to associate director, April 2, 1979, box 2-5-1 "Correspondence, USDOI, ATPO, 1.78–12.79," ATCA. In a letter to Griggs, who was eager to construct his original route, Richie explained that he was "committed to the process we have undertaken of evaluating alternatives with local help and participation." He argued that community-based deliberations would take time and that they needed to give the committee process an opportunity to develop plausible alternatives. Richie wrote, "I think the prognosis is good if we continue to be patient

and to work in good faith with local interests. I don't consider that to be pussy-footing. I hope you don't either." Richie to Griggs, September 25, 1978, box 2-5-1 "Correspondence, USDOI, ATPO, 1.78–12.79," ATCA.

65   Richie to Masland, October 30, 1978, box 2-5-1 "Correspondence, USDOI, ATPO, 1.78–12.79," ATCA.

66   Frank Masland, Jr., to William Goodling, September 7, 1982, CCA.

67   Les Brewer to Richie, April 15, 1980, folder "Cumberland Valley 1980," box "Startzell's Retired Files 58," ATCA.

68   Ibid.

69   Sheldon Brymesser to Russell Dickenson, October 10, 1984, CCA.

70   "Path through the 'Wilderness,'" *Pennsylvania Farmer*, August 9, 1980.

71   Murrel R. Walters III to William Penn Mott, August 14, 1985, CCA; also see Sheldon Brymesser to Cumberland County Commissioners, March 23, 1983, CCA.

72   Richie to John Rausch, October 16, 1978, CCA.

73   ATPO, "Comprehensive Management Plan," September 1981.

74   ATPO, Appalachian Trail Report, 39. Similar letters were written in other locations by farmers such as Jack Casey. In 1982, Casey sold rights to thirteen acres of pasture to the Park Service. The trail led hikers straight through a field of his grazing animals. Casey reported that he enjoyed meeting the hikers and believed that "the continuing use of the land for agriculture and the Appalachian Trail . . . very compatible." Jack Casey to "Whom It May Concern," October 20, 1984, CCA.

75   For more on the Sagebrush Rebellion and reactions to federal land management policies in the West during the late 1970s and early 1980s, see Cawley, *Federal Land, Western Anger*; Klyza, *Who Controls Public Lands?*; Howard E. McCurdy, "Environmental Protection," 85–107. For more on how the politics of designating wilderness areas influenced public land politics in the West, see Turner, *Promise of Wilderness*; Turner, "Specter of Environmentalism," 123–49.

76   Short, *Ronald Reagan*, 13–14.

77   Averill, "Ranger's Son Battling," *Traverse City Record Eagle*, July 31, 1978. Cushman maintained that although he was critical of its policies, he was not an enemy of the National Park Service. His father had been a park ranger in Yosemite, and Cushman claimed that as a boy, he had dreamed of working for the agency.

78   "Land Grab by the Parks," *Newsweek*, August 14, 1978. For examples of landowner resistance to Park Service acquisition efforts in other areas, see Susan Willoughby, "Award Whets [Voyageurs] Park Resistance," *Duluth New-Tribune*, June 25, 1978; David Averill, "Ranger's Son Battling: Cushman Opposes Policies of the National Park Service," *Traverse City Record Eagle*, July 31, 1978; Jim Foley, "Ire in Wilsonia"; Robert Jones, "Policy Shift Angers Park Residents," *Los Angeles Times*, June 11, 1978.

79   David Helvarg, *The War against the Greens: The Wise Use Movement, the New Right, and the Browning of America* (Boulder, CO: Sierra Club Books, 2004), 101. For more on Cushman's background and influence on the property rights movement, also see Jacqueline Vaughn Switzer, *Green Backlash: The History and Politics of*

Environmental Opposition in the U.S. (Boulder, CO: Lynne Rienner Publishers, 1997), 194–95, 252–53.

80   Dick Poland, "Californian Seeks to Calm Trail-Site Feud," *Carlisle Evening News*, February 28, 1979; Deb Cline, "He's Shaking Park Service Tree," *Carlisle Evening Sentinel*, February 27, 1979.

81   Karen Lynch, "CANT Ponders Joining National Group," *Carlisle Evening Sentinel*, March 1, 1979. *Prime Time Sunday* aired a program called "For All People for All Time" on December 16, 1979, that criticized the National Park Service's land acquisition policies in Ohio's Cuyahoga Valley. The show gave landowners along the AT an example of how the national media might be used to help build sympathy for their cause.

82   Pamela Fenicle to Richie, May 5, 1980, CCA.

83   "Viewpoint V: Warren Doyle, 10,000-miler, ALHDA Coordinator, ATC Life Member," n.d., WDC. Also Warren Doyle, interview by author, February 10, 2007.

84   Although he was critical of the National Park Service's land acquisition policies, Doyle maintained that he "seldom, if ever, criticize[d] the condition of the footway" and was "always appreciative of the trail workers efforts." These quotes were written on a letter from Karen Wade to Warren Doyle, Jr., January 4, 1983, WDC.

85   ATPO, Appalachian Trail Report, 30. Shipe's subjects were likely to be biased by the free ice cream and the friendly social exchange that was facilitated by the existing road route.

86   In the effort to reroute the trail off roads and into the woods, two towns were added to the route: Harpers Ferry and Boiling Springs—both of which the trail now crosses through. The ATC headquarters is located in Harpers Ferry, and the mid-Atlantic Regional Office of the ATC is in Boiling Springs—in the Cumberland Valley.

87   Todd Ingberg, Annadale, VA, June 1, 1984, WDC.

88   Richie to Griggs, November 15, 1982, WDC.

89   Ibid.

90   Ibid.

91   Richie to Doyle, January 12, 1983, WDC; Karen Wade to Doyle, January 4, 1983, WDC.

92   Si Kahn, *The Forest Service in Appalachia*, John Whitney Foundation, 1974.

93   Warren Doyle, interview by author, February 10, 2007.

94   Richie to Doyle, January 12, 1983, WDC.

95   Spence, *Dispossessing the Wilderness*; Jacoby, *Crimes against Nature*.

96   For histories of the removals of mountain families in Shenandoah National Park, see Perdue, "Appalachian Fables and Facts," 84–104; Perdue, "To Build a Wall," 48–71; Reeder, *Shenandoah Secrets*; and Floyd, *Lost Trails and Forgotten People*. For examples in the Great Smoky Mountains National Park, see Dunn, *Cades Cove*. It is important to note that, while thousands of people were removed to make the eastern national parks, many were willing to sell their land. Some were even grateful for the opportunity to sell after several years of drought and a decline in soil fertility in the early decades of the twentieth century.

97 See M. E. Reger, Harrison Branch Office, Northwest Arkansas Legal Services to National Park Inholders Assn., August 24, 1978, CCA. For examples of how the Park Service's efforts to acquire land for Voyageurs National Park affected poor, rural communities in northern in Minnesota, see Susan Willoughby, "Award Whets Park Resistance," *Duluth New-Tribune*, June 25, 1978.

98 Sills, "Appalachian Trail in Connecticut," 9.

99 Ibid.

100 Ibid.

101 Landowners in these cases were fundamentally concerned about protecting private property rights—a concept that was not part of most early Native American cultures. For examples of national park inholders comparing themselves to Native Americans, see Robert Jones, "Policy Shift Angers Park Residents," *Los Angeles Times*, June 11, 1978. Charles S. Cushman, founder of the National Park Inholders Association, claimed that inholders were "the Indians of 1978. . . . Only we're getting kicked off the reservations instead of being put on them." Quote from Averill, "Ranger's Son Battling," *Traverse City Record Eagle*, July 31, 1978.

102 "Appalachian National Scenic Trail Status of Protection, March 1984," *Appalachian Trailway News*, May–June 1984.

NOTES TO CHAPTER 6

1 Fox Butterfield, "Landowners Dispute U.S. Attempt to Move Trail," *New York Times*, July 28, 1985.

2 Leaders of the New Right often evoked Revolutionary War images in their rhetoric protesting the power of the centralized state. For details on how the Sagebrush Rebels used Revolutionary War–era symbols, see Short, *Ronald Reagan*, 17.

3 For more on the rise of the New Right in US politics, see McGirr, *Suburban Warriors*; Michael J. Thompson, ed., *Confronting the New Conservatism: The Rise of the Right in America* (New York: New York University Press, 2007). For more on the effect of the New Right on environmental politics in particular, see Turner, *The Promise of Wilderness*; James McCarthy, "Environmentalism, Wise Use, and the Nature of Accumulation in the Rural West," chapter 6 of *Remaking Reality: Nature at the Millennium*, ed. Bruce Baun and Noel Castree (New York: Routledge, 1998); Switzer, *Green Backlash*; Rothman, *Greening of a Nation?*; and Scott Hamilton Dewey, *Don't Breathe the Air: Air Pollution and U.S. Environmental Politics, 1945–1970* (College Station: Texas A&M University Press, 2000).

4 For more on Nixon's environmental policies, see J. Brooks Flippen, *Nixon and the Environment* (Albuquerque: University of New Mexico Press, 2000).

5 Maurice J. Forrester, "Volunteers and the New Federalism," *The Register: A Newsletter of the Appalachian Trail*, vol. 4, no. 2, December 1981, WDC.

6 As quoted in Forrester, "Volunteers and the New Federalism."

7 Short, *Ronald Reagan*, 67.

8 James G. Watt, speech to the National Association of Counties, Louisville, KY, July 12, 1981; James G. Watt, speech to the National Petroleum Council,

Washington, DC, December 3, 1981. As quoted in Short, *Ronald Reagan*, 61.

9 As quoted in Dale Russakoff, "For Want of 14 Miles, Appalachian Trail May Be Lost," *Washington Post*, July 26, 1982.

10 Karen Wade to Honorable M. Caldwell Butler, March 13, 1981, box 2-5-3 "USDOI, ATPO Correspondence, 9.80–11.81," ATCA.

11 ATC, "Federal Budget Proposals Will Cut Deep," *The Register: A Newsletter of the Appalachian Trail* 4, no. 4 (April 1981); Russakoff, "For Want of 14 Miles."

12 Gordon J. Humphrey and Warren B. Rudman to James Watt, June 9, 1981, box DO 1 (65), DOCR.

13 Ibid.

14 Annual Report, Town of Tyringham, FY1984, WDC.

15 Butterfield, "Landowners Dispute U.S. Attempt to Move Trail," *New York Times*, July 28, 1985.

16 Rachel Gottlieb, "Trail Siting Sometimes Rocky: National Park Service Takes 7,513 Acres during Past Decade," *Valley News: Published for the Upper Connecticut River Valley*, September 24, 1990.

17 "Fires, Booby Traps Linked to Angry Tennessee Landowners," *Sunday Patriot News*, March 10, 1991. Today, there is still an infamous trash heap near US 19E, and the local club—the Tennessee Eastman Club—has posted signs in the area warning hikers not to park their cars nearby due to a history of vandalism in the region. Some speculate that the cause of these contemporary acts goes back to angry landowners who were forced off their land. I found no direct evidence to prove—or disprove—that notion.

18 John Kassel, "Appalachian Trail Takes a Quiet Turn," *Valley News: Published for the Upper Connecticut River Valley*, July 19, 1982.

19 Charles Cushman, "Protecting Private Land in the Northeast," excerpts of speech from proceedings of the Fourth Annual New York Conference on Private Property Rights (1999), http://prfamerica.org/speeches/4th/ProtectingPrivate-LandNE.html (accessed July 20, 2011).

20 Karen Wade to "To the Files," December 26, 1980, box 2-5-3 "USDOI, ATPO Correspondence, 9.80–11.81," ATCA.

21 Larry Van Meter, "Resolutions Passed at the 25th Meeting of the Appalachian Trail Conference," September 10, 1985, WDC.

22 George S. Wislocki, executive director, Berkshire Natural Resources Council, to Helen Fenske, assistant commissioner, NJ Department of Environmental Protection, October 31, 1985, ANTAC Greenway Committee, Ray Hunt Papers, ATCA.

23 Dave Richie to Hank Foster, Tom Deans, Dave Sherman, April 9, 1980, box 2-5-2 "USDOI ATPO Correspondence, 1.80–8.80," ATCA.

24 Ibid.

25 Mrs. Laurence Benander to editor of the *Harrisburg Patriot News*, July 22, 1985.

26 Ibid.

27 George Wislocki to Fenske, October 31, 1985.

28 "Public Ownership of AT Is Land Trust Goal," *Appalachian Trailway News*, May–June 1983.

29 "Higher Ground: ATC's Land Trust Turns 20," *Appalachian Trailway News*, November–December 2002. According to the Uniform Relocation Assistance and Real Estate Property Acquisition Policies Act of 1970, when purchasing land from private owners, federal agencies like the National Park Service could not offer landowners less than the fair market value of a property.

30 Bristow to Trust for Appalachian Trail Lands Committee, August 29, 1986, folder "Countryside Ideas," box "Ray Hunt Papers," ATCA.

31 Preston Bristow, Jr., "Countryside Protection and the Appalachian Trail: A New England Feasibility Study, A Vermont Pilot Project," proposal to the ATC BOM, April 15, 1986, folder "Countryside Ideas," box "Ray Hunt Papers," ATCA.

32 Eric Francis, "Planning Options Offered by British Visitors," *Vermont Standard*, July 23, 1987.

33 William G. Hoppes to Charles Sloan, August 4, 1987, folder "Countryside Ideas," box "Ray Hunt Papers," ATCA.

34 Bristow, "Countryside Protection."

35 Marsden Epworth, "Park Service's Plan for Trail Sparks Debate," June 30, 1983, unknown newspaper, WDC.

36 "New Role for Trail Conference," *Courier: The National Park Service Newsletter* 29, no. 3 (March 1984), 1.

37 ATC, "Management of 'Residual' NPS-acquired A.T. Lands by the Appalachian Trail Conference," November 9, 1983.

38 Larry Van Meter, "National Park Service Delegates Management Responsibility to Appalachian Trail Conference," *Appalachian Trailway News*, March–April 1984.

39 ATC, "Park Service Delegates Management Responsibility over 30,000 Trail Acres to Appalachian Trail Conference," press release, n.d., WDC.

40 Judy Jenner, "Dave Richie, 'ATC Strengths Make It Natural for New Role,'" *Appalachian Trailway News*, March–April 1984.

41 Bob Jacobson, "Land Management—The Challenge," speech delivered at the First Appalachian Trail Club presidents meeting, Harpers Ferry, WV, April 27–28, 1985, brief meeting summary, box 9, GATC MSS.

42 ATC, "Management of Public Lands by a Volunteer Organization," prepared for the President's Commission on Americans Outdoors, December 6, 1985, ANTAC Greenway Committee, Ray Hunt Papers, ATCA.

43 "Report of the Long-Range Planning Committee to the Board of Managers, ATC," October 31, 1986, Ray Hunt Papers, ATCA.

44 ATC, "The Evolution of the Appalachian Trail Protection Program and 'Countryside' Conservation," December 6, 1985, ANTAC Greenway Committee, Ray Hunt Papers, ATCA; also see Robert Proudman, "Clubs Provide Eyes and Ears for Complex Program," *Appalachian Trailway News*, July–August 1991.

45 Maurice Forrester, letter to the editor, *The Register: A Newsletter of the Appalachian Trail* 1, no. 2 (February 1980).

46 Ibid.

47 The Wilderness Act of 1964 outlined the process for the first review of roadless areas in the national forests. Known as the Roadless Area Review and Evaluation

(RARE I), the process found that fifty-six million acres could be designated as wilderness. The Forest Service initiated RARE II in 1977 in an effort to comply with standards established by the National Environmental Protection Act. The latter process specifically involved greater public participation. The designation of roadless areas continued to create controversy in the twenty-first century. See Natural Resource Defense Council, http://www.nrdc.org/land/forests/qroadless.asp (accessed July 23, 2008).

48   Whit Benson, GATC Conservation Committee 1983 Report, box 11, GATC MSS.

49   Ibid.

50   Ibid.

51   Jim Botts and Mike Dawson to Southern Regional Management Committee, August 17, 1982, box 11, GATC MSS.

52   Ibid.

53   Some trail leaders argued that small-scale logging in and along the newly acquired corridor would be a good way to generate income for trail maintenance and to fund future acquisitions. In the early 1980s, three leaders in the trail community drafted a position paper on forest management in the AT corridor. The authors claimed that no trees would be cut within one hundred feet of each side of the trail, but outside of the right-of-way, group selection and individual tree harvest—"good and accepted forestry practices"—should be allowed so that "no group of trees so cut shall exceed one-fourth acre in size nor be closer than 150 feet of other groups of trees so cut within a 10-year interval." They also maintained, "Any forest management activities in the corridor must be considered secondary to protection of the Trail and the Trail experience." The clubs would work with professional foresters to identify areas where cutting would be allowed and to develop forest management plans for those areas. "Forest Management within the National Park Service Appalachian Trail Protective Corridor," position paper presented to the New England Regional Management Committee, submitted by David Field, Earl Jette, Roger Sternberg, March 27, 1982, box 11, GATC MSS.

54   David Field, "Sharing the Greenway: The Role of the Trust," Trail Lands: The Newsletter of the Trust for Appalachian Trail Lands 12, no. 2 (Autumn 1995), 9.

55   Rowe to Roddy, February 10, 1994, box 14, CMCA.

56   The combination of citizen and state authority to achieve large-scale land management goals was an expression of reform liberalism that began growing in the late twentieth century. For more on reform liberalism and environmental politics in the late twentieth century, see Turner, Promise of Wilderness, 299–302.

57   In the late 1980s and 1990s, "partnership parks" also became more common as local leaders tried to work with the Park Service to promote economic development. For example, in Salem, Massachusetts, business leaders, nonprofit organizations, and residents partnered with the National Park Service to develop the Salem Maritime National Historic Site. Project participants hoped that the site would be "a catalyst for economic revitalization, tourism, historic preservation,

upgraded transportation systems, and a general improvement in the quality of life for the city of Salem and the surrounding community." Warren Brown, "Public/Private Land Conservation Partnerships in and around National Parks," chapter 5 of *Land Conservation through Public/Private Partnerships*, (Washington, DC: Island Press, 1993), 121.

58 ATC, "Local Management Planning Guide," November 1988.
59 New York–New Jersey Trail Conference, "A.T. Committee Uses $600 Grant for Town Meeting," *Trailwalker: Newsletter of the NYNJTC* (June/July 1989).
60 ATC, "Local Management Planning Guide," November 1988.
61 First Appalachian Trail Club Presidents Meeting, Harpers Ferry, WV, April 27–28, 1985, brief Meeting summary, box 9, GATC MSS. Project leaders emphasized the importance of the acronym KISMIF (Keep it simple and make it fun).
62 Stephen B. Sease to Helen Fenske, October 28, 1985, ANTAC Greenway Committee, Ray Hunt Papers, ATCA.
63 Brian King, "'Conference' to be Renamed "Conservancy' in July," *Appalachian Trailway News*, January–February 2005.
64 Bob Proudman, "Clubs Provide Eyes and Ears for Complex Program," *Appalachian Trailway News*, July–August 1991.
65 See Michael E. Kraft, "Environmental Policy and Congress," in *Environmental Policy: New Directions for the 21st Century*, ed. Norman J. Vig and Michael E. Kraft (Los Angeles: Sage Publications, 2013), 118–19; Robert Gottlieb, *Environmentalism Unbound: Exploring Pathways for Change* (Cambridge, MA: The MIT Press, 2001), 51.
66 *Bert J. Harris, Jr., Private Property Rights Protection Act of 1995*, sec 70.001, 95–181.
67 See http://www.landrights.org/ (accessed July 26, 2011).
68 Brian B. King, "President Clinton, Vice President Gore Bring the World to the Trail: Hours later, House Leader Pledges Final A.T. Funding This Year," *Appalachian Trailway News*, July–August 1998.

NOTES TO CONCLUSION

1 By 2010, the National Park Service, the US Forest Service, and the fourteen states through which the trail passes had successfully acquired 187,435 acres for the trail corridor, and land acquisition was nearly complete. The AT is occasionally relocated and additional adjacent lands are sometimes purchased to protect the viewshed, and to preserve important cultural and natural resources. National Parks Conservation Association, *The Appalachian National Scenic Trail: A Special Report*, March 2010.
2 "Higher Ground: ATC's Land Trust Turns 20," *ATN* (Nov.—Dec. 2002).
3 Kim Williams, "From Trail to Table," *AT Journeys: The Magazine of the Appalachian Trail Conservancy* (July–August 2011), 15.
4 Benton MacKaye, "The Appalachian Trail: A Guide to the Study of Nature," *Scientific Monthly* 34, no. 4 (April 1932): 330–42.
5 Appalachian Trail Conservancy, "Natural and Cultural Resource Management,"

http://www.appalachiantrail.org/what-we-do/conservation/natural-cultural-resource-management (accessed August 14, 2012).

6   Like the ATC and its clubs, increasingly powerful national environmental organizations tried to maintain ties to their dispersed constituencies by having local chapters.

7   The growth in environmental nonprofits in the 1990s seemed to buck the trend that many other types of civic organizations witnessed—a decline in participation and volunteerism, as documented in Robert Putnam's famous book *Bowling Alone: The Collapse and Revival of American Community* (New York: Simon & Schuster, 2000). Several scholars have critiqued Putnam's argument using the examples of the growth in grassroots environmental organizations, where participation increased steadily in the late twentieth century. For example, see Pamela Paxton, "Is Social Capital Declining in the United States? A Multiple Indicator Assessment," *American Journal of Sociology* 105, no. 1 (July 1999): 88–127.

8   Rosemary O'Leary, "Environmental Policy in the Courts," in *Environmental Policy: New Directions for the Twenty-First Century*, edited by Norman Vig and Michael E. Kraft, 7th ed. (Washington, DC: CQ Press, 2010), 125.

9   Deborah Lynn Guber and Christopher Bosso, "Past the Tipping Point? Public Discourse and the Role of the Environmental Movement in the Post-Bush Era," in Vig and Craft, *Environmental Policy*, 58. Also see Guber, *The Grassroots of Green Revolution: Polling in America on the Environment* (Boston: The MIT Press, 2003). For more on the partisan divide in Congress, see Charles R. Shipan and William R. Lowry, "Environmental Policy and Party Divergence in Congress," *Political Research Quarterly* 54 (2001): 245–63.

10   My analysis here draws on the work of political scientists Charles W. Dunn and J. David Woodard, who synthesized the work of a broad cross-section of conservative thinkers and created a list of ten conservative principles. See *The Conservative Tradition in America* (Lantham, MD: Rowman & Littlefield Publishers, 1996), 48. Also see John R. E. Bliese, *The Greening of Conservative America* (Boulder, CO: Westview Press, 2001).

11   Benton MacKaye, "What Is the A.T.?" 1924, box 183, BMP.

12   White, "Are You an Environmentalist?" 171–85.

13   An excellent critique of preservation can be found in Mary M. Berlik, David B. Kittredge, and David R. Foster, "The Illusion of Preservation: A Global Environmental Argument for the Local Production of Natural Resources," *Journal of Biogeography* 29 (2002): 1557–68.

14   Cronon, "Trouble with Wilderness," 85.

15   I first heard the idea of shifting from "NIMBY" to "WHIMBY" while working on a project to develop community-scale biomass energy for heating schools and towns in Vermont. See Tom Tailer in "Biomass in Vermont's Energy Future," video by Biomass Energy Working Group, Montpelier, Vermont, http://www.youtube.com/watch?v=7DotGgi1tn4 (accessed August 14, 2012).

16   MacKaye, "Why an Appalachian Trail?" unpublished draft, February 1922, box 182, BMP.

Selected Bibliography

ABBREVIATIONS

AMC	Appalachian Mountain Club
ANSTAC	Appalachian National Scenic Trail Advisory Council
ATC	Appalachian Trail Conference/Appalachian Trail Conservancy (since 2005)
ATPO	Appalachian Trail Project Office
CANT	Citizens Against New Trail
CCC	Civilian Conservation Corps
GATC	Georgia Appalachian Trail Club
GMC	Green Mountain Club
IWW	International Workers of the World
LASER	League of States Equal Rights
NEPA	National Environmental Policy Act
NPS	National Park Service
NYNJTC	New York–New Jersey Trail Conference
ORRRC	Outdoor Recreation Resources Review Commission
PATC	Potomac Appalachian Trail Club
PRO-TRAIL	Pennsylvanians Rallied on a Trail Route Advocating Improved Location
RARE II	Roadless Area Review and Evaluation II
SMHC	Smoky Mountain Hiking Club
TVA	Tennessee Valley Authority
USDOI	US Department of Interior

MANUSCRIPT COLLECTIONS

ATCA	Appalachian Trail Conference Archives, Appalachian Trail Conference, Charlestown, West Virginia
BMP	Benton MacKaye Papers, Special Collections, Dartmouth College Library, Hanover, New Hampshire
CCA	Cumberland County Archives, Cumberland County Courthouse, Carlisle, Pennsylvania
CMCA	Carolina Mountain Club Archive, Special Collections, D. H. Ramsey Library, University of North Carolina, Asheville, North Carolina

DOCR   Dartmouth Outing Club Records, Rauner Special Collections
              Library, Dartmouth College, Hanover, New Hampshire
GATC MSS   Georgia Appalachian Trail Club Records, Manuscript Collection,
              Georgia Archives, Morrow, Georgia
GNP   Gaylord Nelson Papers, Wisconsin Historical Society,
              Madison, Wisconsin
MHAC   Myron H. Avery Collection, Maine State Library, Augusta, Maine
NBATCP   Natural Bridge Appalachian Trail Club Papers, Jones Memorial
              Library, Lynchburg, Virginia
NYNJTCA   New York–New Jersey Trail Conference Office, Mahwah, New Jersey
WDC   Warren Doyle Collection, Lees McRae College, Banner Elk, North
              Carolina

SELECTED BIBLIOGRAPHY

Adams, David A. *Renewable Resource Policy: The Legal-Institutional Foundations.*
    Washington, DC: Island Press, 1993.
Alagona, Peter S. "Homes on the Range: Cooperative Conservation and Environmen-
    tal Change on California's Privately Owned Hardwood Rangelands." *Environmental
    History* 13, no. 2 (April 2008): 325–50.
Alanen, Arnold & R. Z. Melnick, eds. *Preserving Cultural Landscapes in America.* Balti-
    more: Johns Hopkins University Press, 2000.
Alston, Lee J. "Farm Foreclosures in the United States during the Interwar Period." *The
    Journal of Economic History* 43, no. 4 (December 1983): 885–903.
Ambrose, Jonathon P., and Susan P. Bratton. "Trends in Landscape Heterogeneity along
    the Borders of Great Smoky Mountains National Park." *Conservation Biology* 4 no. 2
    (1990): 135–43.
Anderson, Larry. *Benton MacKaye: Conservationist, Planner, and Creator of the Appala-
    chian Trail.* Baltimore: Johns Hopkins University Press, 2002.
Anderson, Robert L. "Changing Forests and Forest Management Policy in Relation to
    Dealing with Forest Diseases." *Phytopathology* 93 (2003): 1041–43.
Aron, Cindy S. *Working at Play: A History of Vacations in the United States.* New York:
    Oxford University Press, 1999.
Barbour, Michael. "Ecological Fragmentation in the Fifties." In *Uncommon Ground:
    Rethinking the Human Place in Nature.* New York: W. W. Norton, 1995, 233–55.
Bates, David. *Breaking Trail in the Central Appalachians: A Narrative.* Washington, DC:
    Potomac Appalachian Trail Club, 1987.
Bates, J. Leonard. "Fulfilling American Democracy: The Conservation Movement, 1907
    to 1921." *Mississippi Valley Historical Review* 44 (1957): 29–57.
Batteau, Allen. *The Invention of Appalachia.* Tucson: University of Arizona Press, 1990.
Baun, Bruce, and Noel Castree, eds. *Remaking Reality: Nature at the Millennium.* New
    York Routledge, 1998.
Becker, Jane S. *Selling Tradition: Appalachia and the Construction of an American Folk,
    1930–1940.* Chapel Hill: University of North Carolina Press, 1998.

Bentley, Michael L. "The Role of Backcountry Experience in Middle School Environmental Education." PhD diss., University of Virginia, 1985.

Berlik, Mary M., David B. Kittredge, and David R. Foster. "The Illusion of Preservation: A Global Environmental Argument for the Local Production of Natural Resources." *Journal of Biogeography* 29 (2002): 1557–68.

Billings, Dwight B. *The Road to Poverty: The Making of Wealth and Hardship in Appalachia.* Cambridge, NY: Cambridge University Press, 2000.

Billings, Dwight B., Gurney Norman, and Katherine Ledford, eds. *Confronting Appalachian Stereotypes: Back Talk from an American Region.* Lexington: University Press of Kentucky, 1999.

Binkley, Cameron. "The Creation and Establishment of Cape Hatteras National Seashore: The Great Depression through Mission 66." Special report prepared for Southeast Regional Office, Cultural Resource Division, National Park Service, August 2007.

Birchard, William, and Robert Proudman. *Appalachian Trail Design, Construction, and Maintenance.* 2nd ed. Harpers Ferry, WV: Appalachian Trail Conference, 2000.

Bliese, John R. E. *The Greening of Conservative America.* Boulder, CO: Westview Press, 2001.

Bren, Paulena. "Weekend Getaways: The Chata, the Tramp, and the Politics of Private Life in Post-1968 Czechoslovakia." Chapter 7 of *Socialist Spaces: Sites of Everyday Life in the Eastern Bloc.* Oxford: Berg Publishers, 2002.

Brewer, Richard. *Conservancy: The Land Trust Movement in America.* Lebanon, NH: University Press of New England, 2003.

Brown, Margaret Lynn. *The Wild East: A Biography of the Great Smoky Mountains.* Gainesville: University of Florida Press, 2000.

Brown, Warren. "Public/Private Land Conservation Partnerships in and around National Parks." Chapter 5 of *Land Conservation through Public/Private Partnerships.* Washington, DC: Island Press, 1993.

Bryson, Bill. *A Walk in the Woods.* New York: Broadway Books, 1998.

Burch, William R., ed. *Long-Distance Trails: The Appalachian Trail as a Guide to Future Management and Research Needs.* New Haven, CT: School of Forestry and Environmental Studies, Yale University, 1979.

Callicot, J. Baird, and Michael P. Nelson, eds. *The Great New Wilderness Debate.* Athens: University of Georgia Press, 1998.

Carr, Ethan. *Mission 66: Modernism and the National Park Dilemma.* Amherst: University of Massachusetts Press, 2007.

———. *Wilderness by Design: Landscape Architecture and the National Park Service.* Lincoln: University of Nebraska Press, 1998.

Cawley, R. McGreggor. *Federal Land, Western Anger: The Sagebrush Rebellion and Environmental Politics.* Lawrence: University Press of Kansas, 1993.

Clark, Norman. *Mill Town.* Seattle: University of Washington Press, 1970.

Cordell, H. Ken, Carter Betz, J. M. Bowker, et al. *Outdoor Recreation in American Life: A National Assessment of Demand and Supply Trends.* Champaign, IL: Sagamore Publishing, 1999.

Cox, Thomas. *This Well-Wooded Land: Americans and Their Forests from Colonial Times to the Present.* Lincoln: University of Nebraska Press, 1985.

Cronon, William. "The Trouble with Wilderness; or, Getting Back to the Wrong Nature." In *Uncommon Ground: Rethinking the Human Place in Nature*, 69–90. New York: W. W. Norton & Co., 1996.

———, ed. *Uncommon Ground: Rethinking the Human Place in Nature*. New York: W. W. Norton & Co., 1996.

———. "The Uses of Environmental History." *Environmental History Review* 17, no. 3 (Fall 1993): 1–22.

Dana, Samuel, and Sally K. Fairfax. *Forest and Range Policy: Its Development in the United States*. New York: McGraw Hill Book Company, 1980.

Davis, Donald E. *Where There Are Mountains: An Environmental History of the Southern Appalachians*. Athens: University of Georgia Press, 2000.

Dewey, Scott Hamilton. *Don't Breathe the Air: Air Pollution and U.S. Environmental Politics, 1945–1970*. College Station: Texas A&M University Press, 2000.

Dewitt, John. *Civic Environmentalism: Alternatives to Regulation in States and Communities*. Washington, DC: Congressional Quarterly Press, 1994.

Dorman, Robert. *Revolt of the Provinces: The Regionalist Movement in America, 1920–1945*. Chapel Hill: University of North Carolina Press, 1993.

Doyle, Warren E., Jr. "An Outdoor-Challenge Experience and the Affective Development of College Students." PhD diss., University of Connecticut, 1981.

Drake, Brian. "The Skeptical Environmentalist: Senator Barry Goldwater and the Environmental Management State." *Environmental History* 15, no. 4 (Oct. 2010): 587–611.

———. *The Unnatural State: Conservatives, Libertarians, and the Postwar American Environmental Movement*. PhD diss., University of Kansas, 2006.

Dulles, Foster R. *A History of Recreation: America Learns to Play*. Englewood Cliffs, NJ: Prentice-Hall, 1965.

Dunlap, Riley E., and Angela G. Mertig. *American Environmentalism: The U.S. Environmental Movement, 1970–1990*. Philadelphia: Taylor & Francis, 1992.

Dunn, Charles W., and J. David Woodard. *The Conservative Tradition in America*. Lantham, MD: Rowman & Littlefield Publishers, 1996.

Dunn, Durwood. *Cades Cove: The Life and Death of a Southern Appalachian Community, 1818–1937*. Knoxville: University of Tennessee Press, 1988.

Ebenezer, Howard. *Garden Cities of Tomorrow*. London: Swan Sonnenschein & Co., 1902.

Eller, Ron. *Miners, Millhands, and Mountaineers: Industrialization of the Appalachian South, 1880–1930*. Knoxville: University of Tennessee Press, 1982.

Endicott, Eve, ed. *Land Conservation through Public/Private Partnerships*. Washington, DC: Island Press, 1993.

Fairfax, Sally. "Federal-State Cooperation in Outdoor Recreation Policy Formation: The Case of the Appalachian Trail." PhD diss., Duke University, 1973.

Fairfax, Sally, et al. *Buying Nature: The Limits of Land Acquisition as a Conservation Strategy, 1780–2004*. Cambridge, MA: The MIT Press, 2005.

Fitzgerald, Deborah. *Every Farm a Factory: The Industrial Ideal in American Agriculture*. New Haven, CT: Yale University Press, 2003.

Flink, Charles, Kristine Olka, and Robert Searns. *Trails for the Twenty-First Century*. 2nd ed. Washington, DC: Island Press, 2001.

Flippen, J. Brooks. *Nixon and the Environment*. Albuquerque: University of New Mexico Press, 2000.

Floyd, Tom. *Lost Trails and Forgotten People: The Story of Jones Mountain*. Vienna, VA: Potomac Appalachian Trail Club, 1981.

Foresta, Robert A., *America's National Parks and Their Keepers*. Washington, DC: Resources for the Future, 1984.

———. "Transformation of the Appalachian Trail," *Geographical Review* 77, no. 1 (1987): 76–85.

Foster, Charles H. W. *The Appalachian National Scenic Trail: A Time to Be Bold*. Needham, MA: Charles Foster, 1987.

Foster, David. "Conservation Issues and Approaches for Dynamic Cultural Landscapes." *Journal of Biogeography* 29 (2002): 1533–35.

———. "Land-Use History (1730–1990) and Vegetation Dynamics in Central New England, USA." *Journal of Ecology* 80 (1992): 753–72.

Foster, David, and John Aber, eds. *Forests in Time: The Environmental Consequences of 1000 Years of Change in New England*. New Haven, CT: Yale University Press, 2004.

Freed, Jason E. "Creating the Appalachian Trail: Technological Influences on Symbol Production." PhD diss., Clemson University, 2004.

Garvey, Ed. *Appalachian Hiker*. Oakton, VA: Appalachian Books, 1971.

Geddes, Patrick. *Cities in Evolution: An Introduction to the Town Planning Movement and to the Study of Civics*. London: Williams & Norgate, 1915.

Georgia Appalachian Trail Club. *Friendships of the Trail: The History of the Georgia Appalachian Trail Club, 1930–1980*. Rev. ed. Atlanta: Georgia Appalachian Trail Club, 1995.

Gottlieb, Robert. *Environmentalism Unbound: Exploring New Pathways for Change*. Cambridge, MA: The MIT Press, 2001.

———. *Forcing the Spring: The Transformation of the American Environmental Movement*. Washington, DC: Island Press, 2005.

Gough, Robert. *Farming the Cutover: A Social History of Northern Wisconsin, 1900–1940*. Lawrence: University of Kansas Press, 1997.

Gregg, Sara. *Managing the Mountains: Land Use Planning, the New Deal, and the Creation of a Federal Landscape in Appalachia*. New Haven: Yale University Press, 2010.

Guber, Deborah Lynn. *The Grassroots of Green Revolution: Polling in America on the Environment*. Boston: The MIT Press, 2003.

Guber, Deborah Lynn, and Christopher Bosso. "Past the Tipping Point? Public Discourse and the Role of the Environmental Movement in the Post-Bush Era." Chapter 3 of *Environmental Policy: New Directions for the Twenty-First Century*, edited by Norman J. Vig and Michael E. Kraft. 7th ed. Washington, DC: CQ Press, 2010.

Guha, Ramachandra. "Radical American Environmentalism and Wilderness Preservation: A Third-World Critique." *Environmental Ethics* 11 (Spring 1989): 71–83.

Hahn, Steven. "Hunting, Fishing, and Foraging: Common Rights and Class Relations in the Postbellum South." *Radical History Review* 26 (1982): 37–64.

Hart, John. *Walking Softly in the Wilderness*. San Francisco, CA: Sierra Club Books, 1977.

Hart, John F. "Loss and Abandonment of Cleared Farm Land in the Eastern United States." *Annals of the Association of American Geographers* 58, no. 3 (1968.): 417–40.

Harvey, Mark. A *Symbol of Wilderness: Echo Park and the American Conservation Movement.* Albuquerque: University of New Mexico Press, 1994.

———. *Wilderness Forever: Howard Zahniser and the Path to the Wilderness Act.* Seattle: University of Washington Press, 2007.

Hays, Samuel P. *Beauty, Health, and Permanence: Environmental Politics in the United States, 1955–1985.* New York: Cambridge University Press, 1987.

———. *Conservation and the Gospel of Efficiency: The Progressive Conservation Movement, 1890–1920.* Cambridge, MA: Harvard University Press, 1959.

———. *A History of Environmental Politics since 1945.* Pittsburgh: University of Pittsburgh Press, 2000.

Helvarg, David. *The War against the Greens: The Wise Use Movement, the New Right, and the Browning of America.* Boulder, CO: Sierra Club Books, 2004.

Hemmet, Steven A. "Parks, People, and Private Property: The National Park Service and Eminent Domain." *Environmental Law* 16 (1986): 935–61.

Hill, Edwin G. *In the Shadow of the Mountain: The Spirit of the CCC.* Pullman: Washington State University Press, 1990.

Hirt, Paul. *A Conspiracy of Optimism: Management of the National Forests since World War Two.* Lincoln: University of Nebraska Press, 1994.

Ireland, Lloyd C. *Wildlands and Woodlots: The Story of New England's Forests.* Hanover, NH: University Press of New England, 1982.

Jacobs, Harvey. *Who Owns America? Social Conflict over Property Rights.* Madison: University of Wisconsin Press, 1998.

Jacoby, Karl. "Class and Environmental History: Lessons from 'The War in the Adirondacks.'" *Environmental History* no. 2, vol. 3 (1997): 138–59.

———. *Crimes against Nature: Squatters, Poachers, Thieves, and the Hidden History of Conservation.* Berkeley: University of California Press, 2001.

Jensen, Clayne, and Steven Guthrie, eds. *Outdoor Recreation in America.* 6th ed. Champaign, IL: Human Kinetics, 2006.

Johnson, Benjamin Heber, "Conservation, Subsistence, and Class at the Birth of Superior National Forest." *Environmental History* 4, no.1 (1999): 80–99.

Judd, Richard. *Common Lands, Common People: The Origins of Conservation in Northern New England.* Cambridge, MA: Harvard University Press, 1997.

Kahn, Si. *The Forest Service in Appalachia.* New York: John Whitney Foundation, 1974.

Kephart, Horace. *Our Southern Highlanders: A Narrative of Adventure in the Southern Appalachians and a Study of Life among the Mountaineers.* Knoxville: University of Tennessee Press, 1976.

King, Brian, Robert A. Rubin, and Judith A. Jenner. *Trail Years: A History of the Appalachian Trail Conference.* Harpers Ferry, WV: Appalachian Trail Conference, 2000.

Klyza, Christopher McGrory. *Who Controls Public Lands? Mining, Forestry, and Grazing Policies, 1870–1990.* Chapel Hill: University of North Carolina Press, 1996.

Kraft, Michael E. "Environmental Policy and Congress." Chapter 5 of *Environmental Policy: New Directions for the Twenty-First Century,* edited by Norman J. Vig and Michael E. Kraft. 7th ed. Washington, DC: CQ Press, 2010.

Krutko, Erin. "Lewis Mountain: Segregation in Shenandoah National Park." Paper delivered at Designing the Parks Conference, Charlottesville, Virginia, May 21, 2008.

Lambert, Darwin. *The Undying Past of Shenandoah National Park*. Boulder, CO: Robert Rinehart, 1989.

Langston, Nancy. *Forest Dreams, Forest Nightmares: The Paradox of Old Growth in the Inland West*. Seattle: University of Washington Press, 1995.

Leopold, Aldo. *A Sand County Almanac, and Sketches Here and There*. 1949. Reprint, London: Oxford University Press, 1970.

Leuchtenburg, William. *The Perils of Prosperity, 1914–1932*. 2nd ed. Chicago: University of Chicago Press, 1993.

Little, Charles E. *Greenways for America*. Baltimore: Johns Hopkins University Press, 1990.

Louter, David. *Windshield Wilderness: Cars, Roads, and Nature in Washington's National Parks*. Seattle: University of Washington Press, 2006.

Lowery, Gerald. "Benton MacKaye's Appalachian Trail as a Cultural Symbol." PhD diss., Emory University, 1981.

Lubove, Roy. *Community Planning in the 1920s: The Contribution of the Regional Planning Association of America*. Pittsburgh: Pittsburgh University Press, 1964.

MacLeannan, Jamie. "Solitude and Sociability: Social Processes among Appalachian Trail Long-Distance Hikers." PhD diss., Rutgers-State University of New Jersey, 2005.

MacKaye, Benton. "The Appalachian Trail: A Guide to the Study of Nature." *Scientific Monthly* 34, no. 4 (April 1932): 330–42.

———. "An Appalachian Trail: A Project in Regional Planning." *Journal of American Institute of Architects* 9 (October 1921): 325–30.

———. *Employment and Natural Resources: Possibilities of Making New Opportunities for Employment through the Settlement and Development of Agricultural and Forest Lands and Other Resources*. US Department of Labor. Washington, DC: General Printing Office, 1919.

———. "The First Solider Colony—Kapuskasing, Canada." *The Public* 22 (November 15, 1919): 1066–68.

———. *From Geography to Geotechnics*. Edited by Paul T. Bryant. Urbana: University of Illinois Press, 1968.

———. *The New Exploration: A Philosophy of Regional Planning*. Urbana-Champaign: University of Illinois Press, 1962. First published in 1928; reprinted in 1956 with introduction by Lewis Mumford and foreword by David N. Startzell.

———. "Progress on the Appalachian Trail." *Appalachia* 15, no. 3 (December 1922): 244–52.

———. "Recreational Possibilities of Public Forests." *Journal of the New York State Forestry Association* 3, no. 2 (October 1916): 4–10, 29–30.

———. "Some Social Aspects of Forest Management." *Journal of Forestry* 16, no. 2 (February 1918): 210–14.

Maher, Neil. *Nature's New Deal: The Roots of the American Environmental Movement*. New York: Oxford University Press, 2008.

Marzulla, Nancie G. "The Property Rights Movement: How It Began and Where It Is Headed." Chapter 1 of *Land Rights: The 1990s' Property Rights Rebellion*, edited by Bruce Yandle. Lanham, MD: Rowman & Littlefield, 1995.

Massachusetts House. "Special Report of the Department of Natural Resources Relative to the Protection of the Appalachian Trail." House Report No. 4609. Boston, 1968.

Mastran, Shelley Smith, and Nan Lowerre. *Mountaineers and Rangers: A History of Federal Forest Management in the Southern Appalachians, 1900–1981.* US Department of Agriculture, Forest Service, April 1983.

McCarthy, James. "Environmentalism, Wise Use, and the Nature of Accumulation in the Rural West." Chapter 6 of *Remaking Reality: Nature at the Millennium,* edited by Bruce Baun and Noel Castree. New York: Routledge, 1998.

McCurdy, Howard E. "Environmental Protection and the New Federalism." Chapter 4 of *Controversies in Environmental Policy,* edited by Sheldon Kamieniecki. Albany: SUNY Press, 1986.

McGirr, Lisa. *Suburban Warriors: The Origins of the New American Right.* Princeton: Princeton University Press, 2001.

McLaughlin, Jeff. "Hikers Torture Appalachians." *Boston Globe.* June 12, 1972.

Miller, Char. *American Forests: Nature, Culture, and Politics.* Lawrence: University of Kansas Press, 1997.

Minteer, Ben A. *The Landscape of Reform: Civic Pragmatism and Environmental Thought in America.* Cambridge, MA: The MIT Press, 2006.

Mitchell, Robert Cameron, Angela A. Mertig, and Rilet E. Dunlap. "Twenty Years of Environmental Mobilization: Trends among National Environmental Organizations." Chapter 2 of *American Environmentalism: The Environmental Movement, 1970–1990.* Washington, DC: Taylor & Francis, 1992.

Moran, Emilio F., and Elinor Ostrom, eds. *Seeing the Forest and the Trees: Human-Environment Interactions in Forest Ecosystems.* Cambridge, MA: The MIT Press, 2005.

Mumford, Lewis. *The Golden Day: A Study in American Experience and Culture.* New York: Boni and Liveright, 1926.

———. *The Story of Utopias.* New York: Boni and Liveright, 1922.

———. *Technics and Civilization.* New York: Harcourt, Brace and Company, 1934.

———. "The Theory and Practice of Regionalism." *The Sociological Review* 20, no. 1 (January 1928): 18–33.

Myers, Phyllis. "Direct Funding of Nonprofit Land Protection: A New Genre of State Land Conservation Programs." Chapter 11 of *Land Conservation through Public/Private Partnerships.* Washington, DC: Island Press, 1993.

Nash, Roderick. *Wilderness and the American Mind.* 4th ed. New Haven, CT: Yale University Press, 2001.

Neel, Susan Rhoades. "Newton Drury and the Echo Park Dam Controversy." *Forest and Conservation History* 38, no. 2 (April 1994): 56–66.

Neff, Jeff W. *Katahdin: An Historic Journey.* Boston: Appalachian Mountain Club Books, 2006.

Neustadt, Richard E., and Ernest R. May. *Thinking in Time: The Uses of History for Decision Makers.* New York: MacMillan, 1986.

Newfont, Kathryn. *Blue Ridge Commons: Environmental Activism and Forest History in Western North Carolina.* Athens: University of Georgia Press, 2012.

New York–New Jersey Trail Conference. *Vistas and Visions: A History of the New York–New Jersey Trail Conference.* New York: New York–New Jersey Trail Conference, 1995.

Niskanen, William A. *Reaganomics: An Insider's Account of the Policies and the People*. New York: Oxford University Press, 1988.

O'Leary, Rosemary. "Environmental Policy in the Courts." Chapter 6 of *Environmental Policy: New Directions for the Twenty-First Century*, ed. Norman Vig and Michael E. Kraft. 7th ed. Washington, DC: CQ Press, 2010.

Oliver, Duane. *Hazel Creek: From Then til Now*. Maryville, TN: Stinnett Printing Company, 1989.

Parrish, Michael E. *The Anxious Decades: America in Prosperity and Depression, 1920–1941*. New York: W. W. Norton & Company, 1994.

Parsons, Kermit C. "Collaborative Genius: The Regional Planning Association of America." *Journal of the American Planning Association* 60, no. 4 (1994): 462–82.

Paxton, Pamela. "Is Social Capital Declining in the United States? A Multiple Indicator Assessment." *American Journal of Sociology* 105, no. 1 (July 1999): 88–127.

Petzoldt, Paul. *The Wilderness Handbook*. New York: W. W. Norton & Company, 1974.

Perdue, Charles M., and Nancy M. Martin Perdue. "Appalachian Fables and Facts: A Case Study of the Shenandoah National Park Removals." *Appalachian Journal* 7, nos. 1–2 (Autumn/Winter 1979–1980): 84–104.

———. "'To Build a Wall around These Mountains': The Displaced People of Shenandoah." *The Magazine of Albemarle County History* 49 (1991): 48–71.

Phillips, Sarah. *This Land, This Nation: Conservation, Rural America, and the New Deal*. Cambridge: Cambridge University Press, 2007.

Potere, David, et al. "Patterns in Forest Clearing along the Appalachian Trail." *Photogrammetric Engineering and Remote Sensing* (July 2007): 783–91.

Proudman, Robert, and Rueben Rajala. *AMC's Field Guide to Trail Building and Maintenance*. 2nd ed. Boston: Appalachian Mountain Club, 1981.

Pudup, Mary Beth. *Appalachia in the Making: The Mountain South in the Nineteenth Century*. Chapel Hill: University of North Carolina Press, 1995.

Putnam, Robert. *Bowling Alone: The Collapse and Revival of American Community*. New York: Simon & Schuster, 2000.

Reeder, Carolyn, and Jack Reeder. *Shenandoah Secrets: The Story of the Park's Hidden Past*. Vienna, VA: Potomac Appalachian Trail Club, 1998.

Reeves, James L. "A Qualitative Study of Walk with Nature: An Outdoor, Environmental, Experiential Education Program." PhD diss., University of Georgia, 1993.

Reich, Justin. "Re-Creating the Wilderness: Shaping Narratives and Landscapes in Shenandoah National Park." *Environmental History* 6, no. 1 (Jan. 2001): 95–118.

Reiger, John F. *American Sportsmen and the Origins of Conservation*. 3rd ed. Corvallis: Oregon State University Press, 2001.

Rome, Adam. *Bulldozer in the Countryside: Suburban Sprawl and the Rise of American Environmentalism*. Cambridge: Cambridge University Press, 2001.

Rothman, Hal K. *The Greening of a Nation? Environmentalism in the United States since 1945*. New York: Harcourt Brace, 1998.

———. "'A Regular Ding-Dong Fight': The Dynamics of the Park Service–Forest Service Controversy during the 1920s and 1930s." In *American Forests: Nature, Culture, and Politics*, 109–24. Lawrence: University Press of Kansas, 1997.

Runte, Alfred. *National Parks: The American Experience.* 2nd ed. Lincoln: University of Nebraska Press, 1987.

Sale, Kirkpatrick. *The Green Revolution.* New York: Hill and Wang, 1993.

Sax, Joseph L. "Buying Scenery: Land Acquisition for the National Park Service." *Duke Law Journal* 4 (Sept. 1980): 709–40.

———. "Helpless Giants: The National Parks and the Regulation of Private Lands." *Michigan Law Review* 75 (Dec. 1976): 239–74.

Schrepfer, Susan. *Nature's Altars: Mountains, Gender, and American Environmentalism.* Lawrence: University Press of Kansas, 2005.

Scott, James C. *Seeing Like a State: How Certain Schemes to Improve the Human Condition Have Failed.* New Haven: Yale University Press, 1998.

Sellars, Richard West. *Preserving Nature in the National Parks: A History.* New Haven: Yale University Press, 1997.

Shipan, Charles R., and William R. Lowry. "Environmental Policy and Party Divergence in Congress." *Political Research Quarterly* 54 (2001): 245–63.

Short, C. Brant. *Ronald Reagan and the Public Lands: America's Conservation Debate, 1979–1984.* College Station: Texas A&M University Press, 1989.

Shutkin, William. *The Land That Could Be: Environmentalism and Democracy in the Twenty-First Century.* Cambridge, MA: The MIT Press, 2000.

Sidaway, Roger. "Long-Distance Routes in England and Wales—Their History and Pointers for Future Research." In *Long-Distance Trails: The Appalachian Trail as a Guide to Future Research and Management Needs.* New Haven, CT: Studies, Yale University, 1979, 11–27.

Simmons, Dennis E. "Conservation, Cooperation, and Controversy: The Establishment of Shenandoah National Park, 1924–1936." *Virginia Magazine of History* 89, no. 4 (October 1981): 387–404.

Smith, David C. *A History of Lumbering in Maine, 1861–1960.* Orono: University of Maine Press, 1972.

Smith, Daniel S., and Paul C. Hellmund, eds. *Ecology of Greenways.* Minneapolis: University of Minnesota Press, 1993.

Smith, Kimberly K. *African-American Environmental Thought: Foundations.* Lawrence: University of Kansas, 2007.

Smith, Thomas G. *Green Republican: John Saylor and the Preservation of America's Wilderness.* Pittsburgh: University of Pittsburgh Press, 2006.

Spann, Edward K. *Designing Modern America: The Regional Planning Association of America.* Columbus: Ohio State University Press, 1996.

Spence, Mark. *Dispossessing the Wilderness: Indian Removal and the Making of the National Parks.* New York: Oxford University Press, 1999.

Spyker, Stephen K. "Spirituality and Technology on the Appalachian Trail: A Study in Frontiers." PhD diss., Ball State University, 2004.

Sussman, Carl, ed. *Planning the Fourth Migration: The Neglected Vision of the Regional Planning Association of America.* Cambridge, MA: The MIT Press, 1976.

Sutter, Paul S. *Driven Wild: How the Fight against Automobiles Launched the Modern Wilderness Movement.* Seattle: University of Washington Press, 2002.

———. "'A Retreat from Profit': Colonization, the Appalachian Trail, and the Social Roots of Benton MacKaye's Wilderness Advocacy." *Environmental History* 4, no. 4 (1999): 553–77.

Switzer, Jacqueline Vaughn. *Green Backlash: The History and Politics of Environmental Opposition in the U.S.* Boulder, CO: Lynne Rienner Publishers, 1997.

Taylor, Stephen W. *The New South's New Frontier: A Social History of Economic Development in Southwestern North Carolina.* Gainesville: University Press of Florida, 2001.

Thompson, Michael J. ed. *Confronting the New Conservatism: The Rise of the Right in America.* New York: New York University Press, 2007.

Turner, James Morton. "From Woodcraft to 'Leave No Trace': Wilderness, Consumerism, and Environmentalism in Twentieth-Century America." *Environmental History* 7, no. 3 (2002): 462–84.

———. *The Promise of Wilderness: A History of American Environmental Politics, 1964–2004.* Seattle: University of Washington Press, 2012.

———. "'The Specter of Environmentalism': Wilderness, Environmental Politics, and the Evolution of the New Right." *Journal of American History* 96, no. 1 (June 2009): 123–49.

US Congress. *An Act to Amend the National Trails System Act, and for Other Purposes.* Public Law 95-248, 95th Cong., March 21, 1978.

———. *Act to Authorize a Study of the Park, Parkway, and Recreational-Area Programs in the United States, and for Other Purposes.* 49 Stat. 1894, June 23, 1936.

———. *Congressional Record.* 95th Cong., 2d. sess., August 8, 1978, Vol. 124, no. 123.

———. *National Trails System Act.* Public Law 90-543, 90th Cong., October 2, 1968, S. 827.

US Congress. House. Committee on Appropriations. *Department of the Interior and Related Agencies Appropriation Bill, 1979.* 95th Cong., 2d sess., May 24, 1978.

———. Committee on Interior and Insular Affairs. *Land Acquisition Policy and Program of the National Park Service: A Report.* June 4, 1984. Reprinted by the University of Michigan Library.

———. Committee on Interior and Insular Affairs. Subcommittee on National Parks and Recreation. *Statement by Walter Boardman concerning H.R. 4865, A Nationwide System of Trails.* March 6–7, 1967.

———. Committee on Interior and Insular Affairs. Subcommittee on Public Lands on H.R. 8070. *A Bill for the Establishment of a Public Land Law Review Commission to Study Existing Laws and Procedures Relating to the Administration of the Public Lands of the United States,* October 4, 1963.

———. Committee on Roads. *Hearings before the Committee on Roads on H.R. 2142.* 1st Sess., October 24, 1945.

US Congress. Senate. Committee on Energy and Natural Resources. Subcommittee on Parks and Recreation. *Hearings before the Subcommittee on Parks and Recreation on S. 2066, H.R. 8803.* 95th Cong., 1st Sess., Pub. No. 95-81, Washington, DC: General Printing Office, November 1, 1977.

———. Committee on Interior and Insular Affairs. *Hearing of Committee on Interior and Insular Affairs on S. 827.* March 15, 1967.

———. Committee on Interior and Insular Affairs. *Hearings before the Parks and*

Recreation of Subcommittee on S. 622, *The Appalachian Trail*. September 16, 1965.

US Department of the Interior. Bureau of Outdoor Recreation. *Trails for America*. Washington, DC: General Printing Office, 1966.

US Department of the Interior. National Park Service. Appalachian Trail Project Office. *Appalachian Trail Report*, 1985.

————. "Comprehensive Management Plan for the Protection, Management, and Use of the Appalachian National Scenic Trail." Harpers Ferry, West Virginia. September 1981.

————. Northeast Region. *Appalachian Trail Vital Signs, Technical Report NPS/NER/NRTR-2005/026*. November 2005.

————. *Parks for America: A Survey of Park and Related Resources in the Fifty States, and a Preliminary Plan*. Washington, DC: General Printing Office, 1964.

Vig, Norman J., and Michael E. Kraft, eds. *Environmental Policy: New Directions for the Twenty-First Century*, edited by Norman J. Vig and Michael E. Kraft. 7th ed. Washington, DC: CQ Press, 2010.

Walker, Melissa. *All We Knew Was to Farm: Rural Women in the Upcounty South, 1919–1941*. Baltimore: Johns Hopkins University Press, 2000.

Warren, Louis. *The Hunter's Game: Poachers and Conservationists in Twentieth-Century America*. New Haven: Yale University Press, 1997.

Waterman, Laura, and Guy Waterman. *Backwoods Ethics: Environmental Concerns for Hikers and Campers*. Boston, MA: Stone Wall Press, 1979.

————. *Forest and Crag: A History of Hiking, Trail Blazing, and Adventure in the Northeast Mountains*. Boston: Appalachian Mountain Club, 1989.

Wellock, Thomas. *Preserving the Nation: The Conservation and Environmental Movements, 1870–2000*. Wheeling, IL: Harlan Davidson, 2007.

Wessels, Tom. *Reading the Forested Landscape: A Natural History of New England*. Woodstock, VT: The Countryman Press, 2005.

Whisnant, Anne Mitchell. *Super-Scenic Motorway: A Blue Ridge Parkway History*. Chapel Hill: University of North Carolina Press, 2006.

White, Richard, "'Are You an Environmentalist, or Do You Work for a Living?': Work and Nature." In *Uncommon Ground: Rethinking the Human Place in Nature*. New York: W. W. Norton & Co., 1996, 171–85.

Whitney, Gordon G. *From Coastal Wilderness to Fruited Plain: A History of Environmental Change in Temperate North America from 1500 to the Present*. Cambridge: Cambridge University Press, 1994.

Williams, Michael. *Americans and Their Forests: A Historical Geography*. New York: Cambridge University Press, 1992.

Willie, Charles V. *Theories of Human Social Action*. New York: General Hall, 1994.

Wirth, Conrad L. *Parks, Politics, and the People*. Norman: University of Oklahoma Press, 1980.

Yandle, Bruce, ed. *Land Rights: The 1990s' Property Rights Rebellion*. Lanham, MD: Rowman & Littlefield, 1995.

Zealand, Clark T. W. "Decolonizing Experiences: An Ecophenomenological Investigation of the Lived Experience of Appalachian Trail Thru-Hikers." PhD diss., University of Waterloo, Canada, 2007.

Index

A

Adirondack Mountain Club, 36

All-Tramp Soviet, 36

Alpine Club, 19–20

American Land Rights Association. *See* National Park Inholders Association

Anderson, H. C., 42–43

Anderson, Larry, 18

Appalachian Greenway, 106–7, 114–18, 171

Appalachian Highlands Association, 115, 116

Appalachian Long-Distance Hikers Association, 147

Appalachian Mountain Club, 4, 19, 20, 21–22, 23, 36, 40, 106, 120

Appalachian National Park Association, 5, 19, 22

Appalachian National Scenic Trail Advisory Council, 91–92, 98, 100

Appalachian Trail: early trail-building, 20–22, 34–67; economic benefits, 188, 209n70; federal protection of, 69–94; geographic extent and features, 3–4, 11–12, 14, 35, 98, 187, 195–96; herbicides on, 143, 174; increase in number and diversity of users after 1968 Trails Act, 102–7; motorized vehicles on, 95, 96, 107, 148; northern vs. southern, 40–42, 49–51; original purposes, 3, 14, 63–64, 66, 80; postwar administrative difficulties, 98–102; postwar purposes, 69, 78, 80–82, 91, 97, 114; private sector support, 9, 116, 118, 162, 165, 167, 178, 190–91; resistance from landowners

(post-1968), 95–96, 107–111, 136–53, 161–62, 227n34; resistance from New Right, 156–65, 180–82, 186; southern cultural divisions, 47–48, 51–52, 55

Appalachian Trail Community program, 9, 187, 188–89, 193

Appalachian Trail Comprehensive Plan, 176

Appalachian Trail Conference (ATC): early era, 5, 34, 35, 40, 44, 55, 61, 63, 64, 67; postwar era, 9, 68, 73, 75–78, 85, 86–89, 91–92, 98, 100, 111–18, 123–24, 138, 147, 151–52; post-1981, 156–57, 159, 164–65, 169, 172–74, 177–80; post-2000, 186–94

Appalachian Trail Interstate Coalition, 146, 163

Appalachian Trail Landowners Organization, 163, 172

Appalachian Trail Location Advisory Committee, 142

Appalachian Trail Project Office, 120, 125, 128, 131, 150, 159, 166, 172, 178

Appalachian Trailway Agreement, 64–65

Apple Orchard Mountain, 75, 212n26

Acadia National Park, 22, 178

Audubon Society, 77, 86, 113, 115, 117, 190, 216n58

automobiles and the wilderness, 20–21, 82, 103, 202n19, 217n64

Avery, Myron: early career, 42–44, 47–51, 57–64; postwar activities, 71, 73, 75–76, 77, 88–89, 214n48, 215n55

B

Ballard, Edward B., 64–65
Barren Mountain, 136
Bartha, Joseph, 38–39
Bates, David, 53
Baxter, Percival, 62–63
Baxter State Park, 63, 106
Bear Mountain and Harriman State Park, 36
Benander, Mrs. Laurence, 166
Benson, Whit, 175
Big Bald Mountain, 74–75
Big Butt Mountain, 74
Blackburn, George, 87
Blackburn, Ruth, 157
Bliss, Laura, 75
Blue Mountain Eagle Climbing Club, 77
Blue Ridge Mountains, 42
Blue Ridge Parkway, 5, 86–87, 129
Boardman, Walter, 103
Boone, Daniel, 106, 206n29
Boone National Forest, 23
Boynton, Claud C., 49–50
Brackney, Howard, 97
Brewster, Ralph O., 62
Brickner, Roger, 164–65
Bristow, Preston, Jr., 169–71
British conservation models, 19, 170–71
Brothers, Joyce, 135
Brymesser, Sheldon, 143, 187–88
Bryson, Bill, 220n35
Buck, Pearl, 74–75
Bureau of Land Management, 125, 144
Bureau of Outdoor Recreation, 8, 92, 101–2, 115, 158
Byers, Arlene, 141

C

CANT (Citizens Against New Trail), 141, 146, 153, 163, 167, 187
Carson, Rachel, 69, 83
Carter, Jimmy, 110, 156

Casey, Jack, 229n74
Catawba Mountain, 120–21
center-line surveying, 133
Chase, Stuart, 27
Chattahoochee National Forest, 45, 68, 93
Cherokee National Forest, 23, 162
Cioffi, Dave, 163
Civilian Conservation Corps, 5, 35, 59–62, 64, 185
Clean Air Act, 7, 83, 185, 191
Clean Water Act, 7, 185, 191
Clinton, Bill, 180–82
Coe, Jonathan, 136
Coffey, Gannon, 87
Cohutta Mountain, 45-46, 175
Cole, S. L., 207n47
Connecticut Appalachian Trail Landowners Association, 163, 172
conservation, 4, 10-12, 18, 21, 23, 29–30, 34-36, 40, 69, 80, 83, 86, 115, 201n14; and conservatism, 8, 182, 191–93, 200n10; "old" versus "new," 6–7
Cooper, Arthur W., 110–11
Corindia, Alan, 106
Corson, Homer, 42
"creative conservation," 9, 153, 156
Criley, Walter L., 100–101
Cronon, William, 193
Cross, Mrs. Leon, 68
Cushman, Charles, 7, 144–46, 163, 180, 229n77
Czechoslovakia, tramping in, 204n8

D

Dartmouth Outing Club, 95, 138–39, 163
Davidge, Ric, 164
Davis, Fred, 44
Davis, Harry, 57–58
Delmolino, Arthur, 154–55
Demaray, Arthur, 88
Department of the Interior, 23, 26, 91, 92, 97–98, 100, 146-47, 164; under Watt, 8, 115–16, 156–58, 192

Wetstone, Greg, 116
Whalen, William, 135
Whitaker, Charles, 27
White Mountain National Forest, 23
White Mountains, 15, 21, 40, 42, 196
Wilderness Act, 78, 93, 185, 233n47
wilderness preservation, 6, 10, 14, 18, 19, 30,
    34, 69-71, 77-80, 82–83, 193; and integra-
    tion with working and managed lands,
    169–171, 174–77, 184, 193–94
Wilderness Society, 6, 77, 83, 86, 190, 194,
    214n48, 216n58
Willie, Charles V., 30
"wise use" movement, 7, 156, 186
Wislocki, George, 167
Witzerman, Carol, 166

Y

York Footpath Society, 19
Young Men's Hebrew Association, 36

Z

Zon, Raphael, 18